MUCH ADO
ABOUT NOTHING

The RSC Shakespeare

Edited by Jonathan Bate and Eric Rasmussen

Chief Associate Editors: Héloïse Sénéchal and Jan Sewell

Associate Editors: Trey Jansen, Eleanor Lowe, Lucy Munro,
Dee Anna Phares

Much Ado About Nothing

Textual editing: Eric Rasmussen

Introduction and Shakespeare's Career in the Theater: Jonathan Bate

Commentary: Eleanor Lowe and Héloïse Sénéchal

Scene-by-Scene Analysis: Esme Miskimmin

In Performance: Penelope Freedman (RSC stagings), Jan Sewell (overview)

The Director's Cut (interviews by Jonathan Bate and Kevin Wright):
Marianne Elliott, Nicholas Hytner

Playing Beatrice: Harriet Walter

The RSC Shakespeare

William Shakespeare

MUCH ADO
ABOUT NOTHING

Edited by Jonathan Bate and Eric Rasmussen

Introduction by Jonathan Bate

The Modern Library
New York

CONTENTS

Introduction   vii
   Couples   vii
   Tragedy Averted   ix
   Much Ado About Noting   x
   Second Chance   xi
   Double Ending   xv

About the Text   xviii

Key Facts   xxiv

Much Ado About Nothing   1

Textual Notes   93

Scene-by-Scene Analysis   95

***Much Ado About Nothing* in Performance:**
The RSC and Beyond   107
   Four Centuries of *Much Ado*: An Overview   107
   At the RSC   119
   The Director's Cut: Interviews with Marianne
     Elliott and Nicholas Hytner   134
   Harriet Walter on Playing Beatrice   147

Shakespeare's Career in the Theater   154
   Beginnings   154
   Playhouses   156
   The Ensemble at Work   160
   The King's Man   165

Shakespeare's Works: A Chronology   168

Further Reading and Viewing   171

References   173

Acknowledgments and Picture Credits   177

INTRODUCTION

COUPLES

On what basis do you choose a partner with whom to share your life? Sexual desire or social compatibility? Surface appearance or inner character? And how much freedom should young people have in making such an important choice? Is there anything to be said for the older way of doing things whereby parents play a central part in the process of arrangement and approval? These questions are no less pressing in today's multicultural societies than they were in the transitional age during which Shakespeare wrote his plays. And of all those plays, *Much Ado About Nothing* is the one that offers the most modern view of the game of boy meets girl that used to be called courtship.

Shakespeare knew that human motives and interactions are never simple. One of his favorite devices for exploring the complexity of our affairs is the double plot. In ancient Athens, Aristotle had said that a good play needs unity of action in order to keep the audience's focus. Shakespeare defied that rule and opted instead for stereoscopic vision. The double plot of *Much Ado* offers two versions of courtship. We might call them the romantic and the realistic, or the ancient and the modern.

There is an old story that goes back to ancient Greek romance and that reappeared in the early Renaissance. It received its most influential telling in an epic Italian romance by Ludovico Ariosto called *Orlando Furioso*. It tells of how a girl is wrongly accused of infidelity to the man she loves. He is tricked into believing that he has witnessed her letting another man into her bedroom window. The trick is that he is actually witnessing another woman disguised as his beloved. Accusations fly and an unhappy ending seems inevitable, but after various twists and turns the lovers are reunited.

This—adapted through various intermediary versions and reworked with many distinctively Shakespearean touches—is the origin of the Claudio and Hero story about which the play makes much ado. Coming as it does from the romance tradition, the relationship is focused on honor (a girl's chastity is nonnegotiable) and on the combination of idealization and desire that we call "romantic love." One of the intermediate versions of the story, also known to Shakespeare, introduced the element of social class: its main characters are a knightly follower of Piero, King of Aragon, and the daughter of the poor but honorable Lionato de'Lionati of Messina. From here, Shakespeare took a series of questions about what constitutes a *suitable* marriage, how to reconcile the romantic desires of the young with the more down-to-earth matters of status, respect, and money that are of concern to their parents.

Hero is the archetypal romance heroine. Her identity is defined by her sexual honesty: the accusation of infidelity almost literally kills her. Claudio is also bound by traditional notions of honor. Appearance is everything and all that matters is what *men* say. He doesn't believe Hero's denials of the false accusations and neither does his lord, Don Pedro, who makes clear that men must stand together: "I stand dishonoured, that have gone about / To link my dear friend to a common stale" (a "stale" means a whore).

Claudio's friend Benedick is given a choice at the climax of the accusation scene: to stick with the men or to stand up for Hero. The person who forces him to make that choice is Hero's cousin, Beatrice. She knows what is the right thing to do, but cannot do it herself because she is a woman: "Is a not approved in the height a villain, that hath slandered, scorned, dishonoured my kinswoman? O that I were a man! What, bear her in hand until they come to take hands, and then, with public accusation, uncovered slander, unmitigated rancour—O God, that I were a man! I would eat his heart in the market-place." If Benedick is to retain Beatrice's respect, he will have to take on the role that she cannot: he will have to challenge his friend Claudio to a duel.

The glorious relationship between Beatrice and Benedick has no equivalent in any of the older versions of the Claudio and Hero story. It is Shakespeare's unique invention. And it takes over the audience's interest. This is a completely different, completely new, astonishingly modern relationship. The starting point is not sexual desire, not the romantic idea of falling in love at first sight. Nor is it honor or status. Beatrice is an orphan, not a daughter to be married off as a commodity. There is a general assumption that she will end up as an old maid. Her dazzling wit is her only defense against the loneliness of her likely fate.

We all know the problem with the romantic view of love: what is left when the gloss wears off, when the first mad passion is over? We have faith in Beatrice and Benedick because with them it is the other way around. Compatibility comes first, romance later. Their "merry war" of words reveals that they are intellectual equals and mutual respect will flow from there. "In each of them," the actor Harriet Walter notes in her interview on playing the part of Beatrice, "submitting to love was linked with an idea of loss of power and control. But having had such a long drawn-out and often antagonistic courtship, they can be said to really know one another and to have seen the worst of one another." A partnership based on equality and respect, not on idealization or status: that is what makes Beatrice and Benedick so very real and so very modern.

TRAGEDY AVERTED

Comedy is tragedy averted. A young woman prepares herself for marriage. Then we witness the ceremony itself. Whenever we go to a wedding we cannot help relishing the dramatic pause when the priest asks the couple, "If either of you know any inward impediment why you should not be conjoined, I charge you on your souls to utter it." On this occasion the drama turns into a crisis: in front of the whole congregation Claudio the groom accuses Hero the bride of infidelity on the very eve of her wedding day. She faints, he storms out, her father says that he hopes she is dead since she has brought such shame on his household. The play has begun with the end of a war, a move from the language of martial bonding to that of courtship and coupling. Its atmosphere has been all holiday. No more.

The change of mood extends even to the other pair of lovers. The relationship between Benedick and Beatrice has hitherto been characterized by sharp but always lighthearted banter; now Beatrice raises the stakes dramatically, forcing Benedick to choose between love and friendship. Suddenly we have moved into the *Othello*-world of sexual accusation and death threat. Don John, the chief plotter of all the mischief, is no Iago—he is a cardboard cut-out villain, an archetypal melancholy man ("I cannot hide what I am: I must be sad when I have cause, and smile at no man's jests")—so in our rational minds we do not believe he will triumph, but we end the fourth act feeling that a substantial act of atonement will be required of Claudio.

Comedy makes room for little acts of grace; it allows the second chance that tragedy denies. In *Much Ado*, the grace comes from two agencies: the Friar who arranges the mock-death and resurrection of Hero, and the Watchmen who stumble upon the truth of Don John's plot. We expect God to work his benign way through friars. It may seem strange that providence also works by means of the bumbling, malaprop-prone Dogberry. It is, however, one of the laws of the comic universe that appearance ("semblance") is deceptive. Those who think they are clever, like Don John, end up looking foolish; those who we at first think are foolish, like Dogberry, turn out to be peculiarly wise. Their wisdom is that of the heart, not the intellect. Jesus said that to understand the kingdom of heaven one has to make oneself as a child: Dogberry, like Bottom in *A Midsummer Night's Dream*, is one of Shakespeare's natural children. He is "condemned into everlasting redemption" for his simplicity and goodness.

MUCH ADO ABOUT NOTING

The play's title is multiply suggestive. There is much ado about the nothing that Hero has done wrong. Shakespeare often makes "nothing" a euphemism for female genitals, because women lack a male "thing" between their legs, so there is an obscene second sense. "Nothing" seems to have been pronounced "noting," which provides a further rich sense: the play is full of "noting" in the sense of watching and overhearing, whether in the famous scenes in which Benedick and Beatrice are deliberately allowed to overhear conversations of great interest to them, or the plan to let Claudio "witness" the infidelity of his betrothed. Messina is full of hearsay.

Disguise is a closely related motif: Don Pedro woos Hero on behalf of, and in the guise of, Claudio. This plan is eavesdropped upon by scheming Borachio ("Being entertained for a perfumer, as I was smoking a musty room, comes me the prince and Claudio, hand in hand in sad conference. I whipped me behind the arras and there heard it agreed upon that the prince should woo Hero for himself, and having obtained her, give her to Count Claudio") and also misheard by a servant of Leonato's brother ("The prince and Count Claudio, walking in a thick-pleached alley in my orchard, were thus overheard by a man of mine: the prince discovered to Claudio that he loved my niece your daughter and meant to acknowledge it this night in a dance"). In each narrative of noting, an imagined detail—interlaced branches in a garden walk, a musty room hung with tapestry—creates a sense of location even as Shakespeare writes for a bare stage. As befits a work in which prose outweighs verse by a ratio of more than two to one, the texture of the play offers far more realism than romance: instead of the (sometimes parodically overblown) love-poetry we find in many of the other comedies, the focus here is on less hyperbolic but more heartfelt matters such as a bride's delight in the precise fashion and cut of her wedding dress.

It is unlikely to have taken a bright Elizabethan boy actor more than about an hour to learn the little part of Hero. Traditionally the leading actress—Dora Jordan in the eighteenth century, Ellen Terry in the nineteenth, Peggy Ashcroft in the twentieth—has played Beatrice, and one suspects that the Chamberlain's Men's best boy would have done so in the original Shakespearean production. Claudio says of Hero, "Silence is the perfectest herald of joy." She is the embodiment of the silent woman, talked about far more than she talks. Hero says far less than the other major characters, but we hear her name more often than that of any other character. And when we begin to look at her in this light we come to the center of the play, for talking about people is the play's central activity.

SECOND CHANCE

The early nineteenth-century critic William Hazlitt was a great admirer of Hero's fortitude. Writing about *Much Ado* in his book *Characters of Shakespear's Plays* (1817), he noted that "The justification of Hero in the end, and her restoration to the confidence and arms of her lover, is brought about by one of those temporary consignments to the grave of which Shakespeare seems to have been fond." Hazlitt suggested that Shakespeare explained the theory behind this favorite plot twist in a crucial speech of the Friar's:

> She dying, as it must so be maintained,
> Upon the instant that she was accused,
> Shall be lamented, pitied and excused
> Of every hearer, for it so falls out
> That what we have we prize not to the worth
> Whiles we enjoy it; but, being lacked and lost,
> Why, then we rack the value, then we find
> The virtue that possession would not show us
> Whiles it was ours. So will it fare with Claudio:
> When he shall hear she died upon his words,
> Th'idea of her life shall sweetly creep
> Into his study of imagination,
> And every lovely organ of her life
> Shall come apparelled in more precious habit,
> More moving-delicate and full of life,
> Into the eye and prospect of his soul
> Than when she lived indeed.

Silence is associated with death, and Hero's name is also associated with death: it is evocative of the title of the Roman poet Ovid's highly influential tales of deserted and despairing lovers, the *Heroides* (as well as the name of one of the characters in that collection, Hero mourning for her drowned lover, Leander). Death is the logic of the Heroine's exclusion from the first part of the play: in her habitual reticence, she is almost like a dead person from the start. But the Friar's suggestion is a kind of appropriation of death: he recognizes that the kind of death into which Hero has been forced can become the basis for a new life. The moment people believe she really is dead, they will start to value her. His recognition of this is based on what Hazlitt calls the theory behind Shakespeare's predilection for temporary consignments to the grave, namely the intuition of the human tendency not to value someone or something fully until we have lost it.

The idea remained very important to Shakespeare right through to the end of his career. Prospero in *The Tempest* only realizes how much he loves Ariel when he releases him. The point about the temporary consignment to the grave is that it gives a second chance. It allows one to experience the loss that makes one value what one has lost, and then it gives back the lost object. And this time, so the theory goes, one will really value it. "Come, lady, die to live," says the Friar: it is only the apparent death, played out in elaborate fullness, that can provide a sufficiently firm basis for a subsequent fullness of life. When Hero is brought back to the stage, the language dwells sustainedly on this notion of dying to live. Hero dies while her slanders lived and lives once they die.

A temporary consignment to the grave is powerful in a play because a play serves a similar function. Claudio will come to value his Hero through having lived through her death. We will come to value our Heros through living through the stage deaths of others like them. The great sixteenth-century French essayist Michel de Montaigne wrote an essay on Cicero's dictum "That to philosophize is to learn how to die"; Shakespeare would suggest that to play-go is to learn how to live by seeing others pretend to die. As defenders of the stage were quick to point out when the theater was attacked by puritans as immoral, the drama may serve an educative function for the audience. It may make us learn to value life through the surrogate experience of loss. Profound comedy must always be close to tragedy; the apparent death is necessary for the achievement of a comic fullness of life. One way of putting it would be to say that *The Winter's Tale*, with its hinged tragicomic structure, is the logical conclusion of Shakespeare's work. That play is certainly the fully matured reworking of *Much Ado*.

The temporary consignment to the grave is not only an analogue for the audience's experience in the theater, and for the tragic element in comedy, it is also central to most myths and religions. Christ spends three days in the grave; Christianity is built on the idea of dying to oneself in order to achieve fuller life in Christ. Shakespeare made much of certain classical myths of temporary death and rebirth: the dying god, Adonis; Proserpina, goddess of spring, who dies to live and who is the archetype of Marina and Perdita; Orpheus bringing Eurydice back from the underworld. The ultimate original for the Hero plot is a Greek myth, that of Alcestis. Shakespeare could conceivably have known a Latin translation of Euripides' play on the subject, but he certainly received the story at second hand through the prose romances that were the direct sources of *Much Ado*.

The plot of *Alcestis* may be summarized briefly: a man called Admetus is allowed an extra length of life, provided that at the appointed hour of his death someone else can be persuaded to die for him; Admetus' father and mother refuse; Alcestis, his loyal wife, consents and accordingly dies; just after her death, Herakles happens to be passing, on his way to perform one of his labors; despite his wife's recent death, Admetus entertains Herakles in accordance with the laws of hospitality; the latter discovers what has happened and goes to Death, the messenger who is taking Alcestis to the underworld, wrestles her from him and restores her to her husband, who by this time feels guilty and repentant that he has let her die in his place. The story is played out on the level of myth, not in a civic community like Shakespeare's Messina, but the idea of a second chance is the key shared motif.

Much Ado shares with Euripides' *Alcestis* the idea of transformation being wrought by an image of the dead wife working on the mind. Alcestis expires on stage. Euripides gives a strong emphasis to her liminal position, both dead and not dead, no longer living but not yet received into the underworld. A gap is thus left open for recovery and return. When Herakles does return, it is with a veiled woman. Initially he says that it is a woman whom he has won; he asks Admetus to look after her while he goes off to perform his labor. Admetus says that he doesn't want a woman in the house, especially one whose form is so like that of Alcestis. Herakles talks of a potential remarriage and the widower reacts angrily; there is a sense of his being tested and this time not failing. Eventually Admetus gives way to the strong will of Herakles and says he will take the woman into the house. The revelation and reunion then occur. It is a beautiful sequence, close in spirit and style to the reanimation of Hermione in *The Winter's Tale*. Strikingly, though, Alcestis does not speak. This motif is taken into the mythic structure when Herakles explains that she will not be allowed to speak for three days, by which time her obligations to the gods of the underworld will have been washed away. Alcestis functions as the archetypal silenced woman, and in this she is a precedent for the Hero who is allowed to say so little throughout the play and is given only two brief factual speeches on her unveiling at the climax. There are plenty of differences, not least in that there is no accusation of infidelity on Admetus' part. *Alcestis* is not a direct source for the Hero plot; rather, it is a powerful mythic prototype for the silencing of the woman and its extension, her temporary consignment to the grave. As in *All's Well That Ends Well* and *The Winter's Tale*, the actual death of the myth is replaced by a self-conscious stage trick. Superhuman interventions like that of Herakles are replaced by domesticated divine agents: the Friar's scheme in this play, Helen's self-contrived devices in *All's Well*, Paulina's priestess-like art in *The Winter's Tale*. Silence is not given a mythic-religious cause but becomes a psychological and social reality. But the strong sense of a second chance, of dying to live, draws the texts together.

DOUBLE ENDING

If we read Hero as an analogue for the female victims of Ovid's *Heroides*, then Claudio is like one of the men in those poems: thoroughly untrustworthy and self-interested. This would accord with the bad press he's always had: Charles Gildon at the beginning of the eighteenth century accused him of "barbarous" conduct toward Hero, A. C. Swinburne at the end of the nineteenth century called him "a pitiful fellow," and most theatergoers today have little sympathy for him. But if, on the other hand, Hero is an Alcestis, Claudio is an Admetus who repents of and learns from his earlier unfair conduct. To accept the play as romance we have to go with this reading. The Friar's plan has got to work: the mock death must make Claudio see Hero's virtues, must make him into a nobler lover. We must therefore take seriously such lines in the final act as "I have drunk poison whiles he uttered it" and "Sweet Hero! Now thy image doth appear / In the rare semblance that I loved it first." And we must accept the sincerity of Claudio's vow of an annual sackcloth visit to Hero's monument. We must accept the magic of the reunion and, as in *The Winter's Tale*, we must, in the Friar's words, "let wonder seem familiar."

In an Elizabethan collection of romances called *A Petite Pallace of Pettie his Pleasure*, which Shakespeare almost certainly read, the moral of the Admetus and Alcestis story is addressed to women readers: "you should die to yourselves and live to your husbands." An old-fashioned plea for wifely submissiveness. But Shakespeare orders the matter differently: he retains the motif of the woman dying and then living again, but he does so in order that the husbands should die to themselves and live to their wives, for in *Much Ado*, as in *The Winter's Tale*, it is the husband who must be transformed by loss in order that he may become worthy of his wife.

As spectators we have been much more attracted to the witty lovers than the (supposedly) romantic ones. Since we cannot wait for the union of Benedick and Beatrice, we join Claudio in the rush toward it. Only on a second reading or viewing do we stop to worry about the kind of husband he will make for Hero. The question that matters to us is how on earth Beatrice and Benedick will stop insulting each other long enough to agree on a marriage contract. The answer comes from Leonato when he says "Peace! I will stop your mouth"—and forces the lovers into a kiss. We know that the wit-combat will resume, but for a moment at the end of the play we imagine the suspension of all quarrels in a kiss and then a dance. Technically, the Beatrice and Benedick story is a subplot that Shakespeare introduced into a romance story he inherited from Renaissance Italy; theatrically, they steal the show, and the benign plot whereby they are tricked into acknowledging their love for each other is the most memorable thing in the play. The simultaneously ardent and reluctant conjunction of "Signior Mountanto" and "Lady Disdain" helps us to forget about Claudio's deficiencies. Small wonder that King Charles I wrote "Bennedike and Betrice" beneath the title of the play in his copy of Shakespeare's Second Folio and that in the nineteenth century Hector Berlioz dispensed with the other pair altogether in composing his opera *Béatrice et Bénédict*.

Though Don Pedro facilitates Claudio's desire for Hero, it is Beatrice who intrigues him. When he offers to repeat his matchmaking and get her a husband, for a moment he is half-serious in offering her himself. The exchange is one of the loveliest moments anywhere in Shakespearean comedy:

BEATRICE   Good lord, for alliance! Thus goes everyone to the world but I, and I am sunburnt. I may sit in a corner and cry "Hey-ho for a husband!"

DON PEDRO   Lady Beatrice, I will get you one.

BEATRICE   I would rather have one of your father's getting. Hath your grace ne'er a brother like you? Your father got excellent husbands, if a maid could come by them.

DON PEDRO   Will you have me, lady?

BEATRICE   No, my lord, unless I might have another for working days: your grace is too costly to wear every day. But I beseech your grace pardon me. I was born to speak all mirth and no matter.

DON PEDRO   Your silence most offends me, and to be merry best becomes you, for out of question, you were born in a merry hour.

BEATRICE   No, sure, my lord, my mother cried, but then there was a star danced, and under that was I born. Cousins, God give you joy!

Beatrice bookends this encounter with references to the pair who have found love; her merriment in the interim masks a profound loneliness that Don Pedro himself retains at the end of the play. "Prince, thou art sad": says Benedick, "get thee a wife, get thee a wife." Everyone needs to join the dance of matrimony, he suggests—otherwise one will end up a despised exile like Don John. But the note of realism that comes from the grounded prose voice of the sparring partners is sounded one last time, in a lighthearted reference to cuckoldry that simultaneously reactivates and defuses the matter of infidelity that has created all the ado in the first place: "There is no staff more reverend than one tipped with horn." A truce has been called, but the merry and not so merry war between the sexes is always liable to resume. Its only armistice is that of death.

ABOUT THE TEXT

Shakespeare endures through history. He illuminates later times as well as his own. He helps us to understand the human condition. But he cannot do this without a good text of the plays. Without editions there would be no Shakespeare. That is why every twenty years or so throughout the last three centuries there has been a major new edition of his complete works. One aspect of editing is the process of keeping the texts up to date—modernizing the spelling, punctuation, and typography (though not, of course, the actual words), providing explanatory notes in the light of changing educational practices (a generation ago, most of Shakespeare's classical and biblical allusions could be assumed to be generally understood, but now they can't).

But because Shakespeare did not personally oversee the publication of his plays, editors also have to make decisions about the relative authority of the early printed editions. Half the sum of his plays appeared only posthumously, in the elaborately produced First Folio text of 1623, the original "Complete Works" prepared for the press by Shakespeare's fellow actors, the people who knew the plays better than anyone else. The other half had appeared in print in his lifetime, in the more compact and cheaper form of "Quarto" editions, some of which reproduced good quality texts, others of which were to a greater or lesser degree garbled and error-strewn. In the case of a few plays there are hundreds of differences between the Quarto and Folio editions, some of them far from trivial.

If you look at printers' handbooks from the age of Shakespeare, you quickly discover that one of the first rules was that, whenever possible, compositors were recommended to set their type from existing printed books rather than manuscripts. This was the age before mechanical typesetting, where each individual letter had to be picked out by hand from the compositor's case and placed on a stick (upside down and back to front) before being laid on the press. It was an age of murky rush-light and of manuscripts written in a secretary hand that had dozens of different, hard-to-decipher forms. Printers' lives were a lot easier when they were reprinting existing books rather than struggling with handwritten copy. Easily the quickest way to have created the First Folio would have been simply to reprint those eighteen plays that had already appeared in Quarto and only work from manuscript on the other eighteen.

But that is not what happened. Whenever Quartos were used, playhouse "promptbooks" were also consulted and stage directions copied in from them. And in the case of several major plays where a reasonably well-printed Quarto was available, the Folio printers were instructed to work from an alternative, playhouse-derived manuscript. This meant that the whole process of producing the first complete Shakespeare took months, even years, longer than it might have done. But for the men overseeing the project, John Hemings and Henry Condell, friends and fellow actors who had been remembered in Shakespeare's will, the additional labor and cost were worth the effort for the sake of producing an edition that was close to the practice of the theater. They wanted all the plays in print so that people could, as they wrote in their prefatory address to the reader, "read him and again and again," but they also wanted "the great variety of readers" to work from texts that were close to the theater-life for which Shakespeare originally intended them. For this reason, the *RSC Shakespeare*, in both *Complete Works* and individual volumes, uses the Folio as base text wherever possible. Significant Quarto variants are, however, noted in the Textual Notes.

Much Ado About Nothing is one of the plays where the Folio text was printed from the Quarto, though with some reference to a playhouse manuscript, which provided some additional stage directions. Most modern editors use the Quarto as their copy text but import stage directions, act divisions, and some corrections from Folio. Our Folio-led editorial practice follows the reverse procedure, using Folio as copy text, but deploying Quarto as a "control text" that offers assistance in the correction and identification of compositors' errors. Differences are for the most part minor.

The following notes highlight various aspects of the editorial process and indicate conventions used in the text of this edition:

Lists of Parts are supplied in the First Folio for only six plays, not including *Much Ado About Nothing*, so the list here is editorially supplied. Capitals indicate that part of the name which is used for speech headings in the script (thus "BENEDICK a lord from Padua").

Locations are provided by the Folio for only two plays. Eighteenth-century editors, working in an age of elaborately realistic stage sets, were the first to provide detailed locations. Given that Shakespeare wrote for a bare stage and often an imprecise sense of place, we have relegated locations to the explanatory notes at the foot of the page, where they are given at the beginning of each scene where the imaginary location is different from the one before. The whole of *Much Ado* is located in Messina, a city in northeast Sicily.

Act and Scene Divisions were provided in the Folio in a much more thoroughgoing way than in the Quartos. Sometimes, however, they were erroneous or omitted; corrections and additions supplied by editorial tradition are indicated by square brackets. Five-act division is based on a classical model, and act breaks provided the opportunity to replace the candles in the indoor Blackfriars playhouse which the King's Men used after 1608, but Shakespeare did not necessarily think in terms of a five-part structure of dramatic composition. The Folio convention is that a scene ends when the stage is empty. Nowadays, partly under the influence of film, we tend to consider a scene to be a dramatic unit that ends with either a change of imaginary location or a significant passage of time within the narrative. Shakespeare's fluidity of composition accords well with this convention, so in addition to act and scene numbers we provide a *running scene* count in the right margin at the beginning of each new scene, in the typeface used for editorial directions. Where there is a scene break caused by a momentary bare stage, but the location does not change and extra time does not pass, we use the convention *running scene continues*. There is inevitably a degree of editorial judgment in making such calls, but the system is very valuable in suggesting the pace of the plays.

Speakers' Names are often inconsistent in Folio. We have regularized speech headings, but retained an element of deliberate inconsistency in entry directions, in order to give the flavor of Folio.

Verse is indicated by lines that do not run to the right margin and by capitalization of each line. The Folio printers sometimes set verse as prose, and vice versa (either out of misunderstanding or for reasons of space). We have silently corrected in such cases, although in some instances there is ambiguity, in which case we have leaned toward the preservation of Folio layout. Folio sometimes uses contraction ("turnd" rather than "turned") to indicate whether or not the final "-ed" of a past participle is sounded, an area where there is variation for the sake of the five-beat iambic pentameter rhythm. We use the convention of a grave accent to indicate sounding (thus "turnèd" would be two syllables), but would urge actors not to overstress. In cases where one speaker ends with a verse half line and the next begins with the other half of the pentameter, editors since the late eighteenth century have indented the second line. We have abandoned this convention, since the Folio does not use it, and neither did actors' cues in the Shakespearean theater. An exception is made when the second speaker actively interrupts or completes the first speaker's sentence.

Spelling is modernized, but older forms are occasionally maintained where necessary for rhythm or aural effect.

Punctuation in Shakespeare's time was as much rhetorical as grammatical. "Colon" was originally a term for a unit of thought in an argument. The semicolon was a new unit of punctuation (some of the Quartos lack them altogether). We have modernized punctuation throughout, but have given more weight to Folio punctuation than many editors, since, though not Shakespearean, it reflects the usage of his period. In particular, we have used the colon far more than many editors: it is exceptionally useful as a way of indicating how many Shakespearean speeches unfold clause by clause in a developing argument that gives the illusion of enacting the process of thinking in the moment. We have also kept in mind the origin of punctuation in classical times as a way of assisting the actor and orator: the comma suggests the briefest of pauses for breath, the colon a middling one, and a full stop or period a longer pause. Semi-colons, by contrast, belong to an era of punctuation that was only just coming in during Shakespeare's time and that is coming to an end now: we have accordingly only used them where they occur in our copy texts (and not always then). Dashes are sometimes used for parenthetical interjections where the Folio has brackets. They are also used for interruptions and changes in train of thought. Where a change of addressee occurs within a speech, we have used a dash preceded by a period (or occasionally another form of punctuation). Often the identity of the respective addressees is obvious from the context. When it is not, this has been indicated in a marginal stage direction.

Entrances and Exits are fairly thorough in Folio, which has accordingly been followed as faithfully as possible. Where characters are omitted or corrections are necessary, this is indicated by square brackets (e.g. "[*and Attendants*]"). *Exit* is sometimes silently normalized to *Exeunt* and *Manet* anglicized to "remains." We trust Folio positioning of entrances and exits to a greater degree than most editors.

Editorial Stage Directions such as stage business, asides, indications of addressee and of characters' position on the gallery stage are used only sparingly in Folio. Other editions mingle directions of this kind with original Folio and Quarto directions, sometimes marking them by means of square brackets. We have sought to distinguish what could be described as *directorial* interventions of this kind from Folio-style directions (either original or supplied) by placing them in the right margin in a different typeface. There is a degree of subjectivity about which directions are of which kind, but the procedure is intended as a reminder to the reader and the actor that Shakespearean stage directions are often dependent upon editorial inference alone and are not set in stone. We also depart from editorial tradition in sometimes admitting uncertainty and thus printing permissive stage directions, such as an *Aside?* (often a line may be equally effective as an aside or a direct address—it is for each production or reading to make its own decision) or a *may exit* or a piece of business placed between arrows to indicate that it may occur at various different moments within a scene.

Line Numbers in the left margin are editorial, for reference and to key the explanatory and textual notes.

Explanatory Notes at the foot of each page explain allusions and gloss obsolete and difficult words, confusing phraseology, occasional major textual cruces, and so on. Particular attention is given to nonstandard usage, bawdy innuendo, and technical terms (e.g. legal and military language). Where more than one sense is given, commas indicate shades of related meaning, slashes alternative or double meanings.

Textual Notes at the end of the play indicate major departures from the Folio. They take the following form: the reading of our text is given in bold and its source given after an equals sign, with "Q" indicating that it derives from the Quarto of 1600, "F" from the First Folio of 1623, "F2" a reading from the Second Folio of 1632, and "Ed" from the subsequent editorial tradition. The rejected Folio ("F") reading is then given. A selection of Quarto variants and plausible unadopted editorial readings is also included. Thus, for example: "3.1.106, **ta'en** = F. Q = limed." This indicates that at Act 3 Scene 1 line 106 we have retained the Folio reading "ta'en" but that "limed" is an interestingly different reading in the Quarto.

KEY FACTS

MAJOR PARTS: (*with percentage of lines/number of speeches/scenes on stage*) Benedick (17%/134/8), Leonato (13%/120/9), Don Pedro (12%/135/8), Claudio (11%/125/8), Beatrice (10%/106/8), Dogberry (7%/52/4), Hero (5%/44/6), Borachio (5%/23/6), Don John (4%/40/6), Friar Francis (3%/16/2), Margaret (2%/26/3), Antonio (2%/23/4), Ursula (2%/19/3), Conrad (1%/23/1), Verges (1%/18/3), Balthasar (1%/11/2).

LINGUISTIC MEDIUM: 30% verse, 70% prose.

DATE: Late 1598. Not mentioned by Francis Meres in list of Shakespeare's plays in *Palladis Tamis* (registered for publication September 1598), but included part for Will Kemp, who left Shakespeare's acting company in early 1599.

SOURCES: The Hero/Claudio plot of a deception leading to a false supposition of infidelity has many precedents in the sixteenth-century Italian romance tradition; Shakespeare's primary sources seem to have been (1) the tale of Sir Timbreo and Fenicia in Matteo Bandello's *Novelle*, which included characters of Piero King of Aragon and Lionato of Messina (in Italian, 1554, no English translation, but Shakespeare might have known the French translation of Pierre de Belleforest, *Histoires Tragiques*, 1569), and (2) the tale of Renaldo and Ginevra in Ariosto's *Orlando Furioso*, book 5 (English translation by Sir John Harington, 1591). The Beatrice and Benedick plot is Shakespeare's innovation, though witty couples and characters who scorn love only to fall in love themselves have comic precedents, notably in the plays of John Lyly.

TEXT: Quarto published 1600, probably printed from Shakespeare's manuscript or a transcript of it. Generally good quality of printing.

On some occasions, actors' names instead of characters' appear in the speech headings (Kemp for Dogberry and Cowley for Verges). Folio printed from Quarto, though with some reference to a playhouse manuscript; extra stage directions inserted, also act divisions; some corrections and some errors introduced. Our text restores Quarto readings in cases judged to be compositor error, but retains Folio where changes appear to be intentional.

MUCH ADO
ABOUT NOTHING

LIST OF PARTS

DON PEDRO, Prince of Aragon

BENEDICK, a lord from Padua ⎱ companions
CLAUDIO, a lord from Florence ⎰ to Don Pedro

BALTHASAR, a singer, attendant upon Don Pedro

A BOY, servant to Benedick

DON JOHN, illegitimate brother of Don Pedro

BORACHIO ⎱ followers of
CONRAD ⎰ Don John

LEONATO, governor of Messina

INNOGEN, his silent wife

HERO, his daughter

BEATRICE, his niece, an orphan

ANTONIO, an old man, brother of Leonato

MARGARET ⎱ gentlewomen
URSULA ⎰ attendant upon Hero

FRIAR FRANCIS

DOGBERRY, Constable in charge of the Watch

VERGES, Headborough accompanying Dogberry

A SEXTON

WATCHMEN

Attendants and Messengers

Title **NOTHING** puns on "noting" (i.e. musical notation/observation) and on "no thing" (i.e. vagina) **List of parts Headborough** parish officer

Act 1 Scene 1

*Enter Leonato Governor of Messina, Innogen his wife, Hero his daugh-
ter and Beatrice his niece, with a Messenger*

LEONATO   I learn in this letter that Don Peter   *Shows a letter*
of Aragon comes this night to Messina.

MESSENGER   He is very near by this: he was not three leagues off
when I left him.

5   LEONATO   How many gentlemen have you lost in this action?

MESSENGER   But few of any sort, and none of name.

LEONATO   A victory is twice itself when the achiever brings
home full numbers. I find here that Don Peter hath bestowed
much honour on a young Florentine called Claudio.

10   MESSENGER   Much deserved on his part and equally remembered by Don Pedro. He hath borne himself beyond the
promise of his age, doing in the figure of a lamb the feats of a
lion. He hath indeed better bettered expectation than you
must expect of me to tell you how.

15   LEONATO   He hath an uncle here in Messina will be very much
glad of it.

MESSENGER   I have already delivered him letters, and there
appears much joy in him, even so much that joy could not
show itself modest enough without a badge of bitterness.

20   LEONATO   Did he break out into tears?

MESSENGER   In great measure.

LEONATO   A kind overflow of kindness. There are no faces
truer than those that are so washed. How much better is it to
weep at joy than to joy at weeping!

1.1 Location: Messina, city in northeast Sicily   Innogen a character who never speaks:
she may have been created in the writing and omitted in the performance   **Hero** named after
the loyal lover of Leander who killed herself after he drowned swimming the Hellespont to see
her   **Beatrice** from the Latin *beatrix* meaning "she who blesses"   **1 Don Peter** i.e. Don
Pedro   **2 Aragon** kingdom in northern Spain   **3 leagues** a league is about three miles
5 action battle   **6 sort** high rank   **name** reputation/distinction/noble status   **9 Florentine**
person from the city of Florence, in northwest Italy   **11 remembered** rewarded   **12 figure**
form/image   **19 badge of bitterness** i.e. the uncle's **tears** that demonstrate that his joy is
modest   **badge** badge worn by a nobleman's servant (a sign of inferiority and humility)
22 kind natural   **23 truer** more genuine/virtuous/honest

25 **BEATRICE**   I pray you, is Signior Mountanto returned from the wars or no?

MESSENGER   I know none of that name, lady: there was none such in the army of any sort.

LEONATO   What is he that you ask for, niece?

30 **HERO**   My cousin means Signior Benedick of Padua.

MESSENGER   O, he's returned, and as pleasant as ever he was.

BEATRICE   He set up his bills here in Messina and challenged Cupid at the flight: and my uncle's fool, reading the challenge, subscribed for Cupid and challenged him at the

35 bird-bolt. I pray you, how many hath he killed and eaten in these wars? But how many hath he killed? For indeed I promised to eat all of his killing.

LEONATO   Faith, niece, you tax Signior Benedick too much, but he'll be meet with you, I doubt it not.

40 **MESSENGER**   He hath done good service, lady, in these wars.

BEATRICE   You had musty victual and he hath holp to eat it: he's a very valiant trencherman, he hath an excellent stomach.

MESSENGER   And a good soldier too, lady.

45 **BEATRICE**   And a good soldier to a lady. But what is he to a lord?

MESSENGER   A lord to a lord, a man to a man, stuffed with all honourable virtues.

BEATRICE   It is so indeed, he is no less than a stuffed man. But for the stuffing — well, we are all mortal.

---

25 Mountanto from the fencing term "montanto," an upward thrust, suggestive of the verbal dueling Benedick engages in with Beatrice (there may also be a sexual play on "mount on to")   **30 Benedick** from the Latin *benedictus* meaning "blessed"   **Padua** northern Italian city known for its university   **31 pleasant** amusing/merry   **32 bills** notices advertising a public entertainment   **33 Cupid** god of love who shot love-inducing arrows into people's hearts   **flight** archery with flight-arrows (light, well-feathered arrows)   **fool** probably a professional fool employed by Leonato for entertainment   **34 subscribed for** took up the challenge on behalf of   **35 bird-bolt** blunt arrow safe enough to be used by children or fools   **38 Faith** in faith (i.e. truly)   **tax** censure/disparage   **39 meet** even   **41 musty victual** moldy, stale food   **41 holp** helped   **42 valiant trencherman** hearty eater (**valiant** plays on the sense of "courageous" as Beatrice implies that the only thing Benedick tackles with boldness is food) a **trencher** is a wooden plate   **43 stomach** appetite (puns on the sense of "courage")   **45 he to** he compared to   **46 stuffed** full/replete   **48 stuffed man** figure stuffed to resemble a man/man sated with food

50 **LEONATO**   You must not, sir, mistake my niece. There is a kind
of merry war betwixt Signior Benedick and her: they never
meet but there's a skirmish of wit between them.

BEATRICE   Alas, he gets nothing by that. In our last conflict
four of his five wits went halting off, and now is the whole
55 man governed with one: so that if he have wit enough to
keep himself warm, let him bear it for a difference between
himself and his horse, for it is all the wealth that he hath left
to be known a reasonable creature. Who is his companion
now? He hath every month a new sworn brother.

60 **MESSENGER**   Is't possible?

BEATRICE   Very easily possible: he wears his faith but as the
fashion of his hat — it ever changes with the next block.

MESSENGER   I see, lady, the gentleman is not in your books.

BEATRICE   No. An he were, I would burn my study. But I pray
65 you, who is his companion? Is there no young squarer now
that will make a voyage with him to the devil?

MESSENGER   He is most in the company of the right noble
Claudio.

BEATRICE   O lord, he will hang upon him like a disease: he is
70 sooner caught than the pestilence, and the taker runs
presently mad. God help the noble Claudio. If he have caught
the Benedick, it will cost him a thousand pound ere he be
cured.

MESSENGER   I will hold friends with you, lady.

75 **BEATRICE**   Do, good friend.

LEONATO   You'll ne'er run mad, niece.

BEATRICE   No, not till a hot January.

MESSENGER   Don Pedro is approached.

---

51 betwixt between   **54 five wits** five mental faculties (imagination, memory, fantasy,
estimation, common sense)   **halting** limping   **56 difference** in heraldry the sign that
distinguished the junior branch of a family (in this case Benedick)   **58 known . . . creature**
identified as one in possession of the faculty of reason (i.e. human)   **59 sworn brother**
brother-in-arms (one who swore brotherly loyalty and support in combat to a friend)   **61 faith**
fidelity/oath of brotherhood   **62 block** mold for shaping new fashions of hats   **63 books**
good books, favor   **64 An** if   **65 squarer** brawler/quarrelsome rogue   **70 pestilence**
plague/disease   **71 presently** immediately   **72 ere** before   **74 hold** remain   **76 run mad** i.e.
by catching (falling in love with) **the Benedick**

Enter Don Pedro, Claudio, Benedick, Balthasar and John the bastard

DON PEDRO   Good Signior Leonato, are you come to meet your
80   trouble? The fashion of the world is to avoid cost, and you
            encounter it.

LEONATO   Never came trouble to my house in the likeness of
            your grace, for trouble being gone, comfort should remain.
            But when you depart from me, sorrow abides and happiness
85   takes his leave.

DON PEDRO   You embrace your charge too willingly. I think this
            is your daughter.

LEONATO   Her mother hath many times told me so.

BENEDICK   Were you in doubt, sir, that you asked her?

90   LEONATO   Signior Benedick, no, for then were you a child.

DON PEDRO   You have it full, Benedick. We may guess by this
            what you are, being a man. Truly the lady fathers herself. Be
            happy lady, for you are like an honourable father.

BENEDICK   If Signior Leonato be her father, she would not have
95   his head on her shoulders for all Messina, as like him as
            she is.   *Don Pedro and Leonato talk aside*

BEATRICE   I wonder that you will still be talking, Signior
            Benedick: nobody marks you.

BENEDICK   What, my dear Lady Disdain! Are you yet living?

100   BEATRICE   Is it possible disdain should die while she hath such
            meet food to feed it as Signior Benedick? Courtesy itself must
            convert to disdain, if you come in her presence.

BENEDICK   Then is courtesy a turncoat. But it is certain I am
            loved of all ladies, only you excepted: and I would I could find
105   in my heart that I had not a hard heart, for truly I love none.

BEATRICE   A dear happiness to women: they would else have
            been troubled with a pernicious suitor. I thank God and my

---

80 trouble i.e. Don Pedro and his companions who will put Leonato, as host, to the cost and effort of entertaining them   **fashion** usual practice   **82 likeness** appearance   **86 charge** responsibility/expense   **90 for . . . child** i.e. so I had nothing to fear from a seducer such as you   **91 have it full** have been amply answered   **92 fathers herself** i.e. shows who her father is through her resemblance to him   **95 head** i.e. with its white hair   **98 marks** pays attention to   **101 meet** suitable (puns on "meat," which meant food generally)   **103 turncoat** one who changes their appearance or loyalties   **104 would** wish   **106 dear happiness** great good fortune   **107 pernicious** ruinous/wicked

cold blood, I am of your humour for that. I had rather hear
my dog bark at a crow than a man swear he loves me.

110 BENEDICK   God keep your ladyship still in that mind, so some
gentleman or other shall scape a predestinate scratched face.

BEATRICE   Scratching could not make it worse an 'twere such
a face as yours were.

BENEDICK   Well, you are a rare parrot-teacher.

115 BEATRICE   A bird of my tongue is better than a beast of yours.

BENEDICK   I would my horse had the speed of your tongue, and
so good a continuer. But keep your way, a God's name, I have
done.

BEATRICE   You always end with a jade's trick. I know you of old.

120 DON PEDRO   That is the sum of all, Leonato.—   *To the others*
Signior Claudio and Signior Benedick, my dear friend
Leonato hath invited you all. I tell him we shall stay here at
the least a month, and he heartily prays some occasion may
detain us longer. I dare swear he is no hypocrite, but prays
125 from his heart.

LEONATO   If you swear, my lord, you shall   *To Don John*
not be forsworn.— Let me bid you welcome, my lord. Being
reconciled to the prince your brother, I owe you all duty.

DON JOHN   I thank you. I am not of many words, but I thank
130 you.

LEONATO   Please it your grace lead on?

DON PEDRO   Your hand, Leonato. We will go together.

Exeunt all but Benedick and Claudio

CLAUDIO   Benedick, didst thou note the daughter of Signior
Leonato?

135 BENEDICK   I noted her not, but I looked on her.

CLAUDIO   Is she not a modest young lady?

---

108 **humour for that** disposition on that issue   111 **scape** escape   **predestinate** inevitable
112 **an 'twere** if it were   114 **rare parrot-teacher** marvelous chatterer (literally, one who
repeats herself as if teaching a parrot)   115 **beast of yours** i.e. because beasts do not have the
power of speech   117 **so . . . continuer** was able to go on for so long   119 **jade** overused or
worthless horse/whore   **trick** knack (of stopping abruptly)/sexual act   127 **forsworn** proved
wrong   **Being** as you are   135 **noted her not** did not pay her any special attention

BENEDICK   Do you question me as an honest man should do, for my simple true judgement? Or would you have me speak after my custom, as being a professed tyrant to their sex?

140   **CLAUDIO**   No, I pray thee speak in sober judgement.

BENEDICK   Why, i'faith, methinks she's too low for a high praise, too brown for a fair praise, and too little for a great praise. Only this commendation I can afford her, that were she other than she is, she were unhandsome, and being no

145   other but as she is, I do not like her.

CLAUDIO   Thou think'st I am in sport. I pray thee tell me truly how thou lik'st her.

BENEDICK   Would you buy her, that you inquire after her?

CLAUDIO   Can the world buy such a jewel?

150   **BENEDICK**   Yea, and a case to put it into. But speak you this with a sad brow? Or do you play the flouting jack, to tell us Cupid is a good hare-finder and Vulcan a rare carpenter? Come, in what key shall a man take you to go in the song?

CLAUDIO   In mine eye, she is the sweetest lady that ever I

155   looked on.

BENEDICK   I can see yet without spectacles and I see no such matter. There's her cousin, an she were not possessed with a fury, exceeds her as much in beauty as the first of May doth the last of December. But I hope you have no intent to turn

160   husband, have you?

CLAUDIO   I would scarce trust myself, though I had sworn the contrary, if Hero would be my wife.

BENEDICK   Is't come to this? In faith, hath not the world one man but he will wear his cap with suspicion? Shall I never

---

139 after my custom in my usual way/as is my habit   **141 low** short   **high** elevated/ elaborate (puns on the sense of "tall")   **142 brown** brown-haired   **fair** fine/flattering (puns on the sense of "light-complexioned/pale-haired")   **143 afford** offer/allow   **146 in sport** joking, being playful   **150 case** plays on the sense of "vagina" (jewel could also mean "virginity")   **151 sad** serious   **flouting jack** mocking rascal   **152 hare-finder** one with eyesight sharp enough to spot a quick hare (the mockery of a flouting jack as Cupid was blind)   **Vulcan** Roman god of fire, traditionally depicted as a blacksmith   **153 go** be in tune/ harmonize   **158 fury** fierce passion/rage/avenging spirit   **164 wear . . . suspicion** get married and invite suspicion when wearing his cap that it covers horns (signs of being a cuckold — i.e. having an unfaithful wife)

165   see a bachelor of threescore again? Go to, i'faith, an thou
           wilt needs thrust thy neck into a yoke, wear the print of it
           and sigh away Sundays. Look, Don Pedro is returned to seek
           you.

           Enter Don Pedro [and] John the bastard

           DON PEDRO   What secret hath held you here, that you followed
170   not to Leonato's?

           BENEDICK   I would your grace would constrain me to tell.

           DON PEDRO   I charge thee on thy allegiance.

           BENEDICK   You hear, Count Claudio. I can be secret as a dumb
           man, I would have you think so. But on my allegiance, mark
175   you this, on my allegiance — he is in love. With who? Now
           that is your grace's part. Mark how short his answer is: with
           Hero, Leonato's short daughter.

           CLAUDIO   If this were so, so were it uttered.

           BENEDICK   Like the old tale, my lord: 'It is not so, nor 'twas not
180   so, but indeed, God forbid it should be so!'

           CLAUDIO   If my passion change not shortly, God forbid it
           should be otherwise.

           DON PEDRO   Amen, if you love her, for the lady is very well
           worthy.

185   CLAUDIO   You speak this to fetch me in, my lord.

           DON PEDRO   By my troth, I speak my thought.

           CLAUDIO   And in faith, my lord, I spoke mine.

           BENEDICK   And by my two faiths and troths, my lord, I spoke
           mine.

190   CLAUDIO   That I love her, I feel.

           DON PEDRO   That she is worthy, I know.

---

165 threescore sixty   **Go to** away with you (an expression of impatience)   **166 yoke** wooden
apparatus worn on the neck of a captive and used to subdue and prevent escape; a similar
device is used to couple oxen together for plowing   **print** imprint   **167 sigh away Sundays**
which must now be spent dutifully with one's wife   **171 constrain** compel   **172 charge** order
176 part i.e. to ask with who?   **178 If . . . uttered** if this were indeed the case it would be
uttered in this way   **179 'It . . . so!'** the quotation is supposedly from an old story in which it is
uttered by a woman who has discovered that her lover is a robber   **185 fetch me in** trick me
(into confessing)   **186 troth** good faith   **188 my . . . troths** Benedick owes loyalty to both
Claudio, his sworn brother, and to Don Pedro, prince and military leader

BENEDICK   That I neither feel how she should be loved, nor know how she should be worthy, is the opinion that fire cannot melt out of me: I will die in it at the stake.

195   DON PEDRO   Thou wast ever an obstinate heretic in the despite of beauty.

CLAUDIO   And never could maintain his part but in the force of his will.

BENEDICK   That a woman conceived me, I thank her. That she

200   brought me up, I likewise give her most humble thanks. But that I will have a recheat winded in my forehead, or hang my bugle in an invisible baldrick, all women shall pardon me. Because I will not do them the wrong to mistrust any, I will do myself the right to trust none. And the fine is — for the

205   which I may go the finer — I will live a bachelor.

DON PEDRO   I shall see thee, ere I die, look pale with love.

BENEDICK   With anger, with sickness, or with hunger, my lord, not with love: prove that ever I lose more blood with love than I will get again with drinking, pick out mine eyes with a

210   ballad-maker's pen, and hang me up at the door of a brothel-house for the sign of blind Cupid.

DON PEDRO   Well, if ever thou dost fall from this faith, thou wilt prove a notable argument.

BENEDICK   If I do, hang me in a bottle like a cat and shoot at

215   me, and he that hits me, let him be clapped on the shoulder and called Adam.

---

194 stake a wooden post to which **heretics** were tied for burning   **195 heretic** one who holds blasphemous opinions or whose ideas are in opposition to accepted views   **despite** contempt **197 maintain** justify   **in . . . will** by willful obstinacy   **201 recheat** notes sounded on a horn for calling hounds together at a hunt (here symbolic of the cuckolded husband's horns) **winded** blown   **202 bugle** horn (here suggestive of both the cuckold's horn and the penis) **baldrick** shoulder belt used to hold a **bugle** (also suggestive of the vagina, particularly as it is invisible — i.e. hidden)   **204 fine** conclusion   **205 finer** more finely dressed (without a wife to support)   **208 prove** i.e. should you prove   **more . . . drinking** the heavy sighs brought on by love were thought to drain the heart of blood, while drinking wine was believed to fortify the blood flow   **210 ballad-maker** writer of ballads (songs of love)   **hang . . . Cupid** brothels had signs painted on their walls   **211 for** in the place of   **213 argument** topic for discussion **214 hang . . . at me** cats were sometimes suspended in baskets (bottles) and used for archery practice   **216 Adam** a reference to Adam Bell, a famous archer

DON PEDRO   Well, as try. 'In time the savage bull doth bear the yoke.'

BENEDICK   The savage bull may, but if ever the sensible
220   Benedick bear it, pluck off the bull's horns and set them in my forehead, and let me be vilely painted, and in such great letters as they write 'Here is good horse to hire', let them signify under my sign 'Here you may see Benedick the married man.'

225   **CLAUDIO**   If this should ever happen, thou wouldst be horn-mad.

DON PEDRO   Nay, if Cupid have not spent all his quiver in Venice, thou wilt quake for this shortly.

BENEDICK   I look for an earthquake too, then.

230   **DON PEDRO**   Well, you will temporize with the hours. In the meantime, good Signior Benedick, repair to Leonato's, commend me to him, and tell him I will not fail him at supper, for indeed he hath made great preparation.

BENEDICK   I have almost matter enough in me for such an
235   embassage, and so I commit you—

CLAUDIO   To the tuition of God. From my house, if I had it—

DON PEDRO   The sixth of July. Your loving friend, Benedick.

BENEDICK   Nay, mock not, mock not; the body of your discourse is sometime guarded with fragments, and the guards are but
240   slightly basted on neither. Ere you flout old ends any further, examine your conscience. And so I leave you.   *Exit*

---

217 try tell   **'In . . . yoke'** a proverb that may have been popularized by its use in Thomas Kyd's play *The Spanish Tragedy*   **220 pluck . . . forehead** another reference to cuckoldry
221 in . . . write in lettering that is as big as that usually used to write   **223 sign** sign used to advertise a sideshow or public spectacle which consisted of a picture of the attraction with a description written under it   **225 horn-mad** completely mad/enraged (like a charging bull or a furious cuckold)   **227 spent . . . Venice** shot all of his arrows in Venice, famous for its sexual freedom and prostitution (**spent** puns on its sense of "to ejaculate" and arrows are phallic)   **quiver** case for arrows (puns on quake)   **229 look for** await/expect
230 temporize . . . hours become more temperate (milder) with time/waste time or procrastinate (**hours** may pun on "whores")   **232 fail him** i.e. fail to attend   **234 matter** wit/sense   **235 embassage** message/mission   **236 To . . . Benedick** Claudio and Don Pedro imitate the conventional ending of a letter   **tuition** care/guidance   **238 body** basic material
239 guarded with fragments adorned with scraps   **guards . . . neither** ornamental scraps are only loosely stitched on anyway   **240 flout old ends** mock (me) with old tags of letters/ **fragments** of cloth

CLAUDIO   My liege, your Highness now may do me good.

DON PEDRO   My love is thine to teach: teach it but how,
And thou shalt see how apt it is to learn
245   Any hard lesson that may do thee good.

CLAUDIO   Hath Leonato any son, my lord?

DON PEDRO   No child but Hero, she's his only heir.
Dost thou affect her, Claudio?

CLAUDIO   O, my lord,
250   When you went onward on this ended action,
I looked upon her with a soldier's eye
That liked, but had a rougher task in hand
Than to drive liking to the name of love.
But now I am returned, and that war-thoughts
255   Have left their places vacant, in their rooms
Come thronging soft and delicate desires,
All prompting me how fair young Hero is,
Saying I liked her ere I went to wars.

DON PEDRO   Thou wilt be like a lover presently
260   And tire the hearer with a book of words.
If thou dost love fair Hero, cherish it,
And I will break with her and with her father,
And thou shalt have her. Wast not to this end
That thou began'st to twist so fine a story?

265   CLAUDIO   How sweetly you do minister to love,
That know love's grief by his complexion!
But lest my liking might too sudden seem,
I would have salved it with a longer treatise.

DON PEDRO   What need the bridge much broader than the flood?
270   The fairest grant is the necessity.
Look, what will serve is fit: 'tis once, thou lovest,

---

242 do me good help me   244 apt quick/ready   248 affect love/favor   250 ended action
recently ended military action   254 that now that   257 prompting reminding/urging
260 book of words lovers traditionally wrote lots of poetry   262 break broach the matter
264 twist weave   265 minister to tend to/administer a cure to   268 salved accounted
for/applied soothing ointment to   treatise narrative   269 flood river   270 The . . . necessity
the best gift is the gift that is needed   271 what . . . fit whatever is useful and will suffice is
suitable   'tis once once and for all

And I will fit thee with the remedy.
I know we shall have revelling tonight.
I will assume thy part in some disguise
275   And tell fair Hero I am Claudio,
And in her bosom I'll unclasp my heart,
And take her hearing prisoner with the force
And strong encounter of my amorous tale.
Then after, to her father will I break,
280   And the conclusion is, she shall be thine.
In practice let us put it presently.   *Exeunt*

[Act 1 Scene 2]   *running scene 2*

Enter Leonato and an old man [Antonio] brother to Leonato [meeting]

LEONATO   How now, brother, where is my cousin, your son?
Hath he provided this music?

ANTONIO   He is very busy about it. But brother, I can tell you
strange news that you yet dreamt not of.

5   LEONATO   Are they good?

ANTONIO   As the event stamps them, but they have a good
cover: they show well outward. The prince and Count
Claudio, walking in a thick-pleached alley in my orchard,
were thus overheard by a man of mine: the prince discovered
10   to Claudio that he loved my niece your daughter and meant
to acknowledge it this night in a dance, and if he found her
accordant, he meant to take the present time by the top and
instantly break with you of it.

LEONATO   Hath the fellow any wit that told you this?

15   ANTONIO   A good sharp fellow. I will send for him, and question
him yourself.

---

272 fit supply   276 in her bosom privately   unclasp open (as if undoing the clasps of a
book)   278 encounter conversational address/military assault   1.2 1 cousin a general term
for any relative or close friend   5 they i.e. the news   6 As . . . them as the outcome (event)
determines/proves   stamps prints (the book metaphor continues with cover)   7 show well
outward look promising   8 thick-pleached alley walk overarched by densely intertwining
branches   9 discovered revealed   12 accordant of the same opinion/agreeable
take . . . top seize the opportunity   14 wit good sense/acumen

LEONATO   No, no; we will hold it as a dream till it appear itself.
But I will acquaint my daughter withal, that she may be the
better prepared for an answer, if peradventure this be true.
20   Go you and tell her of it.

[Enter Attendants]

Cousins, you know what you have to do.— O, I cry you
mercy, friend, go you with me and I will use your skill.—
Good cousin, have a care this busy time.

[Act 1 Scene 3]   running scene 3

Enter Sir [Don] John the Bastard and Conrad his companion

CONRAD   What the goodyear, my lord, why are you thus out
of measure sad?

DON JOHN   There is no measure in the occasion that breeds,
therefore the sadness is without limit.

5   CONRAD   You should hear reason.

DON JOHN   And when I have heard it, what blessing bringeth it?

CONRAD   If not a present remedy, yet a patient sufferance.

DON JOHN   I wonder that thou — being as thou sayest thou art,
born under Saturn — goest about to apply a moral medicine
10   to a mortifying mischief. I cannot hide what I am: I must be
sad when I have cause, and smile at no man's jests, eat when
I have stomach, and wait for no man's leisure, sleep when I
am drowsy, and tend on no man's business, laugh when I am
merry, and claw no man in his humour.

15   CONRAD   Yea, but you must not make the full show of this till
you may do it without controlment. You have of late stood
out against your brother, and he hath ta'en you newly into

17 hold regard   appear manifests   18 withal with it   19 peradventure perhaps
21 cry you mercy beg your pardon   22 friend i.e. one of the attendants, a musician
1.3 1 What the goodyear what the devil   out of measure immoderately
3 measure proportion/moderation/limit   occasion that breeds circumstances
that provoke (my sadness)   7 present immediate   sufferance endurance
9 Saturn those born under the influence of Saturn were thought to be naturally morose
and melancholy   10 mortifying mischief fatal disease   13 tend on attend/see to
14 claw soothe/flatter   16 controlment restraint   stood ... brother i.e. opposed
Don Pedro in the recent war

his grace, where it is impossible you should take true root but
by the fair weather that you make yourself. It is needful that
you frame the season for your own harvest.

DON JOHN   I had rather be a canker in a hedge than a rose in his
grace, and it better fits my blood to be disdained of all than to
fashion a carriage to rob love from any. In this — though I
cannot be said to be a flattering honest man — it must not be
denied but I am a plain-dealing villain. I am trusted with a
muzzle and enfranchised with a clog: therefore I have
decreed not to sing in my cage. If I had my mouth, I would
bite. If I had my liberty, I would do my liking. In the
meantime, let me be that I am, and seek not to alter me.

CONRAD   Can you make no use of your discontent?

DON JOHN   I will make all use of it, for I use it only. Who comes
here?

Enter Borachio

What news, Borachio?

BORACHIO   I came yonder from a great supper. The prince your
brother is royally entertained by Leonato, and I can give you
intelligence of an intended marriage.

DON JOHN   Will it serve for any model to build mischief on?
What is he for a fool that betroths himself to unquietness?

BORACHIO   Marry it is your brother's right hand.

DON JOHN   Who, the most exquisite Claudio?

BORACHIO   Even he.

DON JOHN   A proper squire! And who, and who? Which way
looks he?

BORACHIO   Marry, on Hero, the daughter and heir of Leonato.

DON JOHN   A very forward March-chick. How came you to this?

---

18 grace favor   **20 frame** create   **21 canker** wild rose (puns on the sense of "cancer")
22 blood disposition/illegitimate status   **of** by   **23 fashion a carriage** invent a
demeanor/behavior   **25 trusted . . . muzzle** like a fierce dog, only trusted when wearing a
muzzle   **26 enfranchised . . . clog** only given liberty with a heavy block of wood tied to my leg
31 use it only am always discontented/discontent is my only resource   **Borachio** from the
Spanish **borracho** meaning "drunkard"   **37 model** architectural plan   **38 unquietness** i.e. a
troubled life   **40 exquisite** accomplished/perfect   **42 proper squire** fine lover (the tone is
contemptuous)   **45 forward** precocious/eager/ardent/presumptuous   **March-chick** very
young thing (could apply to Hero or Claudio, though Claudio seems likely)

BORACHIO   Being entertained for a perfumer, as I was smoking a musty room, comes me the prince and Claudio, hand in hand in sad conference. I whipped me behind the arras and there heard it agreed upon that the prince should woo Hero for

50   himself, and having obtained her, give her to Count Claudio.

DON JOHN   Come, come, let us thither: this may prove food to my displeasure. That young start-up hath all the glory of my overthrow. If I can cross him any way, I bless myself every way. You are both sure, and will assist me?

55   CONRAD   To the death, my lord.

DON JOHN   Let us to the great supper. Their cheer is the greater that I am subdued. Would the cook were of my mind. Shall we go prove what's to be done?

BORACHIO   We'll wait upon your lordship.   *Exeunt*

Act 2 Scene 1   *running scene 4*

Enter Leonato, [Antonio] his brother, [Innogen] his wife, Hero his daughter [attended by Margaret and Ursula], and Beatrice his niece and a Kinsman

LEONATO   Was not Count John here at supper?

ANTONIO   I saw him not.

BEATRICE   How tartly that gentleman looks. I never can see him but I am heart-burned an hour after.

5   HERO   He is of a very melancholy disposition.

BEATRICE   He were an excellent man that were made just in the midway between him and Benedick: the one is too like an image and says nothing, and the other too like my lady's eldest son, evermore tattling.

---

46 **entertained . . . perfumer** employed as burner of sweet-smelling herbs in the rooms of a house   **smoking** perfuming   48 **sad** serious   **arras** large tapestry hung on a wall for insulation (with sufficient space behind it for a man to conceal himself)   52 **start-up** upstart 53 **overthrow** i.e. defeat in the war   **cross** thwart   54 **sure** reliable, loyal   56 **cheer** merriment, joy   57 **subdued** low in spirits/conquered   58 **prove** put to the test/find out by experience   **2.1 Kinsman** like Innogen, a "ghost" character who does not speak 3 **tartly** sourly, bitterly   4 **am heart-burned** suffer heartburn (indigestion)   8 **image** statue **my . . . son** a widow's eldest son (traditionally a favored and indulged child)

10 **LEONATO**   Then half Signior Benedick's tongue in Count
John's mouth, and half Count John's melancholy in Signior
Benedick's face —

BEATRICE   With a good leg and a good foot, uncle, and money
enough in his purse, such a man would win any woman in
15 the world, if he could get her good will.

LEONATO   By my troth, niece, thou wilt never get thee a
husband if thou be so shrewd of thy tongue.

ANTONIO   In faith, she's too curst.

BEATRICE   Too curst is more than curst. I shall lessen God's
20 sending that way, for it is said: 'God sends a curst cow short
horns', but to a cow too curst he sends none.

LEONATO   So, by being too curst, God will send you no horns.

BEATRICE   Just, if he send me no husband, for the which
blessing I am at him upon my knees every morning and
25 evening. Lord, I could not endure a husband with a beard on
his face! I had rather lie in the woollen.

LEONATO   You may light upon a husband that hath no beard.

BEATRICE   What should I do with him? Dress him in my
apparel and make him my waiting-gentlewoman? He that
30 hath a beard is more than a youth, and he that hath no
beard is less than a man: and he that is more than a youth is
not for me, and he that is less than a man, I am not for him.
Therefore I will even take sixpence in earnest of the
bearward and lead his apes into hell.

35 **LEONATO**   Well then, go you into hell.

BEATRICE   No, but to the gate, and there will the devil meet me
like an old cuckold with horns on his head, and say 'Get you
to heaven, Beatrice, get you to heaven, here's no place for
you maids.' So deliver I up my apes, and away to Saint Peter,

---

13 good leg i.e. shapely   **17 shrewd** mischievous/sharp   **18 curst** perverse/shrewish
22 horns in her response Beatrice plays on the senses of "cuckold's horns" and "penis"
23 Just exactly right   **26 the woollen** rough wool blankets (rather than a husband with a
scratchy beard)   **29 apparel** clothing   **33 in earnest** as an advance payment   **the . . . hell**
proverbially, the fate of an old maid was to lead apes in hell   **34 bearward** keeper of bears
(and possibly apes)   **39 maids** virgins   **Saint Peter** heaven's gatekeeper

40   for the heavens. He shows me where the bachelors sit, and
there live we as merry as the day is long.

ANTONIO   Well, niece, I trust you will be ruled   *To Hero*
by your father.

BEATRICE   Yes, faith, it is my cousin's duty to make curtsy and
45   say 'Father, as it please you': but yet for all that, cousin, let
him be a handsome fellow, or else make another curtsy and
say 'Father, as it please me.'

LEONATO   Well, niece, I hope to see you one day fitted with a
husband.

50   BEATRICE   Not till God make men of some other metal than
earth. Would it not grieve a woman to be overmastered with
a piece of valiant dust? To make account of her life to a clod
of wayward marl? No, uncle, I'll none: Adam's sons are my
brethren, and truly I hold it a sin to match in my kindred.

55   LEONATO   Daughter, remember what I told you: *To Hero*
if the prince do solicit you in that kind, you know your
answer.

BEATRICE   The fault will be in the music, cousin, if you be not
wooed in good time. If the prince be too important, tell him
60   there is measure in everything, and so dance out the answer.
For hear me, Hero: wooing, wedding and repenting is as a
Scotch jig, a measure and a cinque-pace: the first suit is hot
and hasty like a Scotch jig, and full as fantastical, the wedding
mannerly-modest as a measure, full of state and ancientry,

---

40 for the heavens a mild exclamation, but also with the sense of "in order to get to heaven" or "away to Saint Peter as one who is in charge of entry to heaven"   **bachelors** unmarried people of both sexes   **48 fitted** supplied (with suggestion of a vagina filled with a penis) **50 metal** material (puns on "mettle" meaning "temperament")   **51 earth** a reference to the Christian notion that God made man from dust (whereas women were formed from one of Adam's ribs)   **53 wayward marl** unreasonable/changeable clay   **54 brethren** brothers **match . . . kindred** marry a relative   **56 solicit** entreat/woo   **kind** manner (i.e. with talk of marriage)   **59 in good time** soon/in time to the music   **important** pressing, urgent **60 measure** moderation (puns on the dance known as a measure)   **62 Scotch jig** a lively dance   **measure** a slow, stately dance   **cinque-pace** a lively dance involving five (**cinque**) steps (**pas**) and pronounced "sink-a-pace" (thus leading to Beatrice's pun on **sink**)   **suit** wooing   **hot** passionate/vigorous   **63 fantastical** imaginative/full of wild movements **64 mannerly-modest** decorously moderate   **state and ancientry** ceremonious dignity and old-fashioned formality

65   and then comes repentance and, with his bad legs, falls into
the cinque-pace faster and faster, till he sinks into his grave.

LEONATO   Cousin, you apprehend passing shrewdly.

BEATRICE   I have a good eye, uncle, I can see a church by
daylight.

70 LEONATO   The revellers are entering, brother. Make good
room.   *All put on their masks*

Enter Prince [Don] Pedro, Claudio, and Benedick, and Balthasar, [Don]
John, [Borachio, Margaret, Ursula and other] Masquers with a drum

                                            Couples pair up and begin dancing

DON PEDRO   Lady, will you walk a bout with your friend?

HERO   So you walk softly, and look sweetly, and say
nothing, I am yours for the walk, and especially when I walk
75   away.

DON PEDRO   With me in your company?

HERO   I may say so when I please.

DON PEDRO   And when please you to say so?

HERO   When I like your favour, for God defend the lute
80   should be like the case.

DON PEDRO   My visor is Philemon's roof, within the house is Jove.

HERO   Why then your visor should be thatched.

DON PEDRO   Speak low, if you speak love.   *They dance aside*

BALTHASAR   Well, I would you did like me.

85 MARGARET   So would not I for your own sake, for I have many ill
qualities.

BALTHASAR   Which is one?

MARGARET   I say my prayers aloud.

BALTHASAR   I love you the better. The hearers may cry 'Amen'.

90 MARGARET   God match me with a good dancer.

BALTHASAR   Amen.

---

65 **bad legs** tottering or perhaps gout-ridden legs resulting from old age   **67 apprehend
passing shrewdly** interpret things very severely/discern things very sharply   **72 friend**
friend/lover   **73 So** so long as   **79 favour** face   **80 case** a metaphorical reference to Don
Pedro's (apparently unattractive) mask   **81 visor** mask   **Philemon's . . . Jove** the peasant
Philemon entertained a disguised Jove (king of the gods) in his humble cottage
82 thatched i.e. like Philemon's cottage — perhaps a suggestion that Don Pedro is bald or
balding, or that his mask lacks hair

MARGARET   And God keep him out of my sight when the dance
is done. Answer, clerk.

BALTHASAR   No more words: the clerk is answered.   *They dance aside*

95   URSULA   I know you well enough, you are Signior Antonio.

ANTONIO   At a word, I am not.

URSULA   I know you by the waggling of your head.

ANTONIO   To tell you true, I counterfeit him.

URSULA   You could never do him so ill-well, unless you were
100   the very man. Here's his dry hand up and down: you are he,
you are he.

ANTONIO   At a word, I am not.

URSULA   Come, come, do you think I do not know you by your
excellent wit? Can virtue hide itself? Go to, mum, you are he.
105   Graces will appear, and there's an end.   *They dance aside*

BEATRICE   Will you not tell me who told you so?

BENEDICK   No, you shall pardon me.

BEATRICE   Nor will you not tell me who you are?

BENEDICK   Not now.

110   BEATRICE   That I was disdainful, and that I had my good wit
out of the 'Hundred Merry Tales' — well, this was Signior
Benedick that said so.

BENEDICK   What's he?

BEATRICE   I am sure you know him well enough.

115   BENEDICK   Not I, believe me.

BEATRICE   Did he never make you laugh?

BENEDICK   I pray you, what is he?

BEATRICE   Why, he is the prince's jester, a very dull fool, only
his gift is in devising impossible slanders. None but libertines
120   delight in him, and the commendation is not in his wit, but

---

93 clerk i.e. a parish clerk who led the responses during a church service   96 At a word in
brief   97 waggling shaking, either the tremblings of old age or a gesture that accompanied
his denial in the previous line   98 counterfeit imitate   99 do . . . ill-well imitate his
inadequacies so well   100 dry hand a result of age   up and down all over/in every
respect   104 mum silence   105 Graces attractive personal qualities/virtues   111 'Hundred
Merry Tales' a popular collection of crude comic anecdotes   118 only his his only
119 impossible unbelievable   libertines those who disregard moral laws and follow their
own inclinations

in his villainy, for he both pleaseth men and angers them, and then they laugh at him and beat him. I am sure he is in the fleet. I would he had boarded me.   *Aside?*

125 **BENEDICK**   When I know the gentleman, I'll tell him what you say.

BEATRICE   Do, do: he'll but break a comparison or two on me, which peradventure — not marked or not laughed at — strikes him into melancholy, and then there's a partridge wing saved, for the fool will eat no supper that night. We
130 must follow the leaders.   *Music*

BENEDICK   In every good thing.

BEATRICE   Nay, if they lead to any ill, I will leave them at the next turning.

Music for the Dance. [Then] exeunt [dancing, all except Don John, Borachio and Claudio]

DON JOHN   Sure my brother is amorous on Hero and   *Aside to*
135 hath withdrawn her father to break with him about   *Borachio*
it. The ladies follow her and but one visor remains.

BORACHIO   And that is Claudio: I know him by his bearing.

DON JOHN   Are not you Signior Benedick?   *To Claudio*

CLAUDIO   You know me well, I am he.

140 **DON JOHN**   Signior, you are very near my brother in his love. He is enamoured on Hero. I pray you dissuade him from her, she is no equal for his birth. You may do the part of an honest man in it.

CLAUDIO   How know you he loves her?

145 **DON JOHN**   I heard him swear his affection.

BORACHIO   So did I too, and he swore he would marry her tonight.

DON JOHN   Come, let us to the banquet.

---

121 villainy wicked humor/discourtesy/low-minded jesting   **pleaseth ... them** i.e. amuses some with his rudeness but angers those he slanders   **122 in the fleet** among the dancers
123 boarded tackled/accosted (puns on the sense of "had sex with")   **126 break** as a lance might in jousting   **comparison** a sneering or unflattering analogy   **128 partridge wing** the part of the bird with virtually no meat on it (Beatrice's comment is sarcastic)   **130 leaders** i.e. of the dance   **134 amorous on** courting   **140 near ... love** i.e. close to/highly regarded by my brother   **148 banquet** wine, fruit and sweetmeats served after the dance

Exeunt [Don John and Borachio]

CLAUDIO   Thus answer I in the name of Benedick,
150   But hear these ill news with the ears of Claudio.
'Tis certain so, the prince woos for himself.
Friendship is constant in all other things
Save in the office and affairs of love.
Therefore all hearts in love use their own tongues,
155   Let every eye negotiate for itself
And trust no agent, for beauty is a witch
Against whose charms faith melteth into blood.
This is an accident of hourly proof,
Which I mistrusted not. Farewell, therefore, Hero!

Enter Benedick

160   BENEDICK   Count Claudio?
CLAUDIO   Yea, the same.
BENEDICK   Come, will you go with me?
CLAUDIO   Whither?
BENEDICK   Even to the next willow, about your own business,
165   count. What fashion will you wear the garland of? About
your neck, like an usurer's chain? Or under your arm, like a
lieutenant's scarf? You must wear it one way, for the prince
hath got your Hero.
CLAUDIO   I wish him joy of her.
170   BENEDICK   Why, that's spoken like an honest drover, so they sell
bullocks. But did you think the prince would have served you
thus?
CLAUDIO   I pray you leave me.
BENEDICK   Ho, now you strike like the blind man: 'twas the boy
175   that stole your meat, and you'll beat the post.

---

152 constant unwavering/faithful   153 office service/business   154 all let all   157 faith
loyalty/integrity   blood desire   158 accident . . . proof event that is shown to be the case
very regularly   159 mistrusted suspected   164 willow a willow garland was an emblem of
unrequited love   166 usurer's chain heavy gold chain worn by wealthy moneylenders
167 lieutenant's scarf sash worn diagonally across the chest as a symbol of rank   170 drover
cattle dealer   so in this way   174 now . . . post i.e. strike out in anger (an allusion to a tale
in which a boy is punished for stealing meat from his blind master, and gets his revenge by
causing the old man to injure himself on a pillar)   175 post pillar/messenger (i.e. Benedick)

CLAUDIO   If it will not be, I'll leave you.   *Exit*

BENEDICK   Alas, poor hurt fowl, now will he creep into sedges.
But that my Lady Beatrice should know me and not know
me! The prince's fool! Ha? It may be I go under that title
180   because I am merry. Yea, but so I am apt to do myself wrong.
I am not so reputed: it is the base, though bitter, disposition
of Beatrice that puts the world into her person and so gives
me out. Well, I'll be revenged as I may.

Enter the Prince [Don Pedro]

DON PEDRO   Now, signior, where's the count? Did you see him?
185   BENEDICK   Troth, my lord, I have played the part of Lady Fame.
I found him here as melancholy as a lodge in a warren. I told
him, and I think I told him true, that your grace had got the
good will of this young lady, and I offered him my company
to a willow-tree, either to make him a garland, as being
190   forsaken, or to bind him a rod, as being worthy to be
whipped.

DON PEDRO   To be whipped? What's his fault?

BENEDICK   The flat transgression of a schoolboy, who, being
overjoyed with finding a bird's nest, shows it his companion,
195   and he steals it.

DON PEDRO   Wilt thou make a trust a transgression? The
transgression is in the stealer.

BENEDICK   Yet it had not been amiss the rod had been made,
and the garland too: for the garland he might have worn
200   himself and the rod he might have bestowed on you, who, as
I take it, have stolen his bird's nest.

DON PEDRO   I will but teach them to sing, and restore them to
the owner.

---

176 If . . . be i.e. if you will not leave me   177 hurt fowl injured bird   sedges coarse rush-like
plants (where a wounded fowl might hide)   178 not know me not know my true nature
180 so in this way (i.e. by being merry)   182 puts . . . out assumes that the world shares her
opinions and represents me in that way   185 Lady Fame i.e. a gossip   Fame rumor
186 lodge . . . warren dwelling (probably of a gamekeeper) in an enclosed area used for
breeding game (i.e. an isolated place)   190 forsaken rejected (by a lover)   bind . . . rod bind
together a bundle of twigs as rod for punishment   193 flat transgression plain sin
196 a trust an act of trust   202 them i.e. the birds

BENEDICK   If their singing answer your saying, by my faith you
205   say honestly.

DON PEDRO   The Lady Beatrice hath a quarrel to you: the
gentleman that danced with her told her she is much
wronged by you.

BENEDICK   O, she misused me past the endurance of a block!
210   An oak but with one green leaf on it would have answered
her. My very visor began to assume life and scold with her.
She told me — not thinking I had been myself — that I was
the prince's jester, and that I was duller than a great thaw,
huddling jest upon jest with such impossible conveyance
215   upon me that I stood like a man at a mark, with a whole
army shooting at me. She speaks poniards, and every word
stabs. If her breath were as terrible as her terminations,
there were no living near her, she would infect to the North
Star. I would not marry her, though she were endowed with
220   all that Adam had left him before he transgressed. She would
have made Hercules have turned spit, yea, and have cleft his
club to make the fire too. Come, talk not of her, you shall find
her the infernal Ate in good apparel. I would to God some
scholar would conjure her, for certainly, while she is here, a
225   man may live as quiet in hell as in a sanctuary, and people
sin upon purpose, because they would go thither: so indeed
all disquiet, horror and perturbation follows her.

Enter Claudio and Beatrice, Leonato [and] Hero

DON PEDRO   Look, here she comes.

---

204 If . . . honestly if what they sing agrees with what you say you have taught them (i.e. to
marry Claudio) then you speak honorably   206 to with   209 misused abused   block block
of wood   213 great thaw the dull period during which roads became muddy and impassable
and people were unable to go out   214 huddling heaping up   impossible conveyance
incredible skill   215 mark archer's target (at which a man would have stood to note
where the arrows landed)   216 poniards daggers   217 terminations terms of expression
220 all . . . transgressed i.e. the delights and dominion of the Garden of Eden before the Fall
221 Hercules . . . too in Greek legend the Queen of Lydia, Omphale, made Hercules dress as a
woman and spin wool while she took over his club and lion's skin; turning a roasting spit was
one of the lowliest domestic tasks   cleft split   223 Ate goddess of discord and vengeance
224 conjure exorcise (the sending of evil spirits back to hell had to be carried out in Latin so a
scholar would be required)   here i.e. on earth   225 sanctuary holy place of safety

BENEDICK   Will your grace command me any service to the
230   world's end? I will go on the slightest errand now to the
Antipodes that you can devise to send me on: I will fetch you
a tooth-picker now from the furthest inch of Asia, bring you
the length of Prester John's foot, fetch you a hair off the
great Cham's beard, do you any embassage to the Pygmies,
235   rather than hold three words' conference with this harpy.
You have no employment for me?

DON PEDRO   None, but to desire your good company.

BENEDICK   O God, sir, here's a dish I love not: I cannot endure
this Lady Tongue.   *Exit*

240   DON PEDRO   Come, lady, come, you have lost the heart of Signior
Benedick.

BEATRICE   Indeed, my lord, he lent it me awhile, and I gave him
use for it, a double heart for his single one: marry, once
before he won it of me with false dice, therefore your Grace
245   may well say I have lost it.

DON PEDRO   You have put him down, lady, you have put him
down.

BEATRICE   So I would not he should do me, my lord, lest I
should prove the mother of fools. I have brought Count
250   Claudio, whom you sent me to seek.

DON PEDRO   Why, how now, count? Wherefore are you sad?

CLAUDIO   Not sad, my lord.

DON PEDRO   How then? Sick?

CLAUDIO   Neither, my lord.

255   BEATRICE   The count is neither sad, nor sick, nor merry, nor
well: but civil count, civil as an orange, and something of a
jealous complexion.

---

231 Antipodes the other side of the world   232 tooth-picker toothpick   233 Prester John
Christian ruler of a wealthy Eastern kingdom   234 Cham Kubla Khan, emperor of the
Mongols   Pygmies race of very small people thought to live in Asia   235 harpy fierce
mythical creature with the face of a woman and body of a bird   243 use financial interest on
a loan (plays on the sense of "usage")   double twice as loving/duplicitous   244 false dice
i.e. false promises, deception   246 put him down defeated him with wit (Beatrice's response
plays on the sense of "sexually subdued")   248 do puns on the sense of "have sex with"
251 Wherefore why   256 civil count grave/sober count (puns on "Seville," the Spanish city
well known as a producer of bitter-tasting oranges)   257 jealous complexion i.e. yellow, a
color associated with melancholy and jealousy

DON PEDRO   I'faith, lady, I think your blazon to be true, though
I'll be sworn, if he be so, his conceit is false. Here, Claudio, I
260   have wooed in thy name, and fair Hero is won: I have broke
with her father, and his good will obtained. Name the day of
marriage, and God give thee joy!

LEONATO   Count, take of me my daughter, and with her my
fortunes. His grace hath made the match, and all grace say
265   'Amen' to it.

BEATRICE   Speak, count, 'tis your cue.

CLAUDIO   Silence is the perfectest herald of joy. I were but little
happy, if I could say how much. Lady, as you are mine, I am
yours. I give away myself for you and dote upon the
270   exchange.

BEATRICE   Speak, cousin, or, if you cannot, stop   *Claudio and Hero*
his mouth with a kiss, and let not him speak neither.   *kiss?*

DON PEDRO   In faith, lady, you have a merry heart.

BEATRICE   Yea, my lord, I thank it, poor fool, it keeps on the
275   windy side of care. My cousin tells him in his ear that he is in
her heart.

CLAUDIO   And so she doth, cousin.

BEATRICE   Good lord, for alliance! Thus goes everyone to the
world but I, and I am sunburnt. I may sit in a corner and cry
280   'Hey-ho for a husband!'

DON PEDRO   Lady Beatrice, I will get you one.

BEATRICE   I would rather have one of your father's getting.
Hath your grace ne'er a brother like you? Your father got
excellent husbands, if a maid could come by them.

285   DON PEDRO   Will you have me, lady?

BEATRICE   No, my lord, unless I might have another for
working days: your grace is too costly to wear every day. But

---

258 **blazon** description   259 **conceit** understanding of things, notion   264 **His grace** i.e.
God   267 **herald** messenger/proclaimer   269 **dote upon** love dearly   275 **windy . . . care**
windward (i.e. advantageous/safe) side of trouble   278 **Good . . . alliance!** Thank God for
family unions/marriage!   **goes . . . world** everyone gets married   279 **sunburnt** Elizabethans
considered a tanned complexion unattractive   280 **'Hey-ho . . . husband!'** a playful
expression of regret that was also the title of a ballad   282 **getting** conception (a punning
response to Don Pedro's sense of "obtain")

I beseech your grace pardon me. I was born to speak all
mirth and no matter.

290 **DON PEDRO** Your silence most offends me, and to be merry best
becomes you, for out of question, you were born in a merry
hour.

BEATRICE No, sure, my lord, my mother cried, but then there
was a star danced, and under that was I born. Cousins, God
295 give you joy!

LEONATO Niece, will you look to those things I told you of?

BEATRICE I cry you mercy, uncle.— By your   *To Don Pedro*
grace's pardon.   *Exit*

DON PEDRO By my troth, a pleasant-spirited lady.

300 **LEONATO** There's little of the melancholy element in her, my
lord: she is never sad but when she sleeps, and not ever sad
then, for I have heard my daughter say, she hath often
dreamt of unhappiness and waked herself with laughing.

DON PEDRO She cannot endure to hear tell of a husband.

305 **LEONATO** O, by no means: she mocks all her wooers out of
suit.

DON PEDRO She were an excellent wife for Benedick.

LEONATO O lord, my lord, if they were but a week married,
they would talk themselves mad.

310 **DON PEDRO** Count Claudio, when mean you to go to church?

CLAUDIO Tomorrow, my lord. Time goes on crutches till love
have all his rites.

LEONATO Not till Monday, my dear son, which is hence a just
seven-night, and a time too brief, too, to have all things
315 answer my mind.

DON PEDRO Come, you shake the head at so long a breathing.
But I warrant thee, Claudio, the time shall not go dully by us.

---

289 matter substance/serious content   **290 Your . . . me** i.e. I would much rather you talked
on than were silent   **291 becomes** suits   **293 cried** i.e. at the pain of labor   **297 cry you
mercy** beg your pardon   **By . . . pardon** with your grace's (Don Pedro's) pardon (for my
departure)   **300 melancholy element** the body was thought to consist of four elements, or
humors, one of which was black bile, an excess of which caused melancholy   **301 ever**
always   **306 suit** courtship   **313 a just seven-night** precisely a week   **316 breathing**
interval   **317 warrant** assure

I will in the interim undertake one of Hercules' labours,
which is to bring Signior Benedick and the Lady Beatrice into
320 a mountain of affection, th'one with th'other. I would fain
have it a match, and I doubt not but to fashion it, if you three
will but minister such assistance as I shall give you direction.

LEONATO   My lord, I am for you, though it cost me ten nights'
watchings.

325 CLAUDIO   And I, my lord.

DON PEDRO   And you too, gentle Hero?

HERO   I will do any modest office, my lord, to help my
cousin to a good husband.

DON PEDRO   And Benedick is not the unhopefullest husband
330   that I know. Thus far can I praise him: he is of a noble strain,
of approved valour and confirmed honesty. I will teach you
how to humour your cousin that she shall fall in love with
Benedick, and I, with your two helps, will so   *To Leonato*
practise on Benedick that, in despite of his   *and Claudio*
335   quick wit and his queasy stomach, he shall fall in love with
Beatrice. If we can do this, Cupid is no longer an archer: his
glory shall be ours, for we are the only love-gods. Go in with
me, and I will tell you my drift.   *Exeunt*

[Act 2 Scene 2]   *running scene 4 continues*

Enter [Don] John and Borachio

DON JOHN   It is so: the Count Claudio shall marry the daughter
of Leonato.

BORACHIO   Yea, my lord, but I can cross it.

DON JOHN   Any bar, any cross, any impediment will be
5   medicinable to me: I am sick in displeasure to him, and

---

318 **Hercules' labours** in Greek legend, Hercules carried out twelve seemingly impossible tasks
(labours) imposed on him by King Eurystheus   320 **fain** gladly   322 **minister** provide
324 **watchings** staying awake   327 **modest** proper, seemly   329 **unhopefullest** least
promising   330 **strain** descent, lineage   331 **approved** tested/proven   **honesty**
honor   334 **practise on** work upon craftily   335 **queasy stomach** feelings of sickness/
delicate stomach/poor appetite (for love and marriage)   338 **drift** plan, intention
2.2 5 medicinable healing

whatsoever comes athwart his affection ranges evenly with mine. How canst thou cross this marriage?

BORACHIO   Not honestly, my lord, but so covertly that no dishonesty shall appear in me.

10   DON JOHN   Show me briefly how.

BORACHIO   I think I told your lordship a year since, how much I am in the favour of Margaret, the waiting gentlewoman to Hero.

DON JOHN   I remember.

15   BORACHIO   I can at any unseasonable instant of the night appoint her to look out at her lady's chamber window.

DON JOHN   What life is in that, to be the death of this marriage?

BORACHIO   The poison of that lies in you to temper. Go you to the prince your brother, spare not to tell him that he

20   hath wronged his honour in marrying the renowned Claudio — whose estimation do you mightily hold up — to a contaminated stale, such a one as Hero.

DON JOHN   What proof shall I make of that?

BORACHIO   Proof enough to misuse the prince, to vex Claudio,

25   to undo Hero, and kill Leonato. Look you for any other issue?

DON JOHN   Only to despite them, I will endeavour anything.

BORACHIO   Go, then, find me a meet hour to draw Don Pedro and the Count Claudio alone. Tell them that you know that Hero loves me, intend a kind of zeal both to the prince and

30   Claudio — as in a love of your brother's honour, who hath made this match, and his friend's reputation, who is thus like to be cozened with the semblance of a maid — that you have discovered thus. They will scarcely believe this without trial: offer them instances, which shall bear no less likelihood

35   than to see me at her chamber window, hear me call

---

6 comes athwart impedes, is an obstacle to   ranges evenly goes smoothly, directly
15 unseasonable inappropriate/odd   16 appoint instruct   18 temper mix   20 renowned
well-reputed/honorable   21 estimation worth   22 stale prostitute   24 vex torment, afflict
25 undo ruin   issue outcome   26 despite spite, wreak malice on   27 meet suitable
draw bring together   29 intend pretend   zeal ardent loyalty   30 as in as follows/such as
31 like likely   32 cozened cheated   semblance outward appearance   33 trial evidence
34 instances proofs

Margaret Hero, hear Margaret term me Claudio, and bring them to see this the very night before the intended wedding — for in the meantime I will so fashion the matter that Hero shall be absent — and there shall appear such seeming
40   truths of Hero's disloyalty that jealousy shall be called assurance and all the preparation overthrown.

DON JOHN   Grow this to what adverse issue it can, I will put it in practice. Be cunning in the working this, and thy fee is a thousand ducats.

45   BORACHIO   Be thou constant in the accusation, and my cunning shall not shame me.

DON JOHN   I will presently go learn their day of marriage.

Exeunt

[Act 2 Scene 3]

Enter Benedick, alone

BENEDICK   Boy!

[*Enter Boy*]

BOY   Signior?

BENEDICK   In my chamber-window lies a book: bring it hither to me in the orchard.

5   BOY   I am here already, sir.

BENEDICK   I know that, but I would have thee hence and here again.   *Exit* [*Boy*]
I do much wonder that one man, seeing how much another man is a fool when he dedicates his behaviours to love, will,
10   after he hath laughed at such shallow follies in others, become the argument of his own scorn by falling in love: and such a man is Claudio. I have known when there was no

38 fashion the matter arrange matters/contrive affairs   **40 jealousy** suspicion
41 preparation i.e. for the wedding   **42 Grow . . . can** no matter how harmful the outcome   **43 working** carrying out of   **44 ducats** gold (sometimes silver) coins used in Europe   **45 constant** unchanging/resolved   **2.3 51 . . . sir** i.e. I will return so quickly that it will seem as if I had never left (in his reply Benedick jestingly takes the Boy literally)
11 argument subject

music with him but the drum and the fife, and now had he
rather hear the tabor and the pipe. I have known when he
15   would have walked ten mile afoot to see a good armour, and
now will he lie ten nights awake carving the fashion of a new
doublet. He was wont to speak plain and to the purpose —
like an honest man and a soldier — and now is he turned
orthography, his words are a very fantastical banquet, just
20   so many strange dishes. May I be so converted and see with
these eyes? I cannot tell: I think not. I will not be sworn, but
love may transform me to an oyster, but I'll take my oath on
it, till he have made an oyster of me, he shall never make me
such a fool. One woman is fair, yet I am well: another is wise,
25   yet I am well: another virtuous, yet I am well: but till all
graces be in one woman, one woman shall not come in my
grace. Rich she shall be, that's certain: wise, or I'll none:
virtuous, or I'll never cheapen her: fair, or I'll never look on
her: mild, or come not near me: noble, or not I for an angel:
30   of good discourse, an excellent musician, and her hair shall
be of what colour it please God. Ha! The prince and Monsieur
Love! I will hide me in the arbour.   *He hides in the arbor*

Enter [Don Pedro], Leonato, Claudio and [Balthasar]

DON PEDRO   Come, shall we hear this music?

CLAUDIO   Yea, my good lord. How still the evening is,
35   As hushed on purpose to grace harmony.

DON PEDRO   See you where Benedick hath hid himself?

CLAUDIO   O, very well, my lord: the music ended,
We'll fit the kid-fox with a pennyworth.

DON PEDRO   Come, Balthasar, we'll hear that song again.

---

13 drum . . . fife i.e. war-like instruments   fife a flute-like instrument   14 tabor . . . pipe i.e.
instruments associated with festivity   tabor a small drum   15 afoot on foot   16 carving
designing   17 doublet close-fitting jacket with flared base   wont accustomed
19 orthography stylistically polished and elaborate   fantastical fanciful, imaginative
22 transform . . . oyster turn me into a lowly creature/silence me as an oyster snaps shut
26 graces virtues   27 grace favor   none have none of her   28 cheapen bid for
29 or come or she shall come   noble puns on the name of a gold coin   angel puns on the
name of a gold coin   35 As as if   37 the music ended i.e. once the music has ended
38 fit . . . pennyworth i.e. give him more than he bargained for   kid-fox cunning young fox

40 **BALTHASAR** O, good my lord, tax not so bad a voice
    To slander music any more than once.
  DON PEDRO It is the witness still of excellency
    To put a strange face on his own perfection.
    I pray thee sing, and let me woo no more.
45 **BALTHASAR** Because you talk of wooing, I will sing,
    Since many a wooer doth commence his suit
    To her he thinks not worthy, yet he woos,
    Yet will he swear he loves.
  DON PEDRO Nay, pray thee come,
50   Or if thou wilt hold longer argument,
    Do it in notes.
  BALTHASAR Note this before my notes:
    There's not a note of mine that's worth the noting.
  DON PEDRO Why, these are very crotchets that he speaks:
55   Note notes, forsooth, and nothing.   *Music*
  BENEDICK Now, divine air! Now is his soul ravished. *Aside*
    Is it not strange that sheep's guts should hale souls out of
    men's bodies? Well, a horn for my money, when all's done.
  BALTHASAR [*Sings*] *the song*
    Sigh no more, ladies, sigh no more,
60   Men were deceivers ever:
    One foot in sea and one on shore,
    To one thing constant never.
    Then sigh not so, but let them go,
    And be you blithe and bonny,
65   Converting all your sounds of woe
    Into hey nonny, nonny.

---

40 **tax** order 42 **It . . . perfection** it is always proof of excellence that it claims not to recognize
its own skill 44 **woo** entreat, coax 47 **her . . . worthy** Balthasar also refers to himself as one
who is an unworthy singer, but whose skills have yet been courted by Don Pedro 54 **crotchets**
whimsical fancies/musical notes 55 **Note . . . nothing** pay attention to your musical notes, in
truth, and nothing else (**nothing** puns on "noting," which was pronounced in a similar manner)
56 **air** melody 57 **sheep's guts** from which an instrument's strings were made **hale** haul
58 **horn** hunting horn, a more masculine instrument (possibly with an unconscious play on
cuckold's horns) 66 **blithe and bonny** joyful and healthily beautiful

Sing no more ditties, sing no moe,
Of dumps so dull and heavy:
The fraud of men was ever so,
70   Since summer first was leafy.
Then sigh not so, etc.

DON PEDRO By my troth, a good song.

BALTHASAR And an ill singer, my lord.

DON PEDRO Ha, no, no, faith: thou sing'st well enough for a
75   shift.

BENEDICK   An he had been a dog that should have   *Aside*
howled thus, they would have hanged him, and I pray God
his bad voice bode no mischief. I had as lief have heard the
night-raven, come what plague could have come after it.

80   DON PEDRO Yea, marry, dost thou hear, Balthasar? I pray thee
get us some excellent music, for tomorrow night we would
have it at the Lady Hero's chamber window.

BALTHASAR The best I can, my lord.

DON PEDRO Do so: farewell.   *Exit Balthasar*
85   Come hither, Leonato. What was it you told me of today, that
your niece Beatrice was in love with Signior Benedick?

CLAUDIO   O, ay! Stalk on, the fowl sits.—   *Aside to Don Pedro*
I did never think that lady would have loved   *Aloud*
any man.

90   LEONATO   No, nor I neither, but most wonderful that she
should so dote on Signior Benedick, whom she hath in all
outward behaviours seemed ever to abhor.

BENEDICK Is't possible? Sits the wind in that corner?   *Aside*

LEONATO   By my troth my lord, I cannot tell what to think of
95   it, but that she loves him with an enraged affection: it is past
the infinite of thought.

DON PEDRO Maybe she doth but counterfeit.

---

67 ditties songs   moe more   68 dumps low spirits (puns on the sense of "sad songs")
74 for a shift for the purpose/for lack of a better alternative   76 An if   78 as lief as soon/rather
79 night-raven the call of which was supposed to foretell disaster   87 Stalk on i.e. as a hunter
would advance upon his prey (a sitting fowl)   90 wonderful extraordinary/astonishing
93 Sits . . . corner? Is that the way the wind is blowing? (i.e. is that the way things are)
95 enraged affection furiously passionate love   97 counterfeit pretend

CLAUDIO   Faith, like enough.

LEONATO   O God! Counterfeit? There was never counterfeit of
100   passion came so near the life of passion as she discovers it.

DON PEDRO   Why, what effects of passion shows she?

CLAUDIO   Bait the hook well, this fish will bite.   *Aside to them*

LEONATO   What effects, my lord? She will sit you — you heard
my daughter tell you how.

105   CLAUDIO   She did indeed.

DON PEDRO   How, how, I pray you? You amaze me: I would have
thought her spirit had been invincible against all assaults of
affection.

LEONATO   I would have sworn it had, my lord, especially
110   against Benedick.

BENEDICK   I should think this a gull, but that the   *Aside*
white-bearded fellow speaks it: knavery cannot sure hide
himself in such reverence.

CLAUDIO   He hath ta'en th'infection — hold it up.   *Aside to them*

115   DON PEDRO   Hath she made her affection known to Benedick?

LEONATO   No, and swears she never will. That's her torment.

CLAUDIO   'Tis true indeed, so your daughter says: 'Shall I,'
says she, 'that have so oft encountered him with scorn, write
to him that I love him?'

120   LEONATO   This says she now when she is beginning to write to
him, for she'll be up twenty times a night, and there will she
sit in her smock till she have writ a sheet of paper: my
daughter tells us all.

CLAUDIO   Now you talk of a sheet of paper, I remember a
125   pretty jest your daughter told us of.

LEONATO   O, when she had writ it, and was reading it over, she
found 'Benedick' and 'Beatrice' between the sheet?

CLAUDIO   That.

LEONATO   O, she tore the letter into a thousand halfpence,
130   railed at herself, that she should be so immodest to write to

---

100 discovers reveals   103 sit you sit   111 gull trick/deception   114 hold it up keep up the
trick/keep going   122 smock slip   128 That (yes) that one   129 halfpence fragments (a
halfpenny was a small coin)   130 railed ranted/chastised abusively

one that she knew would flout her. 'I measure him', says she,
'by my own spirit, for I should flout him if he writ to me, yea,
though I love him, I should.'

CLAUDIO   Then down upon her knees she falls, weeps, sobs,
135   beats her heart, tears her hair, prays, curses: 'O sweet
Benedick! God give me patience!'

LEONATO   She doth indeed, my daughter says so, and the
ecstasy hath so much overborne her that my daughter is
sometime afeard she will do a desperate outrage to herself: it
140   is very true.

DON PEDRO   It were good that Benedick knew of it by some other,
if she will not discover it.

CLAUDIO   To what end? He would but make a sport of it and
torment the poor lady worse.

145   DON PEDRO   An he should, it were an alms to hang him. She's an
excellent sweet lady and, out of all suspicion, she is virtuous.

CLAUDIO   And she is exceeding wise.

DON PEDRO   In everything, but in loving Benedick.

LEONATO   O, my lord, wisdom and blood combating in so
150   tender a body, we have ten proofs to one that blood hath the
victory. I am sorry for her, as I have just cause, being her
uncle and her guardian.

DON PEDRO   I would she had bestowed this dotage on me: I
would have daffed all other respects and made her half
155   myself. I pray you tell Benedick of it and hear what he will
say.

LEONATO   Were it good, think you?

CLAUDIO   Hero thinks surely she will die, for she says she will
die if he love her not, and she will die ere she make her love
160   known, and she will die if he woo her, rather than she will
bate one breath of her accustomed crossness.

---

138 ecstasy frenzy   **overborne** overwhelmed   **139 outrage** violence   **145 alms** charitable
deed   **146 suspicion** doubt   **149 blood** passion/desire   **150 tender** young/delicate
153 dotage great love/infatuation   **154 daffed** doffed (i.e. cast off)   **respects** considerations
made . . . myself i.e. married her   **161 bate** abate, modify

DON PEDRO   She doth well: if she should make tender of her love, 'tis very possible he'll scorn it, for the man, as you know all, hath a contemptible spirit.

165   CLAUDIO   He is a very proper man.

DON PEDRO   He hath indeed a good outward happiness.

CLAUDIO   'Fore God, and in my mind, very wise.

DON PEDRO   He doth indeed show some sparks that are like wit.

LEONATO   And I take him to be valiant.

170   DON PEDRO   As Hector, I assure you: and in the managing of quarrels you may see he is wise, for either he avoids them with great discretion, or undertakes them with a Christian-like fear.

LEONATO   If he do fear God, a must necessarily keep peace. If
175   he break the peace, he ought to enter into a quarrel with fear and trembling.

DON PEDRO   And so will he do, for the man doth fear God, howsoever it seems not in him by some large jests he will make. Well, I am sorry for your niece. Shall we go seek
180   Benedick, and tell him of her love?

CLAUDIO   Never tell him, my lord: let her wear it out with good counsel.

LEONATO   Nay, that's impossible: she may wear her heart out first.

185   DON PEDRO   Well, we will hear further of it by your daughter. Let it cool the while. I love Benedick well, and I could wish he would modestly examine himself, to see how much he is unworthy to have so good a lady.

LEONATO   My lord, will you walk? Dinner is ready.

190   CLAUDIO   If he do not dote on her upon this,   *Aside to them*
I will never trust my expectation.

---

162 make tender of offer   **164 contemptible** contemptuous/scornful   **165 proper** handsome   **166 good outward happiness** pleasingly attractive appearance   **167 'Fore God** an exclamation roughly equivalent to "indeed so, with God as my witness"   **170 Hector** the leader of the Trojans in the Trojan war, known for his bravery   **172 discretion** prudence, good judgment   **178 by** to judge by   **large** coarse/unrestrained   **181 wear it out** outlive it/use it up/grow tired of it   **182 counsel** reflection   **186 the while** in the meantime   **187 modestly** in a reasonable, moderate way   **190 upon** after

DON PEDRO   Let there be the same net spread for   *Aside to them*
  her, and that must your daughter and her gentlewoman
  carry. The sport will be when they hold one an opinion of
195 another's dotage, and no such matter: that's the scene that I
  would see, which will be merely a dumb-show. Let us send
  her to call him in to dinner.

                        Exeunt [Don Pedro, Claudio and Leonato]

BENEDICK   This can be no trick: the conference was   *He comes*
  sadly borne, they have the truth of this from Hero.   *forward*
200 They seem to pity the lady: it seems her affections have the
  full bent. Love me? Why, it must be requited. I hear how I am
  censured: they say I will bear myself proudly, if I perceive the
  love come from her. They say too that she will rather die than
  give any sign of affection. I did never think to marry. I must
205 not seem proud. Happy are they that hear their detractions
  and can put them to mending. They say the lady is fair — 'tis
  a truth, I can bear them witness, and virtuous — 'tis so, I
  cannot reprove it, and wise, but for loving me — by my troth,
  it is no addition to her wit, nor no great argument of her
210 folly, for I will be horribly in love with her. I may chance have
  some odd quirks and remnants of wit broken on me because
  I have railed so long against marriage. But doth not the
  appetite alter? A man loves the meat in his youth that he
  cannot endure in his age. Shall quips and sentences and
215 these paper bullets of the brain awe a man from the career of
  his humour? No, the world must be peopled. When I said I
  would die a bachelor, I did not think I should live till I were
  married. Here comes Beatrice. By this day, she's a fair lady! I
  do spy some marks of love in her.

---

194 carry carry out   **they . . . dotage** each believes that the other is in love   **195 no such matter** in fact there is no truth in it   **196 dumb-show** play acted without words (as Benedick and Beatrice will be speechless)   **199 sadly borne** seriously carried out   **200 have . . . bent** are engaged to their fullest extent (like a bow pulled as far as possible)   **202 censured** judged/criticized   **205 their detractions** criticisms of themselves   **208 reprove** disprove/refute/reject   **209 argument** demonstration/evidence   **211 quirks** quips/witty conceits   **broken** cracked at my expense/snapped like a lance in jousting   **214 sentences** maxims, sayings   **215 paper . . . brain** i.e. words, which cannot hurt   **awe** terrify/restrain   **career . . . humour** pursuit of his inclination   **career** gallop of a horse, as in a tournament

Enter Beatrice

220 BEATRICE   Against my will I am sent to bid you come in to
dinner.

BENEDICK   Fair Beatrice, I thank you for your pains.

BEATRICE   I took no more pains for those thanks than you take
pains to thank me: if it had been painful, I would not have
225 come.

BENEDICK   You take pleasure then in the message?

BEATRICE   Yea, just so much as you may take upon a knife's
point and choke a daw withal. You have no stomach, signior,
fare you well.   *Exit*

230 BENEDICK   Ha! 'Against my will I am sent to bid you come in to
dinner' — there's a double meaning in that. 'I took no more
pains for those thanks than you took pains to thank me' —
that's as much as to say, 'Any pains that I take for you is as
easy as thanks.' If I do not take pity of her, I am a villain; if I
235 do not love her, I am a Jew. I will go get her picture.   *Exit*

Act 3 Scene 1   *running scene 6*

Enter Hero, and two gentlewomen, Margaret and Ursula

HERO   Good Margaret, run thee to the parlour,
There shalt thou find my cousin Beatrice
Proposing with the prince and Claudio.
Whisper her ear, and tell her I and Ursula
5 Walk in the orchard, and our whole discourse
Is all of her. Say that thou overheard'st us,
And bid her steal into the pleachèd bower
Where honeysuckles, ripened by the sun,
Forbid the sun to enter, like favourites,
10 Made proud by princes, that advance their pride
Against that power that bred it: there will she hide her

---

222 **pains** efforts (Beatrice plays on the sense of literal pain in **painful**)   228 **choke** kill/silence
daw jackdaw (proverbially a stupid bird, so also a rude reference to the talkative Benedick)
withal with   **stomach** appetite   235 **Jew** thought by many Elizabethans to be pitiless
picture a miniature, which a lover might wear or carry with him   **3.1 3 Proposing** conversing
10 **advance . . . it** defy the very prince whose favor made them great

To listen our purpose. This is thy office:
Bear thee well in it, and leave us alone.

MARGARET   I'll make her come, I warrant you, presently.

[*Exit*]

15 HERO   Now, Ursula, when Beatrice doth come,
As we do trace this alley up and down,
Our talk must only be of Benedick.
When I do name him, let it be thy part
To praise him more than ever man did merit:
20 My talk to thee must be how Benedick
Is sick in love with Beatrice. Of this matter
Is little Cupid's crafty arrow made,
That only wounds by hearsay.

Enter Beatrice [into the bower]

Now begin:
For look where Beatrice like a lapwing runs
25 Close by the ground to hear our conference.

URSULA   The pleasant'st angling is to see the fish   *To Hero*
Cut with her golden oars the silver stream,
And greedily devour the treacherous bait:
So angle we for Beatrice, who even now
30 Is couchèd in the woodbine coverture.
Fear you not my part of the dialogue.

HERO   Then go we near her, that her ear lose   *To Ursula*
nothing
Of the false sweet bait that we lay for it.   *They approach the bower*
No, truly, Ursula, she is too disdainful: *Aloud*
35 I know her spirits are as coy and wild
As haggards of the rock.

URSULA   But are you sure
That Benedick loves Beatrice so entirely ?

HERO   So says the prince and my new-trothèd lord.

---

12 purpose matter of our conversation   office duty/task   16 trace range through, pass
along   23 hearsay report/rumor/something overheard   24 lapwing bird of the plover
family known for running through the grass in a crouching fashion   27 oars i.e. fins
30 couchèd . . . coverture lying hidden in the thick covering of honeysuckle   35 coy
disdainful   wild unrestrained/wayward/rude/fierce   36 haggards untamed female hawks
38 entirely completely/sincerely   39 new-trothèd i.e. Claudio, newly betrothed

40	URSULA	And did they bid you tell her of it, madam?
	HERO	They did entreat me to acquaint her of it,

But I persuaded them, if they loved Benedick,
To wish him wrestle with affection,
And never to let Beatrice know of it.

45	URSULA	Why did you so? Doth not the gentleman

Deserve as full as fortunate a bed
As ever Beatrice shall couch upon?

	HERO	O god of love! I know he doth deserve

As much as may be yielded to a man.
50   But nature never framed a woman's heart
Of prouder stuff than that of Beatrice.
Disdain and scorn ride sparkling in her eyes,
Misprising what they look on, and her wit
Values itself so highly that to her
55   All matter else seems weak: she cannot love,
Nor take no shape nor project of affection,
She is so self-endeared.

	URSULA	Sure, I think so:

And therefore certainly it were not good
60   She knew his love, lest she make sport at it.

	HERO	Why, you speak truth. I never yet saw man,

How wise, how noble, young, how rarely featured,
But she would spell him backward: if fair-faced,
She would swear the gentleman should be her sister:
65   If black, why, nature, drawing of an antic,
Made a foul blot: if tall, a lance ill-headed:
If low, an agate very vilely cut:
If speaking, why, a vane blown with all winds:
If silent, why, a block movèd with none.

---

45 Doth . . . upon? i.e. doesn't Benedick deserve a wife as good as Beatrice   **46 bed** marriage
bed   **47 couch** lie   **49 yielded** given   **53 Misprising** undervaluing/scorning   **55 weak** of
little worth/contemptible   **56 project** conception, notion   **57 self-endeared** in love with
herself   **62 How** however   **rarely** excellently   **63 spell him backward** declare he is the
opposite   **fair-faced** attractive/light-complexioned   **65 black** dark-complexioned   **antic**
grotesque figure/grinning buffoon   **66 ill-headed** with a poorly made or misshapen head
67 agate an agate stone would often have a tiny figure carved into it before being set in a ring

70   So turns she every man the wrong side out,
          And never gives to truth and virtue that
          Which simpleness and merit purchaseth.

URSULA   Sure, sure, such carping is not commendable.

HERO   No, not to be so odd and from all fashions
75   As Beatrice is cannot be commendable.
          But who dare tell her so? If I should speak,
          She would mock me into air: O, she would laugh me
          Out of myself, press me to death with wit.
          Therefore let Benedick, like covered fire,
80   Consume away in sighs, waste inwardly.
          It were a better death than die with mocks,
          Which is as bad as die with tickling.

URSULA   Yet tell her of it: hear what she will say.

HERO   No, rather I will go to Benedick
85   And counsel him to fight against his passion.
          And truly I'll devise some honest slanders
          To stain my cousin with. One doth not know
          How much an ill word may empoison liking.

URSULA   O, do not do your cousin such a wrong.
90   She cannot be so much without true judgement —
          Having so swift and excellent a wit
          As she is prized to have — as to refuse
          So rare a gentleman as Signior Benedick.

HERO   He is the only man of Italy,
95   Always excepted my dear Claudio.

URSULA   I pray you be not angry with me, madam,
          Speaking my fancy: Signior Benedick,
          For shape, for bearing, argument and valour,
          Goes foremost in report through Italy.

100 HERO   Indeed he hath an excellent good name.

---

72 simpleness plainness/integrity   **purchaseth** earns/deserves   **73 carping** fault-finding
74 odd at odds with   **from** contrary to   **78 press . . . death** pressing a person to death with
heavy weights was the penalty for one who refused to plead guilty or innocent to a crime
79 covered covered with a tightly packed heap of fuel to ensure a long burning time
85 counsel advise   **86 honest slanders** i.e. slanders that will do no serious harm to her
reputation   **92 prized** esteemed, valued   **94 only** i.e. best, unrivaled   **97 fancy** thought/
preference/liking   **98 argument** skill in debate/powers of reasoning

URSULA   His excellence did earn it ere he had it.
    When are you married, madam?

HERO   Why, every day, tomorrow. Come, go in:
    I'll show thee some attires, and have thy counsel   *They step back*

105   Which is the best to furnish me tomorrow.   *from the bower*

URSULA   She's ta'en, I warrant you: we have caught her,
    madam.

HERO   If it prove so, then loving goes by haps:
    Some Cupid kills with arrows, some with traps.

                            Exeunt [Hero and Ursula]

BEATRICE   What fire is in mine ears? Can this be true?   *She comes*

110   Stand I condemned for pride and scorn so much?   *forward*
    Contempt farewell, and maiden pride adieu!
    No glory lives behind the back of such.
    And, Benedick, love on, I will requite thee,
    Taming my wild heart to thy loving hand.

115   If thou dost love, my kindness shall incite thee
    To bind our loves up in a holy band.
    For others say thou dost deserve, and I
    Believe it better than reportingly.   *Exit*

Act 3 Scene 2   *running scene 7*

Enter Prince [Don Pedro], Claudio, Benedick and Leonato

DON PEDRO   I do but stay till your marriage be consummate, and
    then go I toward Aragon.

CLAUDIO   I'll bring you thither, my lord, if you'll vouchsafe
    me.

5   DON PEDRO   Nay, that would be as great a soil in the new gloss of
    your marriage as to show a child his new coat and forbid him
    to wear it. I will only be bold with Benedick for his company,

---

103 **tomorrow** from tomorrow onward   104 **attires** ornamented headdresses with false hair
attached to them   105 **furnish me** fit me out with, clothe me with   107 **haps** chance/
accidents   114 **Taming . . . hand** i.e. as a hawk would learn to obey the falconer   116 **band**
bond (plays on sense of "wedding ring")   118 **reportingly** as it is reported/through hearsay
3.2 1 consummate consummated/accomplished   3 **vouchsafe** permit   7 **only . . . with** be
bold only with (i.e. prevail upon)

for from the crown of his head to the sole of his foot he is all
mirth. He hath twice or thrice cut Cupid's bow-string and
the little hangman dare not shoot at him. He hath a heart as
sound as a bell and his tongue is the clapper, for what his
heart thinks his tongue speaks.

BENEDICK   Gallants, I am not as I have been.

LEONATO   So say I, methinks you are sadder.

CLAUDIO   I hope he be in love.

DON PEDRO   Hang him, truant! There's no true drop of blood in
him to be truly touched with love. If he be sad, he wants
money.

BENEDICK   I have the toothache.

DON PEDRO   Draw it.

BENEDICK   Hang it.

CLAUDIO   You must hang it first, and draw it afterwards.

DON PEDRO   What? Sigh for the toothache?

LEONATO   Where is but a humour or a worm.

BENEDICK   Well, everyone cannot master a grief but he that
has it.

CLAUDIO   Yet say I, he is in love.

DON PEDRO   There is no appearance of fancy in him, unless it be
a fancy that he hath to strange disguises — as to be a
Dutchman today, a Frenchman tomorrow. Unless he have a
fancy to this foolery, as it appears he hath, he is no fool for
fancy, as you would have it to appear he is.

CLAUDIO   If he be not in love with some woman, there is no
believing old signs: a brushes his hat o'mornings, what
should that bode?

10 hangman i.e. executioner   16 truant knave   17 wants lacks   20 Draw extract (Claudio
puns on the sense of "disembowel," sometimes the fate of a hanged man)   21 Hang it an
expression of angry impatience   22 hang it teeth were hung up outside barbers' shops as
advertisements for the dental work that barbers also carried out (though Claudio also refers to
the hanging, and drawing, of a criminal)   24 Where where there   humour . . . worm
toothache was thought to be caused either by the descent from the head into the tooth of one of
the four humors (fluids), or by a worm in the tooth   25 but except   28 fancy love (Don Pedro
goes on to pun on the sense of "whim")   30 Frenchman tomorrow German and Spanish
references follow hereafter in the Quarto (see Textual Notes); Folio's omission of them may have
been to avoid offense at court

DON PEDRO Hath any man seen him at the barber's?

CLAUDIO No, but the barber's man hath been seen with him, and the old ornament of his cheek hath already stuffed tennis-balls.

40 **LEONATO** Indeed, he looks younger than he did, by the loss of a beard.

DON PEDRO Nay, a rubs himself with civet. Can you smell him out by that?

CLAUDIO That's as much as to say the sweet youth's in love.

45 **DON PEDRO** The greatest note of it is his melancholy.

CLAUDIO And when was he wont to wash his face?

DON PEDRO Yea, or to paint himself? For the which, I hear what they say of him.

CLAUDIO Nay, but his jesting spirit, which is now crept into a
50 lute-string and now governed by stops.

DON PEDRO Indeed, that tells a heavy tale for him. Conclude: he is in love.

CLAUDIO Nay, but I know who loves him.

DON PEDRO That would I know too. I warrant, one that knows
55 him not.

CLAUDIO Yes, and his ill conditions, and in despite of all, dies for him.

DON PEDRO She shall be buried with her face upwards.

BENEDICK Yet is this no charm for the toothache. Old signior,
60 walk aside with me: I have studied eight or nine wise words to speak to you, which these hobby-horses must not hear.

[*Exeunt Benedick and Leonato*]

DON PEDRO For my life, to break with him about Beatrice.

---

38 **ornament . . . tennis-balls** filling tennis balls with beard hair seems to have been an actual practice   42 **civet** a musky perfume obtained from the glands of the civet cat   **smell him out** detect the truth/discern his presence by his smell   45 **note** sign   46 **wont** accustomed **wash** clean/perfume   47 **paint** apply cosmetics   50 **lute-string** the lute was considered the instrument of a lover   **governed** controlled/has the musical key determined **stops** frets/restraints/impediments   51 **heavy** sad   56 **ill conditions** bad characteristics **dies** expires/orgasms   58 **face upwards** as a faithful Christian/in a sexual position, under Benedick   59 **Old signior** i.e. Leonato   61 **hobby-horses** jokers   62 **For** upon

CLAUDIO   'Tis even so. Hero and Margaret have by this played
their parts with Beatrice, and then the two bears will not bite
65   one another when they meet.

Enter [Don] John the Bastard

DON JOHN   My lord and brother, God save you.

DON PEDRO   Good den, brother.

DON JOHN   If your leisure served, I would speak with you.

DON PEDRO   In private?

70   DON JOHN   If it please you. Yet Count Claudio may hear, for
what I would speak of concerns him.

DON PEDRO   What's the matter?

DON JOHN   Means your lordship to be married   *To Claudio*
tomorrow?

75   DON PEDRO   You know he does.

DON JOHN   I know not that, when he knows what I know.

CLAUDIO   If there be any impediment, I pray you discover it.

DON JOHN   You may think I love you not: let that appear
hereafter, and aim better at me by that I now will manifest.
80   For my brother, I think he holds you well, and in dearness of
heart, hath holp to effect your ensuing marriage — surely
suit ill spent and labour ill bestowed.

DON PEDRO   Why, what's the matter?

DON JOHN   I came hither to tell you, and, circumstances
85   shortened — for she has been too long a talking of — the
lady is disloyal.

CLAUDIO   Who, Hero?

DON JOHN   Even she: Leonato's Hero, your Hero, every man's
Hero.

90   CLAUDIO   Disloyal?

DON JOHN   The word is too good to paint out her wickedness. I
could say she were worse: think you of a worse title, and I

---

63 by this by this time   **66 God save you** a common greeting   **67 Good den** good evening
68 If . . . served if you have time   **78 let . . . hereafter** whether or not I love you will be
apparent after I have imparted what I have to say   **79 aim . . . manifest** judge me more
effectively according to what I will now reveal to you   **80 holds** regards   **84 circumstances
shortened** in brief/regardless of details   **85 a talking of** the subject of conversation (either
Claudio and Don Pedro's conversation or public gossip)   **91 paint out** convey in full

will fit her to it. Wonder not till further warrant. Go but with
me tonight, you shall see her chamber window entered, even
95   the night before her wedding-day. If you love her then,
tomorrow wed her. But it would better fit your honour to
change your mind.

CLAUDIO   May this be so?

DON PEDRO   I will not think it.

100   DON JOHN   If you dare not trust that you see, confess not that
you know. If you will follow me, I will show you enough,
and when you have seen more and heard more, proceed
accordingly.

CLAUDIO   If I see anything tonight why I should not marry
105   her tomorrow in the congregation where I should wed, there
will I shame her.

DON PEDRO   And, as I wooed for thee to obtain her, I will join
with thee to disgrace her.

DON JOHN   I will disparage her no farther till you are my
110   witnesses. Bear it coldly but till night, and let the issue show
itself.

DON PEDRO   O day untowardly turned!

CLAUDIO   O mischief strangely thwarting!

DON JOHN   O plague right well prevented! So will you say when
115   you have seen the sequel.   *Exeunt*

[Act 3 Scene 3]   *running scene 8*

Enter Dogberry and his compartner [Verges] with the Watch

DOGBERRY   Are you good men and true?

VERGES   Yea, or else it were pity but they should suffer
salvation, body and soul.

---

93 fit suit/adapt   Wonder marvel/be incredulous   warrant proof   96 fit befit
100 If . . . know if you do not dare to admit that what you see with your own eyes is the
case, then you had better say nothing about it/then you know nothing at all   110 Bear it
coldly behave calmly   112 untowardly turned unfavorably changed   113 mischief
misfortune/wickedness   3.3 *Dogberry* named after the berry of the wild cornel or dogwood,
a type of shrub   *Verges* named after verjuice, the bitter juice that comes from unripe fruit
Watch a group of citizens who assisted with local policing   1 true reliable, honest
3 salvation a malapropism—Verges means "damnation"

DOGBERRY   Nay, that were a punishment too good for them, if
5   they should have any allegiance in them, being chosen for
the prince's watch.

VERGES   Well, give them their charge, neighbour Dogberry.

DOGBERRY   First, who think you the most desertless man to be
constable?

10   FIRST WATCHMAN   Hugh Otecake, sir, or George Seacole, for they
can write and read.

DOGBERRY   Come hither, neighbour Seacole. God   *Second*
hath blessed you with a good name: to be a   *Watchman*
well-favoured man is the gift of fortune, but   *steps forward*
15   to write and read comes by nature.

SECOND WATCHMAN   Both which, master constable—

DOGBERRY   You have: I knew it would be your answer. Well, for
your favour, sir, why, give God thanks, and make no boast of
it. And for your writing and reading, let that appear when
20   there is no need of such vanity. You are thought here to be
the most senseless and fit man for the constable of the
watch: therefore bear you the lantern. This is your charge:
you shall comprehend all vagrom men, you are to bid any
man stand, in the prince's name.

25   SECOND WATCHMAN   How if a will not stand?

DOGBERRY   Why, then, take no note of him, but let him go, and
presently call the rest of the watch together, and thank God
you are rid of a knave.

VERGES   If he will not stand when he is bidden, he is none of
30   the prince's subjects.

DOGBERRY   True, and they are to meddle with none but the
prince's subjects. You shall also make no noise in the streets,
for for the watch to babble and talk is most tolerable and not
to be endured.

---

5 allegiance Dogberry means "treachery"   **7 charge** duties/responsibilities   **8 desertless**
Dogberry's error for "deserving"   **10 Otecake** from "oatcake," a cake made of oatmeal
Seacole from "sea coal," a more expensive type of fuel   **14 well-favoured** good-looking
18 favour face/appearance   **21 senseless** Dogberry means "sensible"   **fit** suitable
23 comprehend malapropism for "apprehend"   **vagrom** vagrant   **24 stand** stop
26 take . . . of him pay no attention to him   **31 meddle** be concerned/involved with
33 tolerable Dogberry means "intolerable"

35   WATCHMAN   We will rather sleep than talk: we know what belongs to a watch.

DOGBERRY   Why, you speak like an ancient and most quiet watchman, for I cannot see how sleeping should offend: only have a care that your bills be not stolen. Well, you are to call 40 at all the ale-houses, and bid them that are drunk get them to bed.

WATCHMAN   How if they will not?

DOGBERRY   Why then, let them alone till they are sober: if they make you not then the better answer, you may say they are 45 not the men you took them for.

WATCHMAN   Well, sir.

DOGBERRY   If you meet a thief, you may suspect him, by virtue of your office, to be no true man: and for such kind of men, the less you meddle or make with them, why the more is for 50 your honesty.

WATCHMAN   If we know him to be a thief, shall we not lay hands on him?

DOGBERRY   Truly, by your office, you may, but I think they that touch pitch will be defiled. The most peaceable way for you, if 55 you do take a thief, is to let him show himself what he is, and steal out of your company.

VERGES   You have been always called a merciful man, partner.

DOGBERRY   Truly, I would not hang a dog by my will, much 60 more a man who hath any honesty in him.

VERGES   If you hear a child cry in the night, you must call to the nurse and bid her still it.

WATCHMAN   How if the nurse be asleep and will not hear us?

DOGBERRY   Why then, depart in peace, and let the child wake 65 her with crying, for the ewe that will not hear her lamb when it baas will never answer a calf when he bleats.

---

36 **belongs to** is the responsibility of   37 **ancient** experienced   39 **bills** long-handled weapons with axe-like heads   48 **true** honest   53 **by** according to   54 **pitch** black tar-like substance   **defiled** polluted, soiled   59 **by my will** out of choice   60 **more** Dogberry means "less"   62 **still** quiet/calm

VERGES   'Tis very true.

DOGBERRY   This is the end of the charge: you, constable, are to present the prince's own person. If you meet the prince in
70   the night, you may stay him.

VERGES   Nay, by'r lady, that I think a cannot.

DOGBERRY   Five shillings to one on't, with any man that knows the statues, he may stay him: marry, not without the prince be willing, for indeed the watch ought to offend no man, and
75   it is an offence to stay a man against his will.

VERGES   By'r lady, I think it be so.

DOGBERRY   Ha, ah, ha! Well, masters, good night, an there be any matter of weight chances, call up me. Keep your fellows' counsels and your own, and good night. Come, neighbour.

Starts to go

80   WATCHMAN   Well, masters, we hear our charge. Let us go sit here upon the church-bench till two, and then all to bed.

DOGBERRY   One word more, honest neighbours. I pray you watch about Signior Leonato's door, for the wedding being there tomorrow, there is a great coil tonight. Adieu. Be
85   vigitant, I beseech you.   *Exeunt [Dogberry and Verges]*

Enter Borachio and Conrad

BORACHIO   What, Conrad?

WATCHMAN   Peace! Stir not.   *Aside*

BORACHIO   Conrad, I say!

CONRAD   Here, man, I am at thy elbow.

90   BORACHIO   Mass, and my elbow itched, I thought there would a scab follow.

CONRAD   I will owe thee an answer for that: and now forward with thy tale.

BORACHIO   Stand thee close then under this penthouse, for it
95   drizzles rain, and I will, like a true drunkard, utter all to thee.

---

69 present represent   70 stay detain   71 by'r lady by Our Lady (the Virgin Mary)
73 statues malapropism for "statutes"   marry by the Virgin Mary   78 chances i.e. chances to occur   79 counsels confidences   84 coil bustle   85 vigitant malapropism for "vigilant"
90 Mass by the Mass   91 scab scoundrel/skin disease characterized by a rash or scaliness and itching   94 close concealed   penthouse overhanging part of a building

WATCHMAN   Some treason, masters. Yet stand close.   *Aside*

BORACHIO   Therefore know, I have earned of Don John a
thousand ducats.

CONRAD   Is it possible that any villainy should be so dear?

100 BORACHIO   Thou shouldst rather ask if it were possible any
villainy should be so rich, for when rich villains have need of
poor ones, poor ones may make what price they will.

CONRAD   I wonder at it.

BORACHIO   That shows thou art unconfirmed. Thou knowest

105 that the fashion of a doublet, or a hat, or a cloak, is nothing
to a man.

CONRAD   Yes, it is apparel.

BORACHIO   I mean the fashion.

CONRAD   Yes, the fashion is the fashion.

110 BORACHIO   Tush, I may as well say the fool's the fool. But seest
thou not what a deformed thief this fashion is?

WATCHMAN   I know that Deformed: a has been a vile   *Aside*
thief this seven years, a goes up and down like a gentleman.
I remember his name.

115 BORACHIO   Didst thou not hear somebody?

CONRAD   No, 'twas the vane on the house.

BORACHIO   Seest thou not, I say, what a deformed thief this
fashion is, how giddily a turns about all the hot bloods
between fourteen and five-and-thirty, sometimes fashioning

120 them like Pharaoh's soldiers in the reechy painting, sometime
like god Bel's priests in the old church-window, sometime like
the shaven Hercules in the smirched worm-eaten tapestry,
where his codpiece seems as massy as his club?

---

99 dear costly   104 unconfirmed inexperienced   105 is . . . man does not represent a man's
true self (Conrad, however, understands "is of no importance to a man")   108 fashion i.e. the
style as opposed to garments (apparel) themselves   111 deformed i.e. as fashion is constantly
changing   113 up and down all over the place   118 hot bloods spirited, eager young men
120 Pharaoh's soldiers the soldiers of the Egyptian king who pursued the fleeing Israelites
and were drowned in the Red Sea   reechy smoky/grimy   121 god Bel's priests in the
apocryphal Book of Daniel, the priests of Bel were slain by the king of Persia when Daniel
showed that their god was false   122 smirched soiled/discolored   123 codpiece a
conspicuous attachment, often ornamented, sewn onto the front of breeches over the crotch
massy massive/heavy

CONRAD   All this I see, and I see that the fashion wears out
125   more apparel than the man. But art not thou thyself giddy
         with the fashion too, that thou hast shifted out of thy tale
         into telling me of the fashion?

BORACHIO   Not so, neither. But know that I have tonight
         wooed Margaret, the Lady Hero's gentlewoman, by the
130   name of Hero. She leans me out at her mistress' chamber-
         window, bids me a thousand times good night — I tell this
         tale vilely — I should first tell thee how the prince, Claudio
         and my master, planted and placed and possessed by my
         master Don John, saw afar off in the orchard this amiable
135   encounter.

CONRAD   And thought they Margaret was Hero?

BORACHIO   Two of them did, the prince and Claudio, but the
         devil my master knew she was Margaret, and partly by his
         oaths, which first possessed them, partly by the dark night,
140   which did deceive them, but chiefly by my villainy, which did
         confirm any slander that Don John had made. Away went
         Claudio enraged, swore he would meet her as he was
         appointed next morning at the temple, and there, before the
         whole congregation, shame her with what he saw o'er-
145   night, and send her home again without a husband.

FIRST WATCHMAN   We charge you in the prince's name, stand!

SECOND WATCHMAN   Call up the right master constable. We have
         here recovered the most dangerous piece of lechery that ever
         was known in the commonwealth.

150 FIRST WATCHMAN And one Deformed is one of them. I know him, a
         wears a lock.

CONRAD   Masters, masters—

SECOND WATCHMAN   You'll be made bring Deformed forth, I
         warrant you.

---

126 shifted moved (puns on the senses of "shift" as "underclothing" and as "a change of
clothes")   129 gentlewoman attendant   130 leans me out leans out   133 possessed
informed (with connotations of demonic possession, especially given that Don John is
subsequently referred to as the devil)   134 amiable loving   139 oaths avowals
148 recovered malapropism for "discovered"   lechery malapropism for "treachery"
151 lock lovelock, a fashionable lock of curled hair   153 made made to

155 **CONRAD**   Masters—

FIRST WATCHMAN   Never speak, we charge you. Let us obey you to
go with us.

BORACHIO   We are like to prove a goodly commodity, being
taken up of these men's bills.

160 **CONRAD**   A commodity in question, I warrant you. Come,
we'll obey you.   *Exeunt*

Act 3 Scene 4   *running scene 8*

Enter Hero and Margaret and Ursula

HERO   Good Ursula, wake my cousin Beatrice, and desire
her to rise.

URSULA   I will, lady.

HERO   And bid her come hither.

5 **URSULA**   Well.   *[Exit]*

MARGARET   Troth, I think your other rabato were better.

HERO   No, pray thee good Meg, I'll wear this.

MARGARET   By my troth's not so good, and I warrant your
cousin will say so.

10 **HERO**   My cousin's a fool, and thou art another. I'll wear
none but this.

MARGARET   I like the new tire within excellently, if the hair
were a thought browner, and your gown's a most rare
fashion, i'faith. I saw the Duchess of Milan's gown that they

15 praise so.

HERO   O, that exceeds, they say.

MARGARET   By my troth's but a night-gown in respect of
yours — cloth a gold, and cuts, and laced with silver, set

---

156 obey the First Watchman means "command"   **158 commodity** product/goods bought on
credit   **159 taken up** arrested/received on credit   **bills** long-handled weapons/promissory
notes   **160 in question** subject to legal procedures/sought after/in doubt   **3.4 6 rabato** stiff
linen collar, sometimes used to support a ruff   **12 tire** attire (i.e. headdress)   **within** i.e. in an
inner room   **hair** i.e. false hair on the headdress   **13 rare** splendid   **16 exceeds** excels/is
beyond comparison   **17 respect of** comparison to   **18 cuts** slashes in the fabric of a garment
that reveal differently colored material beneath   **laced** trimmed

with pearls, down sleeves, side sleeves, and skirts, round
20   underborne with a bluish tinsel: but for a fine, quaint,
graceful and excellent fashion, yours is worth ten on't.

HERO   God give me joy to wear it, for my heart is exceeding
heavy.

MARGARET   'Twill be heavier soon by the weight of a man.

25   HERO   Fie upon thee, art not ashamed?

MARGARET   Of what, lady? Of speaking honourably? Is not
marriage honourable in a beggar? Is not your lord
honourable without marriage? I think you would have me
say, saving your reverence, 'a husband'. An bad thinking do
30   not wrest true speaking, I'll offend nobody. Is there any
harm in 'the heavier for a husband'? None, I think, an it be
the right husband and the right wife, otherwise 'tis light and
not heavy. Ask my Lady Beatrice else, here she comes.

Enter Beatrice

HERO   Good morrow, coz.

35   BEATRICE   Good morrow, sweet Hero.

HERO   Why, how now? Do you speak in the sick tune?

BEATRICE   I am out of all other tune, methinks.

MARGARET   Clap's into 'Light o' love' — that goes without a
burden. Do you sing it, and I'll dance it.

40   BEATRICE   Ye light o' love with your heels! Then, if your
husband have stables enough, you'll look he shall lack no
barns.

---

19 down sleeves fitted sleeves that went down to the wrists   side sleeves secondary open
sleeves hanging from the shoulders   round underborne trimmed all the way around (this
could refer either to the skirt or to the visible hem of a petticoat)   20 tinsel silk shot with gold
or silver thread   quaint attractive/elegant/skillfully made   21 on't of it   23 heavy sorrowful
(Margaret plays on the literal sense of "weighed down")   25 Fie upon thee an expression of
disgust or indignation   27 in even in   28 I . . . husband i.e. at this rate, I must even apologize
for mentioning the word "husband"   29 An if   30 wrest distort/misinterpret   31 an if
32 light puns on "sexually loose"   33 else otherwise   34 coz cousin   38 Clap's into let
us start singing   "Light o' love" a popular tune   39 burden a man's part, the bass
accompaniment (Margaret continues to play on the idea of the weight of a man)   dance
playing on the sexual connotations of dancing   40 Ye . . . heels! You're a light-heeled
(i.e. promiscuous) one!   42 barns puns on "bairns" (i.e. children)

MARGARET   O illegitimate construction! I scorn that with my heels.

45   BEATRICE   'Tis almost five o'clock, cousin, 'tis time you were ready. By my troth, I am exceeding ill. Hey-ho!

MARGARET   For a hawk, a horse, or a husband?

BEATRICE   For the letter that begins them all, H.

MARGARET   Well, an you be not turned Turk, there's no more
50   sailing by the star.

BEATRICE   What means the fool, trow?

MARGARET   Nothing I, but God send every one their heart's desire!

HERO   These gloves the Count sent me, they are an
55   excellent perfume.

BEATRICE   I am stuffed, cousin, I cannot smell.

MARGARET   A maid, and stuffed! There's goodly catching of cold.

BEATRICE   O, God help me, God help me! How long have you
60   professed apprehension?

MARGARET   Even since you left it. Doth not my wit become me rarely?

BEATRICE   It is not seen enough, you should wear it in your cap. By my troth, I am sick.

65   MARGARET   Get you some of this distilled *carduus benedictus*, and lay it to your heart: it is the only thing for a qualm.

HERO   There thou prick'st her with a thistle.

BEATRICE   *Benedictus?* Why *benedictus?* You have some moral in this *benedictus.*

---

43 illegitimate construction incorrect interpretation (puns on the notion of illegitimate children)   scorn . . . heels reject that by stamping on or kicking at it   46 Hey-ho! . . . husband? Margaret plays on the title of the well-known ballad   48 H puns on "ache," which was pronounced in the same way as the letter   49 an if   be . . . Turk have not rejected your faith (by rejecting your loathing of love)   50 star the North Star, a reliable indicator for navigators   51 trow I wonder   56 stuffed with a cold (Margaret puns on the senses of "penetrated sexually" and "pregnant")   60 professed apprehension claimed to be witty   62 rarely excellently (Beatrice plays on the sense of "infrequently")   63 in your cap i.e. like a fool's coxcomb (headgear resembling a cock's comb)   65 *carduus benedictus* the "holy thistle," a plant often used in medicine (with an obvious pun on "Benedick")   66 qualm sudden sensation of faintness or nausea

70 MARGARET   Moral? No, by my troth I have no moral meaning, I
meant plain holy-thistle. You may think perchance that I
think you are in love, nay, by'r lady, I am not such a fool to
think what I list, nor I list not to think what I can, nor indeed
I cannot think, if I would think my heart out of thinking,
75 that you are in love or that you will be in love or that you can
be in love. Yet Benedick was such another, and now is he
become a man: he swore he would never marry, and yet now
in despite of his heart, he eats his meat without grudging.
And how you may be converted I know not, but methinks
80 you look with your eyes as other women do.

BEATRICE   What pace is this that thy tongue keeps?

MARGARET   Not a false gallop.

Enter Ursula

URSULA   Madam, withdraw. The prince, the count, Signior
Benedick, Don John, and all the gallants of the town are
85 come to fetch you to church.

HERO   Help me to dress, good coz, good Meg, good Ursula.

[Exeunt]

Act 3 Scene 5

*Enter Leonato, and the Constable [Dogberry] and the Headborough
[Verges]*

LEONATO   What would you with me, honest neighbour?

DOGBERRY   Marry, sir, I would have some confidence with you
that decerns you nearly.

LEONATO   Brief, I pray you, for you see it is a busy time
5 with me.

DOGBERRY   Marry, this it is, sir.

VERGES   Yes, in truth it is, sir.

---

73 list please   **76 such another** i.e. a similar enemy to love   **78 eats . . . grudging** i.e. accepts
his lot without complaining   **82 false gallop** literally, a canter, but Margaret means "I speak
the truth"   **3.5 2 confidence** private conference   **3 decerns** a malapropism for "concerns"

LEONATO   What is it, my good friends?

DOGBERRY   Goodman Verges, sir, speaks a little off the
10   matter — an old man, sir, and his wits are not so blunt as,
God help, I would desire they were, but, in faith, honest as
the skin between his brows.

VERGES   Yes, I thank God, I am as honest as any man living
that is an old man, and no honester than I.

15   DOGBERRY   Comparisons are odorous: *palabras*, neighbour
Verges.

LEONATO   Neighbours, you are tedious.

DOGBERRY   It pleases your worship to say so, but we are the
poor duke's officers. But truly, for mine own part, if I were as
20   tedious as a king, I could find in my heart to bestow it all of
your worship.

LEONATO   All thy tediousness on me, ah?

DOGBERRY   Yea, an 'twere a thousand times more than 'tis, for I
hear as good exclamation on your worship as of any man in
25   the city, and though I be but a poor man, I am glad to hear it.

VERGES   And so am I.

LEONATO   I would fain know what you have to say.

VERGES   Marry, sir, our watch tonight, excepting your
worship's presence, have ta'en a couple of as arrant knaves
30   as any in Messina.

DOGBERRY   A good old man, sir, he will be talking. As they say,
'When the age is in, the wit is out', God help us, it is a world
to see. Well said, i'faith, neighbour Verges. Well, God's a good
man, an two men ride of a horse, one must ride behind. An
35   honest soul, i'faith, sir, by my troth he is, as ever broke bread.
But God is to be worshipped, all men are not alike, alas, good
neighbour.

---

9 Goodman title for a person beneath the rank of gentleman   **10 blunt** Dogberry means
"sharp"   **15 odorous** malapropism for "odious"   *palabras* short for *pocas palabras*, the
Spanish for "few words"   **19 poor duke's officers** Dogberry means "duke's poor officers"
20 tedious Dogberry thinks that the word means something complimentary, such as "rich"
24 exclamation public complaint, but Dogberry means "acclamation"   **28 excepting**
Dogberry means "respecting"   **29 arrant** notorious/absolute   **32 a world** i.e. wondrous
33 a good man i.e. good

LEONATO   Indeed, neighbour, he comes too short of you.

DOGBERRY   Gifts that God gives.

40   LEONATO   I must leave you.

DOGBERRY   One word, sir: our watch, sir, have indeed comprehended two auspicious persons, and we would have them this morning examined before your worship.

LEONATO   Take their examination yourself and bring it me. I
45   am now in great haste, as may appear unto you.

DOGBERRY   It shall be suffigance.

LEONATO   Drink some wine ere you go. Fare you well.

[*Enter a Messenger*]

MESSENGER   My lord, they stay for you to give your daughter to her husband.

50   LEONATO   I'll wait upon them. I am ready.

Exeunt [*Leonato and Messenger*]

DOGBERRY   Go, good partner, go, get you to Francis Seacole, bid him bring his pen and inkhorn to the jail. We are now to examination those men.

VERGES   And we must do it wisely.

55   DOGBERRY   We will spare for no wit, I warrant you. Here's that shall drive some of them to a non-come. Only get the learned writer to set down our excommunication and meet me at the jail.   *Exeunt*

Act 4 Scene 1   *running scene 11*

Enter Prince [*Don Pedro, Don John the*] *Bastard, Leonato, Friar*
[*Francis*], *Claudio, Benedick, Hero and Beatrice* [*and Attendants*]

LEONATO   Come, Friar Francis, be brief: only to the plain form of marriage, and you shall recount their particular duties afterwards.

---

42 **comprehended** malapropism for "apprehended"   **auspicious** malapropism for
"suspicious"   46 **suffigance** malapropism for "sufficient"   52 **inkhorn** inkwell   56 **non-
come** Dogberry probably means "nonplus" (i.e. state of perplexity), but the phrase also
suggests "non compos mentis" (i.e. mad)   57 **excommunication** malapropism for
"communication" (i.e. discussion) or possibly "examination"

FRIAR FRANCIS   You come hither, my lord, to marry this lady.

5   CLAUDIO   No.

LEONATO   To be married to her. Friar, you come to marry her.

FRIAR FRANCIS   Lady, you come hither to be married to this count.

HERO   I do.

10   FRIAR FRANCIS   If either of you know any inward impediment why you should not be conjoined, I charge you on your souls to utter it.

CLAUDIO   Know you any, Hero?

HERO   None, my lord.

15   FRIAR FRANCIS   Know you any, Count?

LEONATO   I dare make his answer, none.

CLAUDIO   O, what men dare do! What men may do! What men daily do, not knowing what they do!

BENEDICK   How now? Interjections? Why then, some be of

20   laughing, as ha, ha, he!

CLAUDIO   Stand thee by, friar. Father, by your leave:
Will you with free and unconstrainèd soul
Give me this maid, your daughter?

LEONATO   As freely, son, as God did give her me.

25   CLAUDIO   And what have I to give you back whose worth
May counterpoise this rich and precious gift?

DON PEDRO   Nothing, unless you render her again.

CLAUDIO   Sweet prince, you learn me noble thankfulness.
There, Leonato, take her back again.   *Hands Hero to Leonato*

30   Give not this rotten orange to your friend.
She's but the sign and semblance of her honour.
Behold how like a maid she blushes here.
O, what authority and show of truth
Can cunning sin cover itself withal!

35   Comes not that blood as modest evidence

4.1 10 inward secret   **21 Stand thee by** stand aside   **by your leave** with your permission (i.e. to call you **Father**)   **26 counterpoise** balance, equal   **27 render her again** give her back   **28 learn** teach   **31 sign and semblance** outward appearance and mere image   **34 withal** with   **35 blood** i.e. blush

To witness simple virtue? Would you not swear,
All you that see her, that she were a maid,
By these exterior shows? But she is none.
She knows the heat of a luxurious bed:
40   Her blush is guiltiness, not modesty.

LEONATO   What do you mean, my lord?

CLAUDIO   Not to be married,
Not to knit my soul to an approvèd wanton.

LEONATO   Dear my lord, if you, in your own proof,
45   Have vanquished the resistance of her youth,
And made defeat of her virginity—

CLAUDIO   I know what you would say: if I have known her,
You will say she did embrace me as a husband,
And so extenuate the 'forehand sin.
50   No, Leonato,
I never tempted her with word too large,
But, as a brother to his sister, showed
Bashful sincerity and comely love.

HERO   And seemed I ever otherwise to you?

55   CLAUDIO   Out on thee, seeming! I will write against it.
You seem to me as Dian in her orb,
As chaste as is the bud ere it be blown.
But you are more intemperate in your blood
Than Venus or those pampered animals
60   That rage in savage sensuality.

HERO   Is my lord well that he doth speak so wide?

LEONATO   Sweet prince, why speak not you?

DON PEDRO   What should I speak?
I stand dishonoured, that have gone about
65   To link my dear friend to a common stale.

---

36 witness bear witness to   **39 luxurious** lecherous   **43 approvèd** proved   **44 in . . . proof**
your own test of her   **47 known** had sex with   **49 extenuate . . . sin** lessen the sin of having
sex before marriage   **51 large** unrestrained/licentious   **53 Bashful** modest/sensitive
comely becoming/proper   **55 write against it** i.e. denounce it publicly   **56 Dian . . . orb**
Diana, goddess of chastity and the moon (her orb)   **57 blown** in bloom   **58 intemperate**
immoderate, unbridled   **blood** sexual desire   **59 Venus** goddess of love   **61 wide** wide of
the mark   **65 stale** prostitute

LEONATO   Are these things spoken, or do I but dream?

DON JOHN   Sir, they are spoken, and these things are true.

BENEDICK   This looks not like a nuptial.

HERO   'True'? O God!

70   CLAUDIO   Leonato, stand I here?
Is this the prince? Is this the prince's brother?
Is this face Hero's? Are our eyes our own?

LEONATO   All this is so, but what of this, my lord?

CLAUDIO   Let me but move one question to your daughter,
75   And by that fatherly and kindly power
That you have in her, bid her answer truly.

LEONATO   I charge thee do so, as thou art my child.   *To Hero*

HERO   O, God defend me, how am I beset!
What kind of catechizing call you this?

80   CLAUDIO   To make you answer truly to your name.

HERO   Is it not Hero? Who can blot that name
With any just reproach?

CLAUDIO   Marry, that can Hero:
Hero itself can blot out Hero's virtue.
85   What man was he talked with you yesternight,
Out at your window betwixt twelve and one?
Now if you are a maid, answer to this.

HERO   I talked with no man at that hour, my lord.

DON PEDRO   Why, then you are no maiden. Leonato,
90   I am sorry you must hear. Upon mine honour,
Myself, my brother and this grievèd count
Did see her, hear her, at that hour last night,
Talk with a ruffian at her chamber window,
Who hath indeed, most like a liberal villain,
95   Confessed the vile encounters they have had
A thousand times in secret.

---

74 **move** put   75 **kindly** natural   78 **beset** assailed, besieged   79 **catechizing** questioning,
a form of instruction used by the Church in which a person answers a set of questions about
the Christian faith   80 **answer . . . name** the first question in the Anglican catechism asks
the respondent his or her name   91 **grievèd** wronged/afflicted with sorrow   94 **liberal**
licentious/unrestrained

DON JOHN   Fie, fie, they are not to be named, my lord,
Not to be spoken of.
There is not chastity enough in language
100   Without offence to utter them. Thus, pretty lady,
I am sorry for thy much misgovernment.
CLAUDIO   O Hero! What a Hero hadst thou been,
If half thy outward graces had been placed
About thy thoughts and counsels of thy heart!
105   But fare thee well, most foul, most fair! Farewell,
Thou pure impiety and impious purity!
For thee I'll lock up all the gates of love,
And on my eyelids shall conjecture hang,
To turn all beauty into thoughts of harm,
110   And never shall it more be gracious.
LEONATO   Hath no man's dagger here a point   *Hero swoons*
for me?
BEATRICE   Why, how now, cousin! Wherefore sink you down?
DON JOHN   Come, let us go. These things, come thus to light,
Smother her spirits up.

                    [*Exeunt Don Pedro, Don John and Claudio*]

115   BENEDICK   How doth the lady?
BEATRICE   Dead, I think. Help, uncle!
Hero! Why, Hero! Uncle! Signior Benedick! Friar!
LEONATO   O fate! Take not away thy heavy hand.
Death is the fairest cover for her shame
120   That may be wished for.
BEATRICE   How now, cousin Hero!
FRIAR FRANCIS   Have comfort, lady.
LEONATO   Dost thou look up?
FRIAR FRANCIS   Yea, wherefore should she not?
125   LEONATO   Wherefore? Why, doth not every earthly thing
Cry shame upon her? Could she here deny
The story that is printed in her blood?

---

101 much misgovernment great misconduct   103 graces virtues/attractions
107 For because of   108 conjecture suspicion   110 gracious attractive/joyful/virtuous
114 spirits vital energies   123 look up revive/look heavenward

Do not live, Hero, do not ope thine eyes,
For did I think thou wouldst not quickly die,
130   Thought I thy spirits were stronger than thy shames,
Myself would on the rearward of reproaches
Strike at thy life. Grieved I, I had but one?
Chid I for that at frugal nature's frame?
O, one too much by thee! Why had I one?
135   Why ever wast thou lovely in my eyes?
Why had I not with charitable hand
Took up a beggar's issue at my gates,
Who smearèd thus, and mired with infamy,
I might have said 'No part of it is mine:
140   This shame derives itself from unknown loins'?
But mine, and mine I loved, and mine I praised,
And mine that I was proud on, mine so much
That I myself was to myself not mine,
Valuing of her — why, she, O, she is fallen
145   Into a pit of ink, that the wide sea
Hath drops too few to wash her clean again,
And salt too little which may season give
To her foul-tainted flesh!
  BENEDICK   Sir, sir, be patient.
150   For my part, I am so attired in wonder,
I know not what to say.
  BEATRICE   O, on my soul my cousin is belied!
  BENEDICK   Lady, were you her bedfellow last night?
  BEATRICE   No, truly not: although until last night,
155   I have this twelvemonth been her bedfellow.
  LEONATO   Confirmed, confirmed! O, that is stronger made
Which was before barred up with ribs of iron.
Would the two princes lie, and Claudio lie,

---

131 on . . . reproaches following this disgrace   132 Grieved . . . one? Did I once grieve that I
only had one child?   133 Chid contended with/chastised   frame plan/scheme of things
138 mired soiled   infamy bad reputation/disgrace   142 mine so . . . her I was so devoted
to and proud of her that I cared nothing for myself   147 season preservative   150 attired
clothed   152 belied slandered

Who loved her so that, speaking of her foulness,
160 Washed it with tears? Hence from her, let her die.
FRIAR FRANCIS   Hear me a little:
For I have only been silent so long,
And given way unto this course of fortune,
By noting of the lady. I have marked
165 A thousand blushing apparitions
To start into her face, a thousand innocent shames
In angel whiteness beat away those blushes,
And in her eye there hath appeared a fire
To burn the errors that these princes hold
170 Against her maiden truth. Call me a fool,
Trust not my reading nor my observations,
Which with experimental seal doth warrant
The tenure of my book: trust not my age,
My reverence, calling, nor divinity,
175 If this sweet lady lie not guiltless here
Under some biting error.
LEONATO   Friar, it cannot be.
Thou seest that all the grace that she hath left
Is that she will not add to her damnation
180 A sin of perjury: she not denies it.
Why seek'st thou then to cover with excuse
That which appears in proper nakedness?
FRIAR FRANCIS   Lady, what man is he you are accused of?
HERO   They know that do accuse me: I know none.
185 If I know more of any man alive
Than that which maiden modesty doth warrant,
Let all my sins lack mercy! O my father,
Prove you that any man with me conversed
At hours unmeet, or that I yesternight

---

163 given way gone along with   165 apparitions appearances   172 Which . . . book
which validates, through the confirmation of experience, all that I have read in books
174 reverence respected state   divinity status as a clergyman/knowledge of theology
176 biting severe/painful   180 perjury swearing something false to be true   182 proper true
186 warrant sanction   189 unmeet unsuitable

190   Maintained the change of words with any creature,
         Refuse me, hate me, torture me to death!
         FRIAR FRANCIS   There is some strange misprision in the princes.
         BENEDICK   Two of them have the very bent of honour,
         And if their wisdoms be misled in this,
195   The practice of it lives in John the bastard,
         Whose spirits toil in frame of villainies.
         LEONATO   I know not. If they speak but truth of her,
         These hands shall tear her. If they wrong her honour,
         The proudest of them shall well hear of it.
200   Time hath not yet so dried this blood of mine,
         Nor age so eat up my invention,
         Nor fortune made such havoc of my means,
         Nor my bad life reft me so much of friends,
         But they shall find, awaked in such a kind,
205   Both strength of limb and policy of mind,
         Ability in means and choice of friends,
         To quit me of them throughly.
         FRIAR FRANCIS   Pause awhile,
         And let my counsel sway you in this case.
210   Your daughter here the princes left for dead:
         Let her awhile be secretly kept in,
         And publish it that she is dead indeed.
         Maintain a mourning ostentation,
         And on your family's old monument
215   Hang mournful epitaphs, and do all rites
         That appertain unto a burial.
         LEONATO   What shall become of this? What will this do?
         FRIAR FRANCIS   Marry, this well carried shall on her behalf
         Change slander to remorse, that is some good.

190 Maintained the change engaged in the exchange   191 Refuse reject/disown
192 misprision mistake, misunderstanding   193 very bent of a total inclination for
195 practice scheming/carrying out   196 frame plotting/creating   199 proudest finest/
most arrogant/most eminent/most vigorous   201 eat eaten   invention inventiveness (to
plan revenge)   202 means resources/wealth   203 reft deprived   204 kind manner
205 policy shrewdness   207 quit . . . throughly avenge myself on them thoroughly
212 publish proclaim/make public   213 mourning ostentation display of mourning
214 monument burial vault   218 carried carried out/managed

220   But not for that dream I on this strange course,
           But on this travail look for greater birth.
           She dying, as it must so be maintained,
           Upon the instant that she was accused,
           Shall be lamented, pitied and excused
225   Of every hearer, for it so falls out
           That what we have we prize not to the worth
           Whiles we enjoy it; but, being lacked and lost,
           Why, then we rack the value, then we find
           The virtue that possession would not show us
230   Whiles it was ours. So will it fare with Claudio:
           When he shall hear she died upon his words,
           Th'idea of her life shall sweetly creep
           Into his study of imagination,
           And every lovely organ of her life
235   Shall come apparelled in more precious habit,
           More moving-delicate and full of life,
           Into the eye and prospect of his soul
           Than when she lived indeed. Then shall he mourn —
           If ever love had interest in his liver —
240   And wish he had not so accusèd her,
           No, though he thought his accusation true.
           Let this be so, and doubt not but success
           Will fashion the event in better shape
           Than I can lay it down in likelihood.
245   But if all aim but this be levelled false,
           The supposition of the lady's death
           Will quench the wonder of her infamy.
           And if it sort not well, you may conceal her,
           As best befits her wounded reputation,

---

220 that i.e. the changing of slander to remorse   221 on this travail as a result of this effort
(travail plays on the sense of "pains of childbirth")   226 prize . . . worth value not at its full
worth   228 rack stretch   233 study of imagination introspective musings   234 organ
aspect, feature   235 apparelled dressed   habit clothing   237 prospect field of view
239 interest in a claim over   liver believed to be the seat of love and passion   242 success
succeeding events   243 event outcome   244 lay . . . likelihood outline its probable outcome
245 aim . . . false intentions except this one are confounded   247 wonder of amazement
at/curiosity about   248 sort turn out

250　　　　In some reclusive and religious life,
　　　　　Out of all eyes, tongues, minds and injuries.
　　　BENEDICK　Signior Leonato, let the friar advise you.
　　　　　And though you know my inwardness and love
　　　　　Is very much unto the prince and Claudio,
255　　　　Yet, by mine honour, I will deal in this
　　　　　As secretly and justly as your soul
　　　　　Should with your body.
　　　LEONATO　Being that I flow in grief,
　　　　　The smallest twine may lead me.
260　FRIAR FRANCIS　'Tis well consented. Presently away,
　　　　　For to strange sores strangely they strain the cure.
　　　　　Come, lady, die to live. This wedding day
　　　　　Perhaps is but prolonged. Have patience and endure.

Exeunt [all but Benedick and Beatrice]

　　　BENEDICK　Lady Beatrice, have you wept all this while?
265　BEATRICE　Yea, and I will weep a while longer.
　　　BENEDICK　I will not desire that.
　　　BEATRICE　You have no reason, I do it freely.
　　　BENEDICK　Surely I do believe your fair cousin is wronged.
　　　BEATRICE　Ah, how much might the man deserve of me that
270　would right her.
　　　BENEDICK　Is there any way to show such friendship?
　　　BEATRICE　A very even way, but no such friend.
　　　BENEDICK　May a man do it?
　　　BEATRICE　It is a man's office, but not yours.
275　BENEDICK　I do love nothing in the world so well as you. Is not
　　　that strange?
　　　BEATRICE　As strange as the thing I know not. It were as
　　　possible for me to say I loved nothing so well as you, but
　　　believe me not: and yet I lie not. I confess nothing, nor I deny
280　nothing. I am sorry for my cousin.
　　　BENEDICK　By my sword, Beatrice, thou lovest me.

---

251 injuries insults　**253 inwardness** intimacy　**258 Being that** since　**flow in grief** overflow
with grief/am overcome with tears　**259 twine** thread　**261 For . . . cure** for extreme/
unusual ills require extreme/unusual remedies　**272 even** direct　**friend** friend/lover

BEATRICE   Do not swear by it and eat it.

BENEDICK   I will swear by it that you love me, and I will make
him eat it that says I love not you.

285 BEATRICE   Will you not eat your word?

BENEDICK   With no sauce that can be devised to it. I protest I
love thee.

BEATRICE   Why then, God forgive me.

BENEDICK   What offence, sweet Beatrice?

290 BEATRICE   You have stayed me in a happy hour: I was about to
protest I loved you.

BENEDICK   And do it with all thy heart.

BEATRICE   I love you with so much of my heart that none is left
to protest.

295 BENEDICK   Come, bid me do anything for thee.

BEATRICE   Kill Claudio.

BENEDICK   Ha, not for the wide world.

BEATRICE   You kill me to deny. Farewell.

BENEDICK   Tarry, sweet Beatrice.

300 BEATRICE   I am gone, though I am here. There is no love in you.
Nay I pray you let me go.

BENEDICK   Beatrice—

BEATRICE   In faith, I will go.

BENEDICK   We'll be friends first.

305 BEATRICE   You dare easier be friends with me than fight with
mine enemy.

BENEDICK   Is Claudio thine enemy?

BEATRICE   Is a not approved in the height a villain, that hath
slandered, scorned, dishonoured my kinswoman? O that I
310 were a man! What, bear her in hand until they come to take
hands, and then, with public accusation, uncovered slander,
unmitigated rancour — O God, that I were a man! I would
eat his heart in the market-place.

BENEDICK   Hear me, Beatrice—

---

282 eat it eat your words   286 protest declare/avow/insist   290 stayed detained, halted
299 Tarry stay/linger   310 bear . . . hand delude her with false hopes   take hands i.e. in
marriage   311 uncovered open, barefaced

315 **BEATRICE** Talk with a man out at a window! A proper saying!

BENEDICK Nay, but Beatrice—

BEATRICE Sweet Hero! She is wronged, she is slandered, she is undone.

BENEDICK Beat—

320 **BEATRICE** Princes and counties! Surely, a princely testimony, a goodly Count Comfit, a sweet gallant, surely! O that I were a man for his sake! Or that I had any friend would be a man for my sake! But manhood is melted into curtsies, valour into compliment, and men are only turned into tongue, and trim

325 ones too. He is now as valiant as Hercules that only tells a lie and swears it. I cannot be a man with wishing, therefore I will die a woman with grieving.

BENEDICK Tarry, good Beatrice. By this hand I love thee.

BEATRICE Use it for my love some other way than swearing by

330 it.

BENEDICK Think you in your soul the Count Claudio hath wronged Hero?

BEATRICE Yea, as sure as I have a thought or a soul.

BENEDICK Enough: I am engaged, I will challenge him. I will

335 kiss your hand, and so leave you. By this hand, Claudio shall render me a dear account. As you hear of me, so think of me. Go comfort your cousin, I must say she is dead: and so farewell.   [*Exeunt separately*]

Act 4 Scene 2   *running scene 12*

Enter the Constables [Dogberry and Verges], Borachio and [Sexton as] the Town Clerk in gowns [with Conrad, and the Watch]

DOGBERRY Is our whole dissembly appeared?

VERGES O, a stool and a cushion for the sexton.

---

315 **A proper saying!** A fine story!   318 **undone** ruined   320 **counties** counts   **testimony** evidence/condemnation of error   321 **Count** plays on the sense of "charge in an indictment" **Comfit** candy/sweet   324 **compliment** etiquette/display   **turned into tongue** are all talk **trim** fine/elegant   326 **swears it** merely swears that the lie is true   334 **engaged** pledged/ accepting of Beatrice's wish   336 **dear** costly/significant   **4.2 Sexton** a church officer 1 **dissembly** malapropism for "assembly"

SEXTON   Which be the malefactors?

DOGBERRY   Marry, that am I and my partner.

5 VERGES   Nay, that's certain, we have the exhibition to
examine.

SEXTON   But which are the offenders that are to be examined?
Let them come before master constable.

DOGBERRY   Yea, marry, let them come before me.   *Borachio and*
10 What is your name, friend?   *Conrad are*
                                                          brought forward
BORACHIO   Borachio.

DOGBERRY   Pray, write down 'Borachio'.— Yours, sirrah?

CONRAD   I am a gentleman, sir, and my name is Conrad.

DOGBERRY   Write down 'master gentleman Conrad'. Masters,
15 do you serve God? Masters, it is proved already that you are
little better than false knaves, and it will go near to be
thought so shortly. How answer you for yourselves?

CONRAD   Marry, sir, we say we are none.

DOGBERRY   A marvellous witty fellow, I assure you. But I will go
20 about with him. Come you hither, sirrah, a word in your ear,
sir: I say to you, it is thought you are false   *To Borachio*
knaves.

BORACHIO   Sir, I say to you we are none.

DOGBERRY   Well, stand aside. 'Fore God, they are both in a tale.
25 Have you writ down that they are none?

SEXTON   Master constable, you go not the way to examine.
You must call forth the watch that are their accusers.

DOGBERRY   Yea, marry, that's the eftest way. Let the watch
come forth. Masters, I charge you, in the prince's name,
30 accuse these men.

FIRST WATCHMAN   This man said, sir, that Don John, the prince's
brother, was a villain.

---

3 malefactors wrongdoers   **5 exhibition** Dogberry means "commission" (i.e. authority to
examine the offenders)   **12 sirrah** sir (contemptuous)   **15 do . . . God** the 1600 Quarto
follows this with an exchange censored from the Folio: Conrad and Borachio reply "Yea, sir, we
hope," to which Dogberry says "Write down that they hope they serve God. And write 'God'
first, for God defend but God should go before such villains." He then continues "Masters . . . ,"
as in Folio   **19 witty** clever/wily   **go about with** get the better of/handle   **24 in a tale** in
agreement   **28 eftest** a nonsense word, which Dogberry intends to mean "easiest/nearest"

DOGBERRY   Write down 'Prince John a villain'. Why, this is flat
perjury, to call a prince's brother villain.

35   BORACHIO   Master constable—

DOGBERRY   Pray thee fellow, peace: I do not like thy look, I
promise thee.

SEXTON   What heard you him say else?

SECOND WATCHMAN   Marry, that he had received a thousand
40   ducats of Don John for accusing the Lady Hero wrongfully.

DOGBERRY   Flat burglary as ever was committed.

VERGES   Yea, by th'mass, that it is.

SEXTON   What else, fellow?

FIRST WATCHMAN   And that Count Claudio did mean, upon his
45   words, to disgrace Hero before the whole assembly, and not
marry her.

DOGBERRY   O villain! Thou wilt be condemned into everlasting
redemption for this.

SEXTON   What else?

50   WATCHMEN   This is all.

SEXTON   And 'this is more, masters, than you can deny.
Prince John is this morning secretly stolen away. Hero was in
this manner accused, in this very manner refused, and upon
the grief of this suddenly died. Master Constable, let these
55   men be bound, and brought to Leonato. I will go before and
show him their examination.   [Exit]

DOGBERRY   Come, let them be opinioned.

VERGES   Let them be in the hands—

CONRAD   Off, coxcomb!

60   DOGBERRY   God's my life, where's the sexton? Let him write
down 'the prince's officer coxcomb'. Come, bind them.—
Thou naughty varlet!

CONRAD   Away! You are an ass, you are an ass.

DOGBERRY   Dost thou not suspect my place? Dost thou not
65   suspect my years? O that he were here to write me down an

---

48 redemption Dogberry means "damnation"   57 opinioned malapropism for "pinioned"
(i.e. bound)   58 Let . . . hands let their hands be tied   59 coxcomb fool   62 naughty wicked
64 suspect malapropism for "respect"

ass! But masters, remember that I am an ass: though it be not written down, yet forget not that I am an ass. No, thou villain, thou art full of piety, as shall be proved upon thee by good witness. I am a wise fellow, and which is more, an
70   officer, and which is more, a householder, and which is more, as pretty a piece of flesh as any in Messina, and one that knows the law, go to, and a rich fellow enough, go to, and a fellow that hath had losses, and one that hath two gowns and everything handsome about him. Bring him
75   away. O that I had been writ down an ass!   *Exeunt*

Act 5 Scene 1   *running scene 13*

Enter Leonato and his brother [Antonio]

ANTONIO   If you go on thus, you will kill yourself,
And 'tis not wisdom thus to second grief
Against yourself.

LEONATO   I pray thee, cease thy counsel,
5   Which falls into mine ears as profitless
As water in a sieve: give not me counsel,
Nor let no comforter delight mine ear
But such a one whose wrongs do suit with mine.
Bring me a father that so loved his child,
10   Whose joy of her is overwhelmed like mine,
And bid him speak of patience,
Measure his woe the length and breadth of mine,
And let it answer every strain for strain,
As thus for thus, and such a grief for such,
15   In every lineament, branch, shape and form.
If such a one will smile and stroke his beard,
Bid sorrow wag, cry 'Hem!' when he should groan,

---

68 piety Dogberry means "impiety"   73 had losses i.e. he was formerly even wealthier
two gowns cloaks were fairly costly, so Dogberry suggests he has reasonably good finances
74 handsome fitting/comfortable   5.1 2 second support   8 suit with correspond to/fit
13 answer requite   strain emotional pang/melody   15 lineament physical feature/
characteristic   branch division/part   17 wag be off   'Hem!' i.e. clear one's throat in
preparation for speech

Patch grief with proverbs, make misfortune drunk
With candle-wasters, bring him yet to me,
20 And I of him will gather patience.
But there is no such man: for, brother, men
Can counsel and speak comfort to that grief
Which they themselves not feel, but tasting it,
Their counsel turns to passion, which before
25 Would give preceptial medicine to rage,
Fetter strong madness in a silken thread,
Charm ache with air and agony with words.
No, no, 'tis all men's office to speak patience
To those that wring under the load of sorrow,
30 But no man's virtue nor sufficiency
To be so moral when he shall endure
The like himself: therefore give me no counsel.
My griefs cry louder than advertisement.

ANTONIO   Therein do men from children nothing differ.

35 LEONATO   I pray thee peace. I will be flesh and blood,
For there was never yet philosopher
That could endure the toothache patiently,
However they have writ the style of gods
And made a push at chance and sufferance.

40 ANTONIO   Yet bend not all the harm upon yourself,
Make those that do offend you suffer too.

LEONATO   There thou speak'st reason. Nay, I will do so.
My soul doth tell me Hero is belied,
And that shall Claudio know, so shall the prince
45 And all of them that thus dishonour her.

Enter Prince [Don Pedro] and Claudio

ANTONIO   Here comes the prince and Claudio hastily.

---

19 **candle-wasters** those who waste candles by staying up late for study or drinking
24 **passion** powerful emotion/rage   25 **preceptial** of precepts (i.e. instructions or rules)
29 **wring** writhe/are oppressed/weep   30 **sufficiency** ability   31 **moral** full of moralizing
advice and opinions   33 **advertisement** advice/admonition/public proclamation
35 **peace** silence   38 **However** however much   **writ . . . of** written in the manner of/
written as if with the authority of   39 **made . . . at** scorned/attacked   **sufferance** suffering/
endurance (of misery)

DON PEDRO Good den, good den.

CLAUDIO Good day to both of you.

LEONATO Hear you, my lords—

50 DON PEDRO We have some haste, Leonato.

LEONATO Some haste, my lord! Well, fare you well, my lord:
Are you so hasty now? Well, all is one.

DON PEDRO Nay, do not quarrel with us, good old man.

ANTONIO If he could right himself with quarrelling,
55 Some of us would lie low.

CLAUDIO Who wrongs him?

LEONATO Marry, thou dost wrong me, thou   *Claudio prepares to*
dissembler, thou: *draw his sword*
Nay, never lay thy hand upon thy sword,
I fear thee not.

60 CLAUDIO Marry, beshrew my hand
If it should give your age such cause of fear:
In faith, my hand meant nothing to my sword.

LEONATO Tush, tush, man, never fleer and jest at me:
I speak not like a dotard nor a fool,
65 As under privilege of age to brag
What I have done being young or what would do
Were I not old. Know, Claudio, to thy head,
Thou hast so wronged my innocent child and me
That I am forced to lay my reverence by,
70 And with grey hairs and bruise of many days,
Do challenge thee to trial of a man.
I say thou hast belied mine innocent child:
Thy slander hath gone through and through her heart,
And she lies buried with her ancestors —
75 O, in a tomb where never scandal slept,
Save this of hers, framed by thy villainy!

CLAUDIO My villainy?

---

50 have are in   52 all is one it's all one/it does not matter   55 Some of us i.e. Don Pedro and
Claudio   58 dissembler deceiver/hypocrite   60 beshrew curse   62 meant . . . sword had
no intentions toward my sword   63 fleer mock, jeer   64 dotard old fool   67 head face
69 reverence respect due to an old man   71 trial . . . man i.e. a duel

	LEONATO	Thine, Claudio, thine, I say.
	DON PEDRO	You say not right, old man.
80	LEONATO	My lord, my lord,

I'll prove it on his body if he dare,
Despite his nice fence and his active practice,
His May of youth and bloom of lustihood.

CLAUDIO   Away! I will not have to do with you.

85 LEONATO   Canst thou so daff me? Thou hast killed my child:
If thou kill'st me, boy, thou shalt kill a man.

ANTONIO   He shall kill two of us, and men indeed:
But that's no matter, let him kill one first.
Win me and wear me, let him answer me.

90   Come follow me, boy, come, sir boy, come follow me:
Sir boy, I'll whip you from your foining fence,
Nay, as I am a gentleman, I will.

LEONATO   Brother—

ANTONIO   Content yourself. God knows I loved my niece,
95   And she is dead, slandered to death by villains,
That dare as well answer a man indeed
As I dare take a serpent by the tongue.
Boys, apes, braggarts, Jacks, milksops!

LEONATO   Brother Antony—

100 ANTONIO   Hold you content. What, man! I know them, yea,
And what they weigh, even to the utmost scruple,
Scrambling, out-facing, fashion-monging boys,
That lie and cog and flout, deprave and slander,
Go anticly, and show outward hideousness,
105   And speak off half a dozen dang'rous words,
How they might hurt their enemies, if they durst,
And this is all.

---

82 nice fence refined and skillful swordsmanship/defensive action (contemptuous)
83 lustihood vigor   85 daff cast aside   89 Win . . . wear me overcome me and then brag
about it, flaunt your prize   91 foining fence thrusting swordsmanship   98 braggarts
boasters   Jacks rascals/louts   milksops effeminate/cowardly men   101 weigh i.e. are
worth   scruple very small measurement of weight   102 Scrambling contentious/uncouth
out-facing defiant/confrontational/bullying   fashion-monging preoccupied with fashion/
dandies   103 cog cheat   flout insult/mock   deprave defame/deride   104 anticly
grotesquely   105 speak off throw out   106 durst dared

LEONATO   But, brother Antony—

ANTONIO   Come, 'tis no matter:

110   Do not you meddle, let me deal in this.

DON PEDRO   Gentlemen both, we will not wake your patience.
My heart is sorry for your daughter's death.
But on my honour, she was charged with nothing
But what was true, and very full of proof.

115   LEONATO   My lord, my lord—

DON PEDRO   I will not hear you.

Enter Benedick

LEONATO   No? Come, brother, away! I will be heard.

ANTONIO   And shall, or some of us will smart for it.

                    Exeunt both [Leonato and Antonio]

DON PEDRO   See, see, here comes the man we went to seek.

120   CLAUDIO   Now, signior, what news?

BENEDICK   Good day, my lord.

DON PEDRO   Welcome, signior: you are almost come to part
almost a fray.

CLAUDIO   We had like to have had our two noses snapped off

125   with two old men without teeth.

DON PEDRO   Leonato and his brother. What think'st thou? Had
we fought, I doubt we should have been too young for them.

BENEDICK   In a false quarrel there is no true valour. I came to
seek you both.

130   CLAUDIO   We have been up and down to seek thee, for we are
high-proof melancholy and would fain have it beaten away.
Wilt thou use thy wit?

BENEDICK   It is in my scabbard: shall I draw it?

DON PEDRO   Dost thou wear thy wit by thy side?

135   CLAUDIO   Never any did so, though very many have been
beside their wit. I will bid thee draw, as we do the minstrels,
draw to pleasure us.

---

111 **wake your patience** disturb your patience further   124 **had . . . have** nearly
125 **with** by   127 **doubt** fear (said with irony)   131 **high-proof** in the highest degree
133 **draw** as one draws a sword   136 **beside their wit** out of their minds (plays on **by thy side**)
draw . . . minstrels draw it as a musician (**minstrel**) would draw out his instrument from its
case or draw a bow across strings

DON PEDRO   As I am an honest man, he looks pale. Art thou sick, or angry?

140   CLAUDIO   What, courage, man! What though care killed a cat, thou hast mettle enough in thee to kill care.

BENEDICK   Sir, I shall meet your wit in the career, an you charge it against me. I pray you choose another subject.

CLAUDIO   Nay then, give him another staff: this last was broke

145   cross.

DON PEDRO   By this light, he changes more and more: I think he be angry indeed.

CLAUDIO   If he be, he knows how to turn his girdle.

BENEDICK   Shall I speak a word in your ear?

150   CLAUDIO   God bless me from a challenge!

BENEDICK   You are a villain. I jest not: I will   *Aside to Claudio* make it good how you dare, with what you dare, and when you dare. Do me right, or I will protest your cowardice. You have killed a sweet lady, and her death shall fall heavy on

155   you. Let me hear from you.

CLAUDIO   Well, I will meet you, so I may have good cheer.

DON PEDRO   What? A feast, a feast?

CLAUDIO   I'faith, I thank him: he hath bid me to a calf's head and a capon, the which if I do not carve most curiously, say

160   my knife's naught. Shall I not find a woodcock too?

BENEDICK   Sir, your wit ambles well, it goes easily.

DON PEDRO   I'll tell thee how Beatrice praised thy wit the other day: I said, thou hadst a fine wit. 'True,' says she, 'a fine little one.' 'No,' said I, 'a great wit.' 'Right,' says she, 'a great gross

---

140 care . . . cat a common proverb   **care** anxiety/sorrow   **141 mettle** spirit, vigor
142 in the career at full gallop, as in a jousting tournament   **an** if   **143 charge** level/advance
in attack   **144 staff** lance   **145 cross** crosswise, in the middle (an indication of clumsiness)
148 turn his girdle a common proverb referring to the turning of one's belt (**girdle**) so that the
buckle is at the back, and meaning "put up with it"   **153 Do me right** give me satisfaction
protest declare   **156 so** provided   **cheer** entertainment   **158 calf's . . . capon** animals
associated with foolishness (the calf) and cowardice (the **capon**, a castrated cockerel)
159 curiously skillfully   **160 woodcock** a bird associated with stupidity   **161 ambles** strolls
(as opposed to moving rapidly)   **easily** in a state of ease/unhurriedly   **163 fine** excellent
(Beatrice's response plays on the senses of "marvelously" and "slender")   **wit** plays on the
sense of "penis"

165   one.' 'Nay,' said I, 'a good wit.' 'Just,' said she, 'it hurts
      nobody.' 'Nay,' said I, 'the gentleman is wise.' 'Certain,' said
      she, 'a wise gentleman.' 'Nay,' said I, 'he hath the tongues.'
      'That I believe,' said she, 'for he swore a thing to me on
      Monday night, which he forswore on Tuesday morning:
170   there's a double tongue, there's two tongues.' Thus did she,
      an hour together, transshape thy particular virtues: yet at
      last she concluded with a sigh, thou wast the properest man
      in Italy.

      CLAUDIO   For the which she wept heartily and said she cared
175   not.

      DON PEDRO   Yea, that she did: but yet for all that, an if she did
      not hate him deadly, she would love him dearly. The old
      man's daughter told us all.

      CLAUDIO   All, all, and moreover, God saw him when he was
180   hid in the garden.

      DON PEDRO   But when shall we set the savage bull's horns on the
      sensible Benedick's head?

      CLAUDIO   Yea, and text underneath, 'Here dwells Benedick
      the married man'?

185   BENEDICK   Fare you well, boy, you know my mind. I will leave
      you now to your gossip-like humour. You break jests as
      braggarts do their blades, which God be thanked, hurt not.
      My lord, for your many courtesies I thank you. I must
      discontinue your company. Your brother the bastard is fled
190   from Messina: you have among you killed a sweet and
      innocent lady. For my Lord Lackbeard there, he and I shall
      meet: and till then, peace be with him.   [Exit]

      DON PEDRO   He is in earnest.

---

167 wise gentleman either said with irony or meaning "old fool"   **hath the tongues** can
speak foreign languages   **169 forswore** swore against/denied   **170 double**
twofold/duplicitous   **171 transshape** transform   **172 properest** most handsome/finest
177 old man's daughter i.e. Hero   **179 God . . . garden** an allusion both to Benedick hiding in
the arbor and to Adam, after his transgression, hiding from God in the Garden of Eden
181 But . . . man Don Pedro and Claudio recall Benedick's earlier statement that this is to be
his fate if he marries   **187 braggarts . . . blades** i.e. as boasters damage or break their swords
themselves to make it look as if they have been fighting   **188 My lord** i.e. Don Pedro

CLAUDIO   In most profound earnest, and I'll warrant you, for
195   the love of Beatrice.

DON PEDRO   And hath challenged thee.

CLAUDIO   Most sincerely.

DON PEDRO   What a pretty thing man is when he goes in his
doublet and hose and leaves off his wit!

*Enter Constable [Dogberry, Verges and the Watch, with] Conrad and
Borachio*

200   CLAUDIO   He is then a giant to an ape, but then is an ape a
doctor to such a man.

DON PEDRO   But, soft you, let me be: pluck up, my heart, and be
sad. Did he not say my brother was fled?

DOGBERRY   Come you, sir: if justice cannot tame you, she shall
205   ne'er weigh more reasons in her balance. Nay, an you be a
cursing hypocrite once, you must be looked to.

DON PEDRO   How now? Two of my brother's men bound?
Borachio one!

CLAUDIO   Hearken after their offence, my lord.

210   DON PEDRO   Officers, what offence have these men done?

DOGBERRY   Marry, sir, they have committed false report,
moreover, they have spoken untruths, secondarily, they are
slanders, sixth and lastly, they have belied a lady, thirdly,
they have verified unjust things, and to conclude, they are
215   lying knaves.

DON PEDRO   First, I ask thee what they have done, thirdly, I ask
thee what's their offence, sixth and lastly, why they are
committed, and to conclude, what you lay to their charge.

CLAUDIO   Rightly reasoned, and in his own division. And by
220   my troth, there's one meaning well suited.

---

199 hose breeches   200 He . . . man he (i.e. one who has left off his wit) is then a hero (giant)
in the eyes of a fool (ape), but in fact the fool is a learned person (doctor) in comparison to
him   202 soft you wait a moment   pluck up rouse/collect yourself   203 sad serious
205 reasons plays on "raisins," then pronounced in a similar manner   balance scales, which
Justice is traditionally depicted as carrying   206 cursing swearing, or Dogberry may mean
"accursed"   209 Hearken inquire   211 false report slander/untruths   213 slanders
Dogberry means "slanderers"   219 division logical order

DON PEDRO   Who have you offended, masters, that you are thus
bound to your answer? This learned constable is too cunning
to be understood. What's your offence?

BORACHIO   Sweet prince, let me go no farther to mine answer.
225   Do you hear me, and let this count kill me. I have deceived
even your very eyes. What your wisdoms could not discover,
these shallow fools have brought to light, who in the night
overheard me confessing to this man, how Don John your
brother incensed me to slander the Lady Hero, how you were
230   brought into the orchard and saw me court Margaret in
Hero's garments, how you disgraced her when you should
marry her. My villainy they have upon record, which I had
rather seal with my death than repeat over to my shame. The
lady is dead upon mine and my master's false accusation,
235   and briefly, I desire nothing but the reward of a villain.

DON PEDRO   Runs not this speech like iron through   *To Claudio*
your blood?

CLAUDIO   I have drunk poison whiles he uttered it.

DON PEDRO   But did my brother set thee on to this?   *To Borachio*

BORACHIO   Yea, and paid me richly for the practice of it.

240   DON PEDRO   He is composed and framed of treachery,
And fled he is upon this villainy.

CLAUDIO   Sweet Hero! Now thy image doth appear
In the rare semblance that I loved it first.

DOGBERRY   Come, bring away the plaintiffs. By this time our
245   sexton hath reformed Signior Leonato of the matter. And
masters, do not forget to specify, when time and place shall
serve, that I am an ass.

VERGES   Here, here comes master Signior Leonato, and the
sexton too.

Enter Leonato [and Antonio, with the Sexton]

---

222 bound on the way/tied up   **answer** trial   **cunning** ingenious/knowledgeable
229 incensed incited   **243 semblance** image   **244 plaintiffs** Dogberry means "defendants"
(a plaintiff is a complainant)   **245 reformed** malapropism for "informed"

250 LEONATO   Which is the villain? Let me see his eyes,
         That, when I note another man like him,
         I may avoid him. Which of these is he?
     BORACHIO   If you would know your wronger, look on me.
     LEONATO   Art thou the slave that with thy breath hast killed
255   Mine innocent child?
     BORACHIO   Yea, even I alone.
     LEONATO   No, not so, villain, thou beliest thyself:
         Here stand a pair of honourable men,
         A third is fled, that had a hand in it.
260   I thank you, princes, for my daughter's death.
         Record it with your high and worthy deeds,
         'Twas bravely done, if you bethink you of it.
     CLAUDIO   I know not how to pray your patience,
         Yet I must speak. Choose your revenge yourself,
265   Impose me to what penance your invention
         Can lay upon my sin. Yet sinned I not
         But in mistaking.
     DON PEDRO   By my soul, nor I.
         And yet, to satisfy this good old man,
270   I would bend under any heavy weight
         That he'll enjoin me to.
     LEONATO   I cannot bid you bid my daughter live —
         That were impossible — but I pray you both,
         Possess the people in Messina here
275   How innocent she died, and if your love
         Can labour aught in sad invention,
         Hang her an epitaph upon her tomb,
         And sing it to her bones, sing it tonight:
         Tomorrow morning come you to my house,
280   And since you could not be my son-in-law,
         Be yet my nephew. My brother hath a daughter,
         Almost the copy of my child that's dead,

---

258 honourable men i.e. Don Pedro and Claudio   265 Impose me to impose on me
274 Possess inform   276 aught at all, to any extent   invention inventiveness/imagination

And she alone is heir to both of us:
Give her the right you should have giv'n her cousin,
285 And so dies my revenge.

CLAUDIO   O noble sir,
Your over-kindness doth wring tears from me!
I do embrace your offer and dispose
For henceforth of poor Claudio.

290 LEONATO   Tomorrow then I will expect your coming,
Tonight I take my leave. This naughty man
Shall face to face be brought to Margaret,
Who I believe was packed in all this wrong,
Hired to it by your brother.

295 BORACHIO   No, by my soul, she was not,
Nor knew not what she did when she spoke to me,
But always hath been just and virtuous
In anything that I do know by her.

DOGBERRY   Moreover, sir, which indeed is not under white and
300 black, this plaintiff here, the offender, did call me ass. I
beseech you let it be remembered in his punishment. And
also the watch heard them talk of one Deformed: they say he
wears a key in his ear and a lock hanging by it, and borrows
money in God's name, the which he hath used so long and
305 never paid that now men grow hard-hearted and will lend
nothing for God's sake. Pray you examine him upon that
point.

LEONATO   I thank thee for thy care and honest pains.

DOGBERRY   Your worship speaks like a most thankful and
310 reverend youth, and I praise God for you.

LEONATO   There's for thy pains.   *Gives money*

DOGBERRY   God save the foundation!

LEONATO   Go, I discharge thee of thy prisoner, and I thank
thee.

---

284 right puns on "rite"   288 dispose you may dispose   293 packed implicated/acting as an
accomplice   299 under . . . black in writing   302 they . . . it Dogberry's misunderstanding of
the First Watchman's claim that Deformed wears a lock   304 in God's name the usual plea of
a beggar   312 God . . . foundation! the usual response of one receiving alms from a charitable
foundation

315   DOGBERRY   I leave an arrant knave with your worship, which I
beseech your worship to correct yourself, for the example of
others. God keep your worship! I wish your worship well.
God restore you to health! I humbly give you leave to depart,
and if a merry meeting may be wished, God prohibit it!
320   Come, neighbour.

LEONATO   Until tomorrow morning, lords, farewell.

Exeunt [Dogberry and Verges]

ANTONIO   Farewell, my lords: we look for you tomorrow.

DON PEDRO   We will not fail.

CLAUDIO   Tonight I'll mourn with Hero.

325   LEONATO   Bring you these fellows on.— We'll talk with
Margaret,   *To the Watch*
How her acquaintance grew with this lewd fellow.

Exeunt [separately]

Act 5 Scene 2   *running scene 14*

Enter Benedick and Margaret [meeting]

BENEDICK   Pray thee, sweet Mistress Margaret, deserve well at
my hands by helping me to the speech of Beatrice.

MARGARET   Will you then write me a sonnet in praise of my
beauty?

5   BENEDICK   In so high a style, Margaret, that no man living
shall come over it, for in most comely truth thou deservest it.

MARGARET   To have no man come over me? Why, shall I always
keep below stairs?

BENEDICK   Thy wit is as quick as the greyhound's mouth, it
10   catches.

MARGARET   And yours as blunt as the fencer's foils, which hit
but hurt not.

---

318 **give you** Dogberry means "ask your"   319 **prohibit** Dogberry means "permit"   322 **look for** expect   326 **lewd** wicked/base   **5.2 2 the speech of** speak with   5 **style** poetic style (puns on "stile")   6 **come over** surpass/surmount (Margaret plays on the sense of "mount sexually")   **comely** proper/pleasing   8 **keep below stairs** remain (unmarried) in the servants' quarters   10 **catches** seizes (its prey)   11 **foils** swords with blunt edges

BENEDICK   A most manly wit, Margaret, it will not hurt a
woman: and so, I pray thee call Beatrice, I give thee the
15   bucklers.

MARGARET   Give us the swords, we have bucklers of our own.

BENEDICK   If you use them, Margaret, you must put in the
pikes with a vice, and they are dangerous weapons for maids.

MARGARET   Well, I will call Beatrice to you, who I think hath
20   legs.   *Exit Margaret*

BENEDICK   And therefore will come.

> The god of love,   *Sings*
> That sits above,
> And knows me, and knows me,
25   > How pitiful I deserve—

I mean in singing; but in loving, Leander the good
swimmer, Troilus the first employer of panders, and a
whole bookful of these quondam carpet-mongers, whose
names yet run smoothly in the even road of a blank verse,
30   why, they were never so truly turned over and over as my
poor self in love. Marry, I cannot show it in rhyme, I have
tried: I can find out no rhyme to 'lady' but 'baby' — an
innocent rhyme: for 'scorn,' 'horn' — a hard rhyme: for
'school,' 'fool' — a babbling rhyme: very ominous endings.
35   No, I was not born under a rhyming planet, for I cannot
woo in festival terms.

Enter Beatrice

Sweet Beatrice, wouldst thou come when I called thee?

BEATRICE   Yea, signior, and depart when you bid me.

BENEDICK   O, stay but till then!

---

14 give . . . bucklers surrender   **16 swords** with phallic connotations   **bucklers** small
shields with spikes in their centers/vaginas   **18 pikes** the shield's spikes/penises   **vice** screw
(with sexual connotations)   **21 come** a possible pun on "orgasm"   **22 The . . . deserve** the
lyrics to a well-known Elizabethan song   **25 How . . . singing** how much pity I deserve for my
poor singing   **26 Leander . . . swimmer** Leander regularly swam across the Hellespont to see
his lover Hero, until one night he drowned   **27 Troilus . . . panders** Troilus was helped in his
love affair with Cressida by the go-between (**pander**) Pandarus, though Cressida eventually
rejected him   **28 quondam carpet-mongers** former ladies' men   **33 innocent** simple/
foolish   **hard** poor/erect (playing on the phallic connotations of **horn**)   **36 festival** merry/
lighthearted/celebratory

40 **BEATRICE**   'Then' is spoken: fare you well now. And yet ere I go, let me go with that I came, which is, with knowing what hath passed between you and Claudio.

BENEDICK   Only foul words: and thereupon I will kiss thee.

BEATRICE   Foul words is but foul wind, and foul wind is but foul 45 breath, and foul breath is noisome: therefore I will depart unkissed.

BENEDICK   Thou hast frighted the word out of his right sense, so forcible is thy wit. But I must tell thee plainly, Claudio undergoes my challenge, and either I must shortly hear from 50 him, or I will subscribe him a coward. And I pray thee now tell me, for which of my bad parts didst thou first fall in love with me?

BEATRICE   For them all together, which maintained so politic a state of evil that they will not admit any good part to 55 intermingle with them. But for which of my good parts did you first suffer love for me?

BENEDICK   'Suffer love'! A good epithet! I do suffer love indeed, for I love thee against my will.

BEATRICE   In spite of your heart, I think. Alas, poor heart! If 60 you spite it for my sake, I will spite it for yours, for I will never love that which my friend hates.

BENEDICK   Thou and I are too wise to woo peaceably.

BEATRICE   It appears not in this confession. There's not one wise man among twenty that will praise himself.

65 **BENEDICK**   An old, an old instance, Beatrice, that lived in the time of good neighbours. If a man do not erect in this age his own tomb ere he dies, he shall live no longer in monuments than the bells ring, and the widow weeps.

BEATRICE   And how long is that, think you?

---

41 **that I came** that which I came for   45 **noisome** noxious   50 **subscribe** state/declare in writing   53 **politic** prudent   56 **suffer** experience/permit (Benedick puns on the senses of "feel pain" and "endure")   61 **friend** lover   63 **confession** statement/declaration/admission   65 **instance** saying/argument   66 **time . . . neighbours** good old days (when neighbors were friendly)   67 **tomb** i.e. memorial   **monuments** memory   68 **bells . . . weeps** i.e. the duration of the funeral and mourning period

70   BENEDICK   Question: why, an hour in clamour and a quarter in
rheum. Therefore is it most expedient for the wise, if Don
Worm, his conscience, find no impediment to the contrary,
to be the trumpet of his own virtues, as I am to myself. So
much for praising myself, who I myself will bear witness is
75   praiseworthy. And now tell me, how doth your cousin?

BEATRICE   Very ill.

BENEDICK   And how do you?

BEATRICE   Very ill too.

Enter Ursula

BENEDICK   Serve God, love me and mend. There will I leave you
80   too, for here comes one in haste.

URSULA   Madam, you must come to your uncle — yonder's
old coil at home: it is proved my Lady Hero hath been falsely
accused, the prince and Claudio mightily abused, and Don
John is the author of all, who is fled and gone. Will you come
85   presently?

BEATRICE   Will you go hear this news, signior?

BENEDICK   I will live in thy heart, die in thy lap, and be buried in
thy eyes. And moreover, I will go with thee to thy uncle's.

Exeunt

Act 5 Scene 3

running scene 15

*Enter Claudio, Prince [Don Pedro] and three or four with tapers [fol-
lowed by Balthasar and Musicians]*

CLAUDIO   Is this the monument of Leonato?

LORD   It is, my lord.

CLAUDIO   [*Reads the*] *epitaph*
'Done to death by slanderous tongues
Was the Hero that here lies:

---

70 **Question** you have asked a question, here follows the answer   **clamour** noise of the bells
71 **rheum** tears   **Don . . . conscience** conscience was often imaged as a gnawing worm
82 **old coil** great turmoil   87 **die** puns on the sense of "orgasm"   88 **eyes** puns on the sense
of "vagina"

5   Death, in guerdon of her wrongs,
       Gives her fame which never dies.
       So the life that died with shame
       Lives in death with glorious fame.'
       Hang thou there upon the tomb,
10   Praising her when I am dumb.
       Now, music, sound, and sing your solemn hymn.

BALTHASAR   [*Sings the*] *song*
       Pardon, goddess of the night,
       Those that slew thy virgin knight,
       For the which, with songs of woe,
15   Round about her tomb they go.
       Midnight, assist our moan,
       Help us to sigh and groan,
       Heavily, heavily:
       Graves, yawn and yield your dead,
20   Till death be utterèd,
       Heavily, heavily.

CLAUDIO   Now, unto thy bones good night!
       Yearly will I do this rite.

DON PEDRO   Good morrow, masters, put your torches out.
25   The wolves have preyed, and look, the gentle day
       Before the wheels of Phoebus round about
       Dapples the drowsy east with spots of grey.
       Thanks to you all, and leave us. Fare you well.

CLAUDIO   Good morrow, masters: each his several way.

30 DON PEDRO   Come, let us hence, and put on other weeds,
       And then to Leonato's we will go.

CLAUDIO   And Hymen now with luckier issue speed's
       Than this for whom we rendered up this woe.   *Exeunt*

---

5 guerdon recompense   6 fame renown/reputation   12 goddess . . . night Diana, goddess of
the moon and of chastity   13 virgin knight i.e. her follower, Hero   26 wheels of Phoebus
wheels of the chariot of Phoebus, the sun god   30 weeds clothes   32 Hymen god of
marriage   speed's speed us (i.e. make us prosper)

Act 5 Scene 4   *running scene 16*

Enter Leonato, Benedick, [Beatrice,] Margaret, Ursula, old man [Anto-
nio], Friar [Francis and] Hero

FRIAR FRANCIS   Did I not tell you she was innocent?

LEONATO   So are the prince and Claudio, who accused her
Upon the error that you heard debated.
But Margaret was in some fault for this,

5   Although against her will, as it appears
In the true course of all the question.

ANTONIO   Well, I am glad that all things sort so well.

BENEDICK   And so am I, being else by faith enforced
To call young Claudio to a reckoning for it.

10   LEONATO   Well, daughter, and you gentlewomen all,
Withdraw into a chamber by yourselves,
And when I send for you, come hither masked.
The prince and Claudio promised by this hour
To visit me. You know your office, brother:

15   You must be father to your brother's daughter,
And give her to young Claudio.   *Exeunt Ladies*

ANTONIO   Which I will do with confirmed countenance.

BENEDICK   Friar, I must entreat your pains, I think.

FRIAR FRANCIS   To do what, signior?

20   BENEDICK   To bind me, or undo me — one of them.
Signior Leonato, truth it is, good signior,
Your niece regards me with an eye of favour.

LEONATO   That eye my daughter lent her: 'tis most true.

BENEDICK   And I do with an eye of love requite her.

25   LEONATO   The sight whereof I think you had from me,
From Claudio and the prince: but what's your will?

BENEDICK   Your answer, sir, is enigmatical.
But for my will, my will is your good will

5.4 3 Upon as a result of   **debated** discussed   **5 against her will** unintentionally
6 question questioning/investigation   **8 else** otherwise   **faith** i.e. his promise to Beatrice
9 reckoning settling of accounts (i.e. a duel)   **17 confirmed countenance** resolute
appearance/demeanor   **20 undo** ruin/untie   **28 for** as for   **is** is that

May stand with ours, this day to be conjoined
30 In the state of honourable marriage,
In which, good friar, I shall desire your help.
LEONATO   My heart is with your liking.
FRIAR FRANCIS   And my help.
Enter Prince [Don Pedro] and Claudio, with Attendants
DON PEDRO   Good morrow to this fair assembly
35 LEONATO   Good morrow, prince, good morrow, Claudio:
We here attend you. Are you yet determined
Today to marry with my brother's daughter?
CLAUDIO   I'll hold my mind, were she an Ethiope.
LEONATO   Call her forth, brother: here's the friar ready.
                                            [*Exit Antonio*]
40 DON PEDRO   Good morrow, Benedick. Why, what's the matter,
That you have such a February face,
So full of frost, of storm and cloudiness?
CLAUDIO   I think he thinks upon the savage bull.
Tush, fear not, man: we'll tip thy horns with gold,
45 And all Europa shall rejoice at thee,
As once Europa did at lusty Jove,
When he would play the noble beast in love.
BENEDICK   Bull Jove, sir, had an amiable low,
And some such strange bull leaped your father's cow,
50 And got a calf in that same noble feat
Much like to you, for you have just his bleat.
*Enter brother [Antonio], Hero, Beatrice, Margaret, [and] Ursula [the
ladies all masked]*
CLAUDIO   For this I owe you: here comes other reck'nings.
Which is the lady I must seize upon?
ANTONIO   This same is she, and I do give you her.
55 CLAUDIO   Why, then she's mine. Sweet, let me see your face.
LEONATO   No, that you shall not, till you take her hand
Before this friar and swear to marry her.

---

38 Ethiope Ethiopian   **45 Europa** Europe   **46 Europa . . . love** in the form of a bull Jove
carried off the princess Europa   **52 owe you** i.e. owe you a response

CLAUDIO   Give me your hand before this holy friar.
              I am your husband, if you like of me.
60 HERO   And when I lived, I was your other wife:
              And when you loved, you were my other husband.   *Unmasks*
    CLAUDIO   Another Hero?
    HERO   Nothing certainer.
              One Hero died defiled, but I do live,
65   And surely as I live, I am a maid.
    DON PEDRO The former Hero! Hero that is dead!
    LEONATO   She died, my lord, but whiles her slander lived.
    FRIAR FRANCIS   All this amazement can I qualify,
              When after that the holy rites are ended,
70   I'll tell you largely of fair Hero's death.
              Meantime let wonder seem familiar,
              And to the chapel let us presently.
    BENEDICK Soft and fair, friar. Which is Beatrice?
    BEATRICE I answer to that name. What is your will?   *Unmasks*
75 BENEDICK Do not you love me?
    BEATRICE Why, no, no more than reason.
    BENEDICK Why then, your uncle, and the prince, and Claudio
              Have been deceived: they swore you did.
    BEATRICE Do not you love me?
80 BENEDICK Troth, no, no more than reason.
    BEATRICE Why then, my cousin, Margaret and Ursula
              Are much deceived, for they did swear you did.
    BENEDICK They swore you were almost sick for me.
    BEATRICE They swore you were well-nigh dead for me.
85 BENEDICK 'Tis no matter. Then you do not love me?
    BEATRICE No, truly, but in friendly recompense.
    LEONATO   Come, cousin, I am sure you love the gentleman.
    CLAUDIO   And I'll be sworn upon't that he loves her,
              For here's a paper written in his hand,   *Shows a paper*
90   A halting sonnet of his own pure brain,
              Fashioned to Beatrice.

---

68 qualify moderate   **70 largely** in full   **73 soft and fair** hold on a moment   **81 cousin**
i.e. Hero   **87 cousin** Beatrice is his niece but **cousin** could refer to any relative

HERO   And here's another   *Shows another paper*
Writ in my cousin's hand, stolen from her pocket,
Containing her affection unto Benedick.

95   BENEDICK   A miracle! Here's our own hands against our
hearts. Come, I will have thee, but by this light I take thee for
pity.

BEATRICE   I would not deny you, but by this good day I yield
upon great persuasion, and partly to save your life, for I was
100   told you were in a consumption.

LEONATO   Peace! I will stop your mouth.

Makes Beatrice and Benedick kiss

DON PEDRO   How dost thou, 'Benedick, the married man'?

BENEDICK   I'll tell thee what, prince: a college of wit-crackers
cannot flout me out of my humour. Dost thou think I care
105   for a satire or an epigram? No. If a man will be beaten with
brains, a shall wear nothing handsome about him. In brief,
since I do purpose to marry, I will think nothing to any
purpose that the world can say against it, and therefore
never flout at me for what I have said against it, for man is
110   a giddy thing, and this is my conclusion. For thy part,
Claudio, I did think to have beaten thee, but in that thou
art like to be my kinsman, live unbruised and love my
cousin.

CLAUDIO   I had well hoped thou wouldst have denied Beatrice,
115   that I might have cudgelled thee out of thy single life to make
thee a double-dealer, which out of question thou wilt be, if
my cousin do not look exceeding narrowly to thee.

BENEDICK   Come, come, we are friends. Let's have a dance ere
we are married, that we may lighten our own hearts and our
120   wives' heels.

LEONATO   We'll have dancing afterward.

---

100 **in a consumption** wasting away   103 **college** assembly/fellowship   104 **flout** mock
106 **shall . . . him** i.e. for fear of attracting attention or having his dress sense mocked
110 **giddy** unstable/flighty   112 **like** likely   115 **cudgelled** beaten   116 **double-dealer**
married man/unfaithful husband   119 **lighten . . . heels** make our wives' heels nimble
through dancing/make our wives sexually eager

BENEDICK   First, of my word: therefore play, music. Prince,
thou art sad: get thee a wife, get thee a wife. There is no staff
more reverend than one tipped with horn.

Enter a Messenger

125 MESSENGER   My lord, your brother John is ta'en in flight,
And brought with armèd men back to Messina.

BENEDICK   Think not on him till tomorrow.
I'll devise thee brave punishments for him.
Strike up, pipers!   *Dance [and exeunt]*

---

123 sad grave/mournful   **no . . . horn** another reference to cuckoldry   **128 brave** fine

TEXTUAL NOTES

Q = First Quarto text of 1600
F = First Folio text of 1623
F2 = a correction introduced in the Second Folio text of 1632
Ed = a correction introduced by a later editor
SD = stage direction
SH = speech heading (i.e. speaker's name)

List of parts = Ed

1.1.35 bird-bolt *spelled* Burbolt *in* F   **42 eat** = Q. F = ease   **79 are you come** =
Q. F = you are come   **89 sir** = Q. *Not in* F   **115 yours** = Q. F = your
120 That = Q. F = This   **188 spoke** = Q. F = speake   **262–63 and . . . her** =
Q. *Not in* F   **205 you do** = Q. F = doe you

1.2.3 SH ANTONIO = Ed. F = *Old. (throughout scene)*   **4 strange** = Q. *Not in* F
6 event = F2. F = events   **8 my** = F. Q = mine   **9 thus** = F. Q = thus much
1.3.6 bringeth = F. Q = brings   **7 yet** = F. Q = at least   **18 true root** = Q. F =
root   **31 will make** = F. Q = make   **48 me behind** = Q. F = behind

2.1.27 upon = F. Q = on   **34 bearward** *spelled* Berrord *in* F   **47 Father** = Q.
F *omits*   **52 account** = F. Q = an account   **66 sinks** = F. Q = sincke
71 SD [Don] John   = Ed. F = *or dumbe Iohn*   **72 a bout** = Ed. F = about
81 Jove = Q. F = Loue   **84, 87, 89 SH BALTHASAR** = Ed. F = *Bene.*
121 pleaseth = F. Q = pleases   **165 count** = F. Q = county   **of** = Q.
F = off   **187 think I told** = Q. F = thinke, told   **188 good will** = Q. F = will
190 a rod = F. Q = vp a rod   **213 and** = F. *Not in* Q   **217 her terminations**
= Q. F = terminations   **239 this** = F. Q = my   **243 his single** = Q. F = a
single   **256–57 a jealous** = F. Q = that iealous   **276 her heart** = Q. F =
my heart   **315 my mind** = Q. F = mind

2.2.27 Don = Q. F = on   **40 truths** = F. Q = truth   **45 thou** = F. Q = you

2.3.29 I for = Q. F = for   **32 SD** *Balthasar*   = Ed. F = *Iacke Wilson (apparently
the actor who played Balthasar)*   **41–42 To . . . excellency** *mistakenly
printed twice in* F   **44 woo** = Q. F = woe   **59 SH BALTHASAR** = Ed. *Not
in* F   **69 was** = Q. F = were   **125 told us of** = F. Q = told of vs   **143 but
make** = F. Q = make but   **169 SH LEONATO** = F. Q = *Claudio*   **171 see** = F.
Q = say   **172–73 Christian-like** = F. Q = most christianlike   **179 seek** =
Q. F = see   **188 to . . . good** = F. Q = so good   **193 gentlewoman** = F. Q =
gentlewomen   **200–1 the full** = F. Q = their full

3.1.0 SD *gentlewomen* = Q. F = *Gentlemen*   **60 she make** = F. Q = sheele
make   **81 than** = Q. F = to   **106 ta'en** = F. Q = limed

3.2.30 Frenchman tomorrow = F. Q *continues* or in the shape of two coun-
tries at once, as a Germaine from the waste downward, all slops, and a
Spaniard from the hip upward, no dublet: unlesse . . . you would have it
appeare he is **51 Conclude** = F. Q = conclude, conclude

3.3.33 talk = F. Q = to talke **35 SH WATCHMAN** F's *Watch. does not distinguish between the first and second watchmen* **40 bid them** = F. Q = bid
those **73 statues** = Ed. F = statute **113 years** = F. Q = yeere **124 and
I see** = Q. F = and see **136 they** = Q. F = thy **156 SH FIRST WATCH-
MAN** = Ed. F *gives the speech to Conrad*

3.4.41 look = F. Q = see

3.5.7 SH VERGES = Ed. F = *Headb. (throughout scene)* **9 off** *spelled* of
in F **23 times** = F. Q = pound **48 as may** = F. Q = as it may
53 examination = Q. F = examine **those men** = F. Q = these men

4.1.18 not . . . do = Q. *Not in* F **77 do so** = Q. F = do **89 you are** = F.
Q = are you **98 spoken** = F. Q = spoke **131 rearward** = Q. F = reward
138 smearéd = F. Q = smirched **158 two princes** = Q. F = Princes
167 beat = Q. F = beare **210 princes** = Ed. F = Princesse **282 swear by
it** = F. Q = sweare **298 deny** = F. Q = deny it **335 leave** = F. Q = I leave

4.2.1 SH DOGBERRY = Ed. F = *Keeper.* **2 SH VERGES** = Ed. F = *Cowley
(apparently the actor who played Verges)* **4 SH DOGBERRY** = Ed. F =
Andrew. **9 SH DOGBERRY** = Ed. F = *Kemp. (throughout rest of scene)*
(Will Kempe was apparently the actor who played Dogberry) **15 serve
God? Masters** = F. Q = serue God? *Both* Yea sir we hope. *Kem* [*i.e. Kempe*]
Write downe, that they hope they serue God: and write God first, for God
defend but God shoulde go before such villaines: maisters **55 Leonato** =
F. Q = Leonatoes **58 SH VERGES** = Ed. F = *Sex*[ton]. Q = *Couley (actor
playing Verges)* **59 SH CONRAD Off** = Ed. Q/F *continue previous speech of
Coxcombe* **65 O that** = Q. F = O that **71 any in** = F. Q = anie is in

5.1.7 comforter = Q. F = comfort **8 do** = Q. F = doth **17 Bid** = Ed. Q/F =
And **68 my** = F. Q = mine **105 off** = Ed. F = of **163 says** = F. Q = said
248 SH VERGES = Ed. F = *Con. 2* **254 thou** = Q. F = thou thou

5.2.29 names = Q. F = name **31 in** = Q. *Not in* F **33 hard rhyme** = Q.
F = hard time **35 for** = F. Q = nor **67 monuments** = F. Q = monument

5.3.3 SH CLAUDIO = Ed. *Not in* F **10 dumb** = F. Q = dead **12 SH
BALTHASAR** = Ed. *Not in* F **21 Heavily, heavily** = Q. F = Heavenly,
heavenly **22 SH CLAUDIO** = Ed. F = *Lo.*

5.4.7 sort = F. Q = sorts **33 my help.** = F. Q = my helpe. Heere comes the
Prince and Claudio, **50 And got** = Q. F = A got **54 SH ANTONIO** = Ed.
F = *Leo.* **64 died defiled** = Q. F = died **83 swore you** = F. Q = swore
that you **84 swore you** = F. Q = swore that you **85 no matter** = F.
Q = no such matter **101 SH LEONATO** = F. *Most eds assign to*
BENEDICK **109 what I have** = Q. F = I have

SCENE-BY-SCENE ANALYSIS

ACT 1 SCENE 1

The play opens at the house of Leonato, Governor of Messina. A Messenger arrives to inform Leonato, Hero, and Beatrice that Don Pedro, Prince of Aragon, is to arrive there from a recent war, accompanied by his illegitimate brother, Don John, and two young noblemen, Claudio and Benedick. We are introduced to all of the main characters and essential information is conveyed about events prior to the action of the play. Several key themes, such as love, marriage, deception, and secrecy, are established, as are the recurrent motifs concerning fashion, value/"worth," and images of animals and cuckolding.

Lines 1–78: The Messenger brings the news of Don Pedro's imminent arrival and Beatrice inquires after "Signior Mountanto," meaning Benedick. She continues to criticize him to the Messenger, who is confused by her attitude. Leonato explains that there is a long-standing battle of wits between Beatrice and Benedick.

Lines 79–132: Don Pedro and his party arrive. Initial pleasantries are exchanged and, while Leonato and Don Pedro talk aside, Beatrice and Benedick insult each other in a fast-paced, witty exchange in which they both assert their dislike of the opposite sex. The simultaneous antagonism and attraction that exists between these two characters is clearly established in their first "skirmish of wit," and forms the basis for much of the verbal, "high" comedy in the play. Don Pedro then announces that Leonato has invited himself, Claudio, and Benedick to stay for at least a month. Leonato extends this invitation to Don John and we learn that there has previously been conflict between the two brothers, although they are now "reconciled."

Lines 133–168: When they are alone, Claudio asks Benedick his opinion of Hero. Benedick dismisses her and compares her to Beatrice, who "exceeds her in beauty." Although he qualifies this with a comment on Beatrice's temper, it suggests that he may feel some attraction. Claudio praises Hero as "sweet," "modest," and "worthy." The ambiguity of the term "worth" is sustained throughout the remainder of the scene.

Lines 169–281: Don Pedro returns and Claudio confesses that he loves Hero. Benedick continues to reject marriage and women and asserts his intention to remain a bachelor. He leaves with a message for Leonato. Don Pedro meanwhile confirms that Hero is Leonato's heir, reminding the audience that marriage is also a financial contract, and offers to woo her on Claudio's behalf, "in some disguise."

ACT 1 SCENE 2

Antonio reveals that his servant overheard Don Pedro and Claudio discussing Hero, introducing the device of concealed overhearing or observation that runs throughout the play. It also establishes the ongoing theme of misunderstanding, as Antonio's servant has reported that it is Don Pedro, not Claudio, who is in love with Hero. Leonato resolves to tell Hero of the prince's intentions so that she may give him the right answer.

ACT 1 SCENE 3

Lines 1–32: Don John discusses his mood and his situation with Conrad, who encourages him to conceal his true feelings toward Don Pedro and wait for an opportunity to act against him. Don John claims that he cannot hide what he is, "a plain-dealing villain," and refuses to alter his sour appearance.

Lines 33–59: Borachio arrives with the news of Claudio's intention to marry Hero. As before, this information has been obtained by eavesdropping, but this time it has been correctly understood. We learn that Claudio was instrumental in Don John's downfall. Conrad and Borachio pledge to help Don John prevent the marriage.

ACT 2 SCENE 1

The setting of the dance allows several smaller scenes-within-a-scene as different pairs or groups of characters are focused on in turn. These exchanges use dramatic irony to present comic situations and misunderstandings, and further the progress of the plots that have emerged so far. The masking of the characters allows for visual comedy in addition to the witty dialogue, and serves as a physical representation of the themes of deception and secrecy.

Lines 1–71: Leonato, Antonio, Hero, and Beatrice wait for the prince and his party to arrive. They discuss Don John's bitter temperament, and Beatrice jokes that the ideal man would be a combination of Don John and Benedick—one says too little and the other too much. This leads to a more general discussion of men and marriage, with Beatrice demonstrating her wit and professing similar opinions to those of Benedick in Act 1 Scene 1, asserting that she will not marry. Leonato reminds Hero of her duty to accept Don Pedro if he should propose, reinforcing the differences between the two cousins: Beatrice appears relatively free in terms of both speech and decision but Hero is subject to her father's authority and, in fact, says nothing throughout the whole exchange.

Lines 72–83: Don Pedro asks Hero to dance with him. Their conversation is romantic, but Hero tells him she cannot give him an answer until she knows who he is.

Lines 84–94: Margaret rebuffs Balthasar's advances.

Lines 95–105: Antonio denies his true identity to Ursula who claims she knows him by the marks of his old age, such as his "dry hand," but then gives a more tactful reason—he cannot hide his "excellent wit."

Lines 106–133: Benedick use his anonymity to verbally abuse Beatrice, pretending to report an insult by someone else. Beatrice pretends not to know she is talking to Benedick and criticizes him at length, suggesting that he overestimates his own wit and that others find him "a very dull fool."

Lines 134–148: Don John and Borachio pretend to believe that Claudio is Benedick and ask to speak to him as a friend of Don Pedro's. They tell him that Don Pedro is in love with Hero and means to marry her, and ask "Benedick" to warn the prince against this as she is not his equal.

Lines 149–183: Claudio's soliloquy reveals that he believes that Don Pedro has won Hero for himself. This reveals a gullible and jealous side to his personality. Benedick enters, and, apparently laboring under the same misconception as Claudio, offers to fashion him a willow garland—the emblem of a forsaken lover. Claudio leaves and Benedick reflects on Beatrice's earlier criticism.

Lines 184–239: Don Pedro, Leonato, and Hero enter, looking for Claudio. Benedick tells them that Claudio believes that the prince has wooed Hero for himself, and is told that this is not true: Hero is intended for Claudio. Don Pedro reports that the gentleman that danced with Beatrice told her that she is "much wronged" by Benedick, who makes a furious speech about how, conversely, she "misused" him and how much he dislikes her. As Beatrice enters, bringing Claudio, he begs Don Pedro to send him on an errand "to the world's end," so that he may avoid her. The prince refuses, but Benedick leaves anyway.

Lines 240–298: Don Pedro comments to Beatrice that she has lost Benedick's heart, and she comments that in the past "he lent it" to her, suggesting a previous attachment between them. Beatrice says that she has brought Claudio, commenting on his jealous disposition. Don Pedro explains that he has Leonato's consent to Claudio marrying Hero, and the lovers exchange vows, although, again, Hero is silent—Beatrice supplies her words. Beatrice then claims to regret her single status, and Don Pedro makes her a half-joking offer of marriage. Beatrice refuses on the grounds that, like a good suit of clothes, he is too expensive to "wear every day." She then apologizes to him for being "all mirth and no matter," before Leonato sends her off on an errand.

Lines 299–338: The assembled characters discuss Beatrice's lively disposition and her single state. Don Pedro comments that she would be "an excellent wife for Benedick." Claudio states his intention to marry Hero the next day, but Leonato says that they must wait a week. Don Pedro suggests that they pass this time by making Benedick and Beatrice fall in love. Everyone agrees to help.

ACT 2 SCENE 2

Borachio shows Don John how he can prevent Claudio's marriage to Hero and injure Don Pedro and Leonato. Don John will tell Claudio and Don Pedro that Hero is unfaithful and show them a scene that Borachio will stage at Hero's window, in which he will play out a lovers' encounter with Margaret, calling her "Hero" throughout. Hero's honor will be ruined, as will that of her father, Claudio, and Don Pedro.

ACT 2 SCENE 3

Theatrical self-awareness is sustained through the next three scenes, as different characters are set up to observe the "dramas" that are being played to deceive them. The first of these is the duping of Benedick in the garden of Leonato's house. The dramatic irony and Benedick's asides add to the comedy, and the theme of deception is reinforced by the sustained trapping imagery.

Lines 1–32: Benedick's soliloquy focuses on the change in Claudio since he fell in love. He contemplates whether he himself will ever be "converted," dwelling on the virtues that his ideal woman would have. He sees the other men and hides in the arbor.

Lines 33–84: Don Pedro and Claudio establish that Benedick is listening, then talk of love and request Balthasar to play a love song, the words of which reinforce the theme of deception. Benedick's asides are cynical and prosaic.

Lines 85–197: After Balthasar has left, Don Pedro, Claudio, and Leonato discuss the fact that Beatrice is in love with Benedick and cannot tell him. They agree that he should not know because he would only "torment" Beatrice. They discuss Beatrice's many virtues, and Benedick's unworthiness. There are asides between the characters as they gauge Benedick's response, and from Benedick, who suspects it is a "gull," but decides it cannot be because Leonato is a part of the conversation.

Lines 198–219: In one short soliloquy Benedick undergoes a rapidly changing array of emotions and self-analysis, and a complete reversal of opinion with regard to Beatrice. Believing that Beatrice loves him, he resolves to bear the mockery he will receive after having "railed so long against marriage" and to return her love.

Lines 220–235: Beatrice comes to call Benedick for dinner. Her responses to his pleasantries are ill tempered, but he persists in reading nonexistent double meanings into her words, and finding evidence of her love.

ACT 3 SCENE 1

Lines 1–33: Hero directs Margaret to go and tell Beatrice that she and Ursula are discussing her in the orchard. She then primes Ursula as to what their conversation must be about—praising Benedick and discussing his love for Beatrice. They see Beatrice enter and conceal herself, and move so that she can overhear them. They use similar images of trapping to those in the previous scene.

Lines 34–108: They discuss Benedick's love for Beatrice and the fact that Hero has supposedly refused to tell Beatrice because "she cannot love" and her response would be to "make sport" of Benedick. They list Benedick's virtues and Hero resolves to tell Benedick to "fight against his passion." They leave to choose a wedding outfit for Hero.

Lines 109–118: Beatrice declares she will "requite" Benedick's love in a speech that, like his in Act 2 Scene 3, shows change and increased self-awareness.

ACT 3 SCENE 2

We do not watch the deceptive performance staged by Borachio. Instead, we see Don John prepare Don Pedro and Claudio to witness it.

Lines 1–61: Don Pedro intends to leave for Aragon once Claudio's marriage is accomplished, taking Benedick with him for company. Benedick enters, claiming to have toothache. Don Pedro, Claudio, and Leonato tease him, saying he shows all the signs of being in love—changing his clothes, shaving his beard, using perfume and, above all, being melancholy. Benedick asks to speak to Leonato in private and they leave.

Lines 62–115: Don John approaches and, having acknowledged that Claudio distrusts him, tells them that Hero is "disloyal" and offers to show them the evidence that night at Hero's window. Claudio and Don Pedro seem reluctant to believe him at first, but by the end of the scene they have vowed to publicly disgrace her if they see proof that Don John is telling the truth.

ACT 3 SCENE 3

Lines 1–85: The master constable, Dogberry, and parish officer, Verges, issue instructions to the Watch. The Watchmen are revealed to be incompetent and stupid, and the nonsensical comedy that is created is compounded by Dogberry's hyperbolic and inaccurate vocabulary, in particular his use of malapropisms. Dogberry's final instruction is to keep an eye on Leonato's house, because of all the wedding preparations.

Lines 86–161: Borachio and Conrad enter, drunk, and the Watch overhear their conversation as Borachio recounts to Conrad his part in the deception of Don Pedro and Claudio. He describes how Don John incited Don Pedro and Claudio with "oaths," and then how his own performance in leaving Hero's window convinced them. He reports that Claudio has sworn to shame Hero in church the next day. The Watch arrest them, despite not understanding all that they have heard.

ACT 3 SCENE 4

Margaret helps Hero to dress for her wedding, while Ursula goes to wake Beatrice. As they discuss clothes, and Margaret makes innuendoes about Hero's impending loss of virginity, Beatrice enters. Like Benedick in Act 3 Scene 2, she puts her melancholy down to illness. Margaret teases her, suggesting that she is in love, and dropping hints about Benedick. Ursula tells them that the men have come to take Hero to church and they withdraw to help her finish dressing.

ACT 3 SCENE 5

Dogberry and Verges go to inform Leonato of the arrest of Borachio and Conrad and the revelation of Don John's plot. Leonato is impatient and too busy to listen to their "tedious," long-winded beginning and is called away to the wedding before they can tell him.

ACT 4 SCENE 1

Lines 1–114: All the characters assemble for the marriage of Hero and Claudio, and Leonato tells the Friar to keep the service brief. Claudio asks if Leonato gives Hero freely to him and, reinforcing the theme of "worth" from earlier, asks what he can give in return for "this rich and precious gift." Don Pedro suggests that all he can do is return the gift. Claudio does so, denouncing Hero as an "approvèd wanton," who has only the appearance of modesty and chastity. Initially, Leonato thinks that Claudio himself has taken Hero's virginity, but Claudio denies this. Hero suggests that Claudio must be ill to speak so falsely. Leonato appeals to Don Pedro, who claims that he has been dishonored by helping to link Claudio to "a common stale."

Claudio asks Hero what man she spoke with at her window the previous night. Hero answers "no man," in one of the few lines she speaks in the whole scene. Claudio, believing what he saw, recounts it to the assembled company, adding that the man has confessed to many previous sexual encounters with Hero. He rejects Hero once more and declares that he will never love again. Hero faints and Don Pedro, Claudio, and Don John leave.

Lines 115–263: Beatrice tries to help Hero, fearing she may be dead. Leonato says that it would be better if she was and prays that she does not wake up, regretting that he ever had a child. At this point, he is torn between the public and domestic elements of his life: his social position and honor, and his love for his only child. Beatrice insists that Hero is "belied." The Friar intervenes, saying that he observed Hero's expressions throughout and that he believes her to be innocent and that Claudio and Don Pedro are deceived. He questions Hero, who denies everything. Benedick suggests that Don John may be responsible. Leonato threatens to kill those who have wronged Hero, but the Friar suggests that they pretend she has died as a result of the slander while they find out the truth. Failing this, Hero can be placed quietly in a convent. He argues that Hero's "death" will create remorse in Claudio and, even if they cannot prove her innocence, pity "will quench the wonder of her infamy." Leonato agrees and Benedick vows to keep the secret.

Lines 264–338: Once alone, Benedick attempts to comfort Beatrice and reassure her that be believes Hero is innocent. She wishes that there was a man who could help, but when Benedick offers, she says it is not his "office." He then declares his love for her, and after some procrastination, she returns it. He asks her to bid him to do anything for her, but when she tells him to "Kill Claudio," he refuses. She threatens to leave and insists again that Hero is wronged and that Claudio is a villain, wishing she were a man so that she might be revenged. Benedick is torn between the bond of male friendship and his love for Beatrice, but eventually agrees to challenge Claudio.

ACT 4 SCENE 2

Borachio and Conrad are interrogated before the Sexton. Again, the process is prolonged by Dogberry's comic self-importance and long-windedness. He selects nonsensical extracts from the proceedings and insists that they are written down, including Conrad's insult that he is "an ass." The Sexton gets to the truth, reporting that the public disgrace of Hero has taken place, that Hero has died as a result, and that Don John has left in secrecy. He states his intention to show Leonato the evidence of the interrogation, and instructs the constable to bring Borachio and Conrad.

ACT 5 SCENE 1

Lines 1–45: Leonato rejects Antonio's attempts to comfort him, and resolves to tell Claudio and Don Pedro that they have slandered Hero.

Lines 46–192: Don Pedro and Claudio are in a hurry and do not wish to quarrel with Leonato, but he accuses them of "villainy" and threatens to fight Claudio. Claudio dismisses his challenge, but Antonio then joins in. Don Pedro refuses to fight two old men and will not listen to Leonato, who leaves with Antonio as Benedick arrives. Don Pedro and Claudio attempt to joke with Benedick as before about love and Beatrice, but he will not respond, and the male camaraderie that previously existed between the three men is awkwardly absent. He quietly challenges Claudio to a duel, and then leaves, telling them that they have "killed a sweet and innocent lady" and that Don John has left Messina.

Lines 193–326: Dogberry and Verges enter, leading Borachio and Conrad. Don Pedro and Claudio inquire why they are bound, and Borachio interrupts Dogberry's confused response and confesses. The revelation of the truth affects Claudio as though he had "drunk poison," as he simultaneously experiences shame, grief, and love for Hero. Leonato returns with the Sexton and demands to see the villain. Borachio owns up, but Leonato points out that Don Pedro and Claudio had a part in it as well. Claudio asks that Leonato choose his punishment. Leonato says that he must tell everyone of Hero's innocence, hang an epitaph on Hero's tomb, and marry his niece in place of Hero the next day. Claudio agrees. Borachio establishes Margaret's innocence of her part in the plot and is taken away.

ACT 5 SCENE 2

Benedick tells Margaret to send Beatrice to him and, while he waits, attempts to compose a love song. As he laments his inability to do so,

Beatrice enters and asks what has happened between him and Claudio. When he replies "Only foul words," she refuses to kiss him and starts to leave. He tells her that he has challenged Claudio and they talk in romantic terms but conclude they are "too wise to woo peaceably," as they cannot avoid jibing at each other. Ursula comes to tell them that Hero is proved innocent and that they are to go to Leonato.

ACT 5 SCENE 3

Claudio hangs the epitaph on Hero's tomb, declaring her innocence. Balthasar sings a "solemn hymn" and Claudio vows to perform the same rite every year. They leave to prepare for Claudio's wedding to Leonato's "niece."

ACT 5 SCENE 4

The lovers are united in marriage, a symbol of order restored. Masks are used again, but the removal of the masks represents the revelation of truths and the end of deception. The only question we may be left with is whether Claudio deserves Hero.

Lines 1–33: Leonato sends the women to mask themselves and consents to Benedick's request to marry Beatrice. The Friar agrees to perform the ceremony.

Lines 34–51: Don Pedro and Claudio arrive and Claudio declares his intention to go through with the marriage.

Lines 52–129: The women enter, masked, and Claudio asks to see the face of the one he is to marry. Leonato insists he must swear to marry her before he sees her. He does so and Hero reveals her face. Claudio and Don Pedro are amazed and Leonato briefly tells of the deception, which the Friar says can be explained after the ceremony. Benedick asks Beatrice if she loves him. She denies it, and he says that Leonato, Don Pedro, and Claudio swore she did. She asks him the same question and he also denies it. They begin to argue, but Claudio produces a sonnet that Benedick has written for Beatrice, and Hero a love letter that Beatrice has written to Benedick. Beatrice continues to wrangle but Leonato says he will stop her mouth by making her and Benedick kiss. Don Pedro teases Benedick for going back on his word and choosing to marry, but Benedick just recommends that he get himself a wife, adding that he will devise "brave punishments" for Don John later. They all dance.

MUCH ADO ABOUT NOTHING IN PERFORMANCE: THE RSC AND BEYOND

The best way to understand a Shakespeare play is to see it or ideally to participate in it. By examining a range of productions, we may gain a sense of the extraordinary variety of approaches and interpretations that are possible—a variety that gives Shakespeare his unique capacity to be reinvented and made "our contemporary" four centuries after his death.

We begin with a brief overview of the play's theatrical and cinematic life, offering historical perspectives on how it has been performed. We then analyze in more detail a series of productions staged over the last half-century by the Royal Shakespeare Company. The sense of dialogue between productions that can only occur when a company is dedicated to the revival and investigation of the Shakespeare canon over a long period, together with the uniquely comprehensive archival resource of promptbooks, program notes, reviews, and interviews held on behalf of the RSC at the Shakespeare Birthplace Trust in Stratford-upon-Avon, allows an "RSC stage history" to become a crucible in which the chemistry of the play can be explored.

We then go to the horse's mouth. Modern theater is dominated by the figure of the director. He or she must hold together the whole play, whereas the actor must concentrate on his or her part. The director's viewpoint is therefore especially valuable. Shakespeare's plasticity is wonderfully revealed when we hear the directors of two highly successful productions answering the same questions in very different ways. And finally, we offer the actor's perspective: a view of the play through the eyes of Beatrice.

FOUR CENTURIES OF *MUCH ADO*: AN OVERVIEW

Much Ado has been popular since it was first written around 1598. The title page of the 1600 Quarto announces it had been "*sundrie times publikely* acted by the right honorable, the Lord Chamberlaine his seruants." The substitution of "Kemp" for Dogberry and "Cowley" for Verges in speech headings helps date the play[1] and also tell us that the leading comedian with Shakespeare's company, the Chamberlain's (subsequently the King's) Men, William Kempe, played the part of Dogberry and another comic actor, Richard Cowley, played Verges. The next references suggest the reason for its popularity. It was one of twenty plays performed at court to celebrate the marriage of James I's daughter Elizabeth to Frederick V, Elector of Palatine, in 1613 which included not only *Much ado abowte nothinge* but also *Benedicte and Betteris*, both titles assumed to refer to Shakespeare's play. Charles I scribbled "Bennedike and Betrice" against *Much Ado* in his copy of the 1632 Second Folio of Shakespeare's plays, and the poet Leonard Digges wrote in the prefatory poem to his 1640 edition of Shakespeare's poems:

> . . . let but Beatrice
> And *Benedicke* be seene, loe in a trice
> The Cockpit, Galleries, Boxes, all are full.

After the closure of the theaters in 1642 and their reopening in 1660 at the Restoration, the play was assigned to Sir William Davenant's company. Davenant incorporated the ever-popular Beatrice and Benedick into his improbable adaptation of *Measure for Measure*, *The Law Against Lovers* (1662), in which Benedick becomes Angelo's younger brother and leads an insurrection against the prison to free Claudio. Beatrice, now a wealthy heiress, is sister to Juliet, and Angelo's ward. A younger sister, Viola, dances a sarabande with castanets. Angelo, disgusted by the low morals of women in his society, claims to have been merely testing Isabella, whom he finally marries. Benedick marries Beatrice, and the duke retires to a monastery. Samuel Pepys records he thought it "a good play and well performed."[2] Charles Johnson subsequently incorporated a number of Benedick's lines into his 1723 adaptation of *As You Like It, Love in a Forest*. In 1737 James Miller also amalgamated *Much Ado* with Molière's *Princess d'Elide* in his comedy *The Universal Passion*, in which Benedick and Beatrice become Lord Proteus and Delia.

There were a handful of productions of Shakespeare's play in the early eighteenth century, but it was David Garrick's Drury Lane production of 1748 that reestablished it firmly in the popular repertoire, a place it has retained ever since. Garrick continued to play Benedick in frequent revivals to great popular acclaim until his retirement from the stage in 1776; Arthur Murphy, actor, writer, and Garrick's biographer, called it "one of Mr Garrick's best Parts in Comedy."[3] His most celebrated Beatrice was Hannah Pritchard, whose performance was "so fine that every scene between her and the great Garrick was a continued struggle for superiority, in which the spectators could not award preference."[4] Garrick was still charming audiences in the part the year before his retirement:

> In the dance in *Much Ado About Nothing*, he excels all the rest by the agility of his springs . . . In his face all can observe, without any refinement of feature, the happy intellect in his unruffled brow, and the alert observer and wit in the lively eye, often bright with roguishness. His gestures are so clear and vivacious as to arouse in one similar emotions.[5]

Garrick's lively performance contrasted with John Philip Kemble's more serious production and stately Benedick. Using a bowdlerized text, Kemble was partnered by a number of successful Beatrices including the future King William's mistress, Dorothea Jordan. His brother, Charles Kemble, had more success in the part which he, too, played for over thirty years from 1803 to 1836 in productions that featured a number of distinguished Beatrices, including Anne Brunton, Helen Faucit, and his own daughter, Fanny Kemble. William Charles Macready also produced the play and played Benedick. Charles Kean's spectacular staging at the Princess's Theatre in 1858 included "a sunset view of the port of Messina, the sun gradually disappearing in the west, casting its declining rays on the houses and ships. Then the moon rose on a brilliant masquerade scene with variegated lights from garden and bridge lamps that shone through the arches of the palace."[6]

The most successful nineteenth-century production, however, was Henry Irving's at the Lyceum with Ellen Terry as Beatrice. It was universally admired:

The sumptuous revival by Mr Henry Irving of this wise and witty comedy has, at any rate, proved to the public satisfaction that Shakespeare, if properly understood, is an evergreen.[7]

The settings were the most sumptuous and picturesque. I can remember none more beautiful even at the Lyceum; the Bay of Messina with Leonato's Marble Palace; the Garden; the Church; the Ballroom—never was mounting more appropriate and helpful, and the result was triumphant. As I have heard others say, and as I have always myself maintained: "The most completely satisfying entertainment I have ever known in the theater."[8]

It was the central performances of Terry and Irving that captivated audiences, though. Irving was credited with a new reading of Benedick: "He conceived the character on completely new lines and gave the play a new vitality. His Benedick was an eccentric, a fantastic, an oddity, but *preux chevalier* [valiant knight]; always."[9] But as Bram Stoker, Irving's dresser, observed, Terry "was born for the part" of Beatrice. Praise of her performance was unstinting:

Merriment is the abiding quality of Miss Ellen Terry's Beatrice. She is Shakespeare's "pleasant-spirited lady"; she was born in a "merry hour"; we know that a "star danced, and under that was she born"; she has a "merry heart," and the actress leans charmingly on this view of the character. All the people about the court love Beatrice, as well they may. They know her antipathy to the rougher sex is only skin deep, and they trick her into matrimony. She is no virago or vixen, but a smiling, chaffing, madcap girl, whose laughter and high spirits are next door to tears.[10]

Terry herself was more critical: "there was very much to admire in Henry Irving's Benedick. But he gave me little help. Beatrice must be swift, swift, swift! Owing to Henry's rather finicking, deliberate method as Benedick, I could never put the right pace into my part."[11] She also objected to a number of the traditional gags Irving continued to employ, but was impressed by the young Johnston Forbes-Robertson's Claudio in which she thought he revealed "a touch of Leontes."[12] She was happier with the 1891 revival: "Henry has vastly improved upon his old rendering . . . acts larger now."

Terry reprised the role in 1903 with Oscar Ashe as Benedick in a production by her son Edward Gordon Craig. Its "bare and impressionistic setting"[13] contrasted with the lavish spectacle of previous productions. The critic J. C. Trewin describes how "Gordon Craig indicated the church simply by the widening light that illuminated the many colors of a huge cross. Otherwise he used only curtains that hung in folds and were painted with pillars."[14] Even the acerbic George Bernard Shaw was impressed as he confided in a letter to Terry: "I went to see Much Adoodle-do yesterday evening. It is a shocking bad play . . . ," but he admits: "I have never seen the church scene go before—didnt [sic] think it could go, in fact."[15] The production recouped the losses Terry and Gordon Craig made on their other production—Ibsen's The Vikings. The advent of modernist writers such as Ibsen and the theatrical experiments of William Poel's Elizabethan Stage Society, which attempted to produce Shakespeare's plays under something approaching original staging conditions, suggest a new theatrical mood. Nevertheless, initial response to Poel's production at the Royal Court was cool: The Times thought it "owed more to . . . antiquarian interest than to the histrionic talents of the players," and was "painfully slow."[16]

Herbert Beerbohm Tree staged a lavish Victorian-style spectacular at His Majesty's the following year. Of Beerbohm Tree's Benedick, George Bernard Shaw said: "I defy anybody not to be amused by him. When he is not amusingly good from Mr Tree's point of view he is amusingly bad from the classical Shakespearian point of view . . . It is, in its way, colossal." He admired Winifred Emery's Beatrice though, clearly conceived in reaction to Terry's charm in the part: "she was clever enough to play Lady Disdain instead of playing for sentimental sympathy; and the effect was keenly good and original." This is his ironic judgment:

All the lovely things Shakespear [sic] dispensed with are there in bounteous plenty. Fair ladies, Sicilian landscapes,

Italian gardens, summer nights and dawns (compressed into five minutes), Renascential splendours, dancing, singing, masquerading, architecture, orchestration carefully culled from Wagner, Bizet, and German, and endless larks in the way of stage business devised by Mr Tree, and carried out with much innocent enjoyment, which is fairly infectious on the other side of the footlights . . . On the whole, my advice is, go and see it: you will never again have the chance of enjoying such an entertainment.[17]

Shaw was correct in his assessment of modern theatrical trends, and the numerous productions of the early twentieth century employed the pared-down style advocated by Poel and Harley Granville Barker, which eliminated many of the traditional gags and stage business that Ellen Terry had complained of and allowed for a faster-paced, fluid acting style using a fuller text.

The play was regularly produced in London and Stratford under directors such as Ben Greet, Harcourt Williams, William Bridges-Adams, Iden Payne, and Hugh Hunt, with a variety of distinguished actors including Sybil Thorndike, Lewis Casson, Edith Evans, Baliol Holloway, Fabia Drake, Alec Clunes, Robert Donat, George Hayes, and Margaretta Scott, and including a postwar production with William Devlin's Dogberry as an air raid warden on a bicycle.

The most successful postwar production was undoubtedly John Gielgud's in 1949, which was still enjoying critical acclaim five years later:

This production by Sir John Gielgud, with sets and dresses by Mr Mariano Andreu, is attaining to a sort of classic status. Five years ago it delighted Stratford, happily introducing Miss Peggy Ashcroft to the festival; two years later, coming to the Phoenix theatre with Miss Diana Wynyard as Beatrice, it delighted London; and now it brings Miss Ashcroft and Sir John Gielgud together again . . . The producer, who is also the principal actor, has had to reckon with many different actors; but his production somehow has a perennial freshness.[18]

1. John Gielgud's 1949 Stratford production with Diana Wynyard as Beatrice and Anthony Quayle as Benedick was the most successful postwar
production: Gielgud himself took over the role of Benedick two years later
with Peggy Ashcroft as Beatrice.

Gielgud's unequivocally romantic production set in the Renaissance
continued touring successfully until 1959. Gielgud stated his personal preference for productions set in their original period,[19] but
nevertheless, since then many of the most successful productions of
Much Ado have been updated and moved around geographically,
partly at least as a response to the greater attention that has been
focused on the Claudio–Hero plot and the need to find a cultural
ambience that might explain if not excuse Claudio's callous treatment of Hero and Leonato's response to her slander. These productions have attracted a mixed critical reception. John Houseman and
Jack Landau transported their 1957 American Shakespeare Festival
production, which starred Katharine Hepburn and Alfred Drake, to
"the American-Spanish Southwest about a hundred years ago." The
well-known critic Brooks Atkinson continued: "It is a brisk idea for

one excellent reason. Katharine Hepburn is very much the modern actress. The hard surface of modern wit, the brittle remarks, the sophisticated eyes become her, as do the flowing costumes and the Spanish headdresses with which Rouben Ter-Arutinian has draped her."[20] While Atkinson thought it all worked except Dogberry as a western sheriff, Henry Hewes thought the opposite: "The nicest performance in the show comes from Larry Gates as Dogberry, the muddled Western Sheriff."[21]

Critics were similarly divided about Douglas Seale's 1958 Shakespeare Memorial Theatre production, which V. S. Pritchett argued "impudently twitches the Bard into light opera" and moves the play forward to 1850 and the Italy of Verdi and Rossini: "This is to the advantage of the comedy which gains Romantic verve and settles for the picturesque; but a disadvantage to the melodramatic conspiracy."[22] The Times' critic, however, came to precisely the opposite conclusion: "The period chosen was a source of profit to the more serious scenes. It was easier than usual to take Don John's conspiracy at its face value when Don John looked and behaved as he did, as Mr Richard Johnson did, as though he had walked straight out of a portrait by Delacroix."[23] And while Pritchett admired the performances of Googie Withers as Beatrice and Michael Redgrave as Benedick, Alan Brien complained that they were "almost buried beneath all this meringue . . . Beatrice becomes a rattling bore whose spinsterhood is only too understandable. Michael Redgrave, too, seems uneasy inside this nineteenth-century Italian joker."[24]

Michael Langham's production for the Stratford Festival, Ontario, of 1958, also set in "the Europe of the last century in a sort of Viennese-operetta style,"[25] was warmly reviewed, especially the performances of Christopher Plummer as Benedick and Eileen Herlie as Beatrice, but less well received when it transferred to the Royal Shakespeare Theatre in 1961 with Geraldine McEwan as Beatrice. In his 1965 National Theatre production, Franco Zeffirelli had

the dazzlingly simple idea of placing it exactly where Shakespeare laid it himself: not in an elocutory limbo, which is where it usually happens, but in Messina . . . the moment the play is

2. Rachel Kempson as Ursula, Geraldine McEwan as Hero, and Zoe Caldwell as Margaret "almost buried beneath all this meringue" in Douglas Seale's 1958 "light opera" production at Stratford.

localized, it meshes as precisely as a watch. Instead of being the proponent of a distant love ethic that now lies pickled in troubadour poetry, Hero becomes a wretchedly believable girl trapped in perfectly recognizable Sicily where the same ferocious code of chastity endures to this day.[26]

Not everyone was convinced. *The Times'* critic complained that

Zeffirelli's Sicily has enormous charm. A nattily uniformed town band parades its streets blaring forth crudely harmonized marches: the troops swagger back from the war in dress swords and plumed pill-box hats and are mobbed by a welcoming crowd of frock-coated civilians. And as for the civic statuary, Zeffirelli has provided it in the shape of self-assembling monuments—ethereal girls who drift on and freeze into Ondines at the base of a fountain, and an unearthly warrior who clambers onto a pedestal and takes up a martial stance as a local hero covered in bird droppings . . . But where, meanwhile, is the play?[27]

There were also criticisms of Robert Graves' textual revisions aimed at clarifying some of the denser language. B. A. Young, however, found it

full of superb comic acting. I am no longer able to write with restraint about Maggie Smith; I can only say that the part of Beatrice might have been written for her. Robert Stephens makes Benedick a provincial Italian wide boy, who soon exchanges his uniform for a variety of sharp suits; he plays the part with sensitivity and wit, and speaks his lines most musically. Albert Finney's Don Pedro . . . is a gorgeous comic creation.[28]

A. J. Antoon set his 1972 New York Shakespeare Festival production in small-town Middle America:

This is a pre–World War I America—marked by chauvinism, self-confidence and suddenly requited love. The gentlemen wear spats and carry pocket flasks. The ladies sneak a shared cigarette, and clear the smoke away before the father of the house enters. Almost everyone is inhibited by social conventions—yet everyone is having a glorious time. As sparklers flare, the couples dance Donald Saddler [ballroom] dances by the light of Japanese lanterns—and the Central Park moon could be part of the set.[29]

Some critics admired the updating and performances of Sam Waterston as Benedick and Kathleen Widdoes as Beatrice, with Dogberry and the Watch played as Keystone Kops. Stanley Kauffman thought it changed "the Beatrice and Benedick backchat into very recognizable Yankee sass, without altering a word," as well as enabling him to use "American actors as Americans instead of as fake Britishers and failed classicists."[30] Others, such as H. R. Coursen, were unconvinced:

For some incomprehensible reason, this *Much Ado* is set in 1910 America. The production is defeated at the outset by its conception. Aristocratic love and Italianate intrigue collide in mid-air with small-town America, bands, balloons, and Blue Ribbon Beer. Language, "By my troth," clashes with spats and gramophones, turkey trots, and Keystone Cops.[31]

John Barton's successful 1976 RSC production, discussed in detail below, meanwhile set the play in the India of the British Raj, creating a similarly removed, claustrophobic environment. Jerry Turner transported the play to seventeenth-century Holland in his 1977 American Conservatory Theatre production, while John Bell's production with the Nimrod Theatre Company in Adelaide, Australia, used a circus atmosphere. Terrence Knapp's Tokyo production set the play in late nineteenth-century Japan and employed a cultural vocabulary of Japanese references, while Dana Larson Evans offered a futuristic, space-age vision at California's Grove Shakespeare Festival in 1980.

Terry Hands' 1982 production for the RSC marked a revival of the play's lush romanticism, in contrast to Gerald Freedman's 1988 New York Shakespeare Festival production, described as:

A high-spirited romp from beginning to end, this "Much Ado" opens with a mock sword fight; ferociously engaged with his soldierly colleague Claudio, Mr [Kevin] Kline's Benedick immediately displays the dazzling physical virtuosity that has so often characterized his performances . . . his Benedick may be brilliant, but he is also vain and hilariously foolish. As he whirls about the stage, Blythe Danner's Beatrice pointedly refuses to look up from her book—but even before she and Benedick commence their verbal volleys, the potential heat of their ultimate destiny is obvious.[32]

In the same year, Judi Dench directed a warmly received production for Kenneth Branagh's newly formed Renaissance Theatre Company, with Branagh himself as Benedick and Samantha Bond as Beatrice. The simplicity of its staging and conception was in marked contrast to Di Trevis' production at the RSC. Since then *Much Ado* has continued its merry war in countless theaters all over the world, including Richard Monette's modern, cosmopolitan 1998 Stratford Ontario production. Peter Meineck directed Robert Richmond's version of the play for New York's Aquila Theater in 2001, turning it "into a spoof of 1960s–70s TV and film secret agents."[33] Greg Doran's brilliant Sicilian RSC production was staged in 2002, the same year as Mark Lamos' Hartford Stage/Shakespeare Theater production set "mostly in the garden of an English country house in the 1920s."[34] Daniela Varon's 2003 production at the Founders' Theater in Lenox, Massachusetts, again set the play in a Messina "inspired by popular images of Sicily in the 1950s, . . . steeped in the culture of violence and family loyalty associated with the Mafia."[35]

A play that has enjoyed such continuous popularity in the theater would seem an obvious candidate for screen treatment. The earliest was Phillips Smalley's 1913 American silent version. There was an East German version in 1963 and two Russian films in 1956 and 1973. A number of successful stage productions were filmed, including Zeffirelli's 1965 National Theatre production with Maggie Smith and Robert Stephens, as well as Joseph Papp's 1973 New York Shakespeare Festival production. Musical adaptations include Hector Berlioz's acclaimed *Béatrice et Bénédict* (1862) and the 2006 American musical adaptation *The Boys Are Coming Home*, set in the Second World War. The most successful film adaptation, though, is undoubtedly Kenneth Branagh's 1993 film set, as Branagh describes in his introduction to the screenplay, in an "imaginary world [which] could have existed almost anytime between 1700 and 1900":

> It was distant enough to allow the language to work without the clash of period anachronisms and for a certain fairy tale quality to emerge. This fairy tale idea seemed to spring naturally out of the countryside in which we were working. We were in Tuscany, central Italy, a magical landscape of vines and olives that seemed untouched by modern life. Lusher and more verdant than Sicily (Shakespeare's setting), it allowed us to create a visual idyll in which this cautionary tale might be told.[36]

AT THE RSC

Much Ado About Nothing is among the most performed of Shakespeare's plays and regarded as a "banker" by theater managers. Critical, as well as popular, focus is invariably on the performances of the actors playing Beatrice and Benedick, on the nature of their relationship and the quality of their repartee. *Much Ado* was chosen as the opening production at the freshly named Royal Shakespeare Theatre (RST) under the new management of Peter Hall as artistic director, and Trevor Nunn made it his first production when he took over as artistic director in 1968. The RSC has mounted twelve productions since 1961: two touring productions, nine at the RST and one at the Swan Theatre—Marianne Elliott's production for the 2006/07 Complete Works season was widely regarded as one of the season's jewels, as well as being a strong box-office success.

When and Where Messina?

Much Ado has the highest prose content of all the plays except *The Merry Wives of Windsor* and it is, perhaps, the immediacy, freshness, and informality of the dialogue that has led directors, for the most part, to move the play away from its Elizabethan origins to later periods. RSC productions have been set in the Regency and Victorian periods, during the British Raj in India, in the 1930s, 1940s, and 1950s. Sets have rarely made much of the specifically Sicilian location of Messina, though Stephen Brimson Lewis designed a sunbaked piazza for Gregory Doran's 2002 production at the RST.

Regency and Victorian Settings

Michael Langham's 1961 production, designed by Desmond Heeley, was played against a backdrop of a towering Italian house of honeydew-colored stone and set in the early nineteenth century, with the women dressed in graceful, high-waisted, neoclassical dresses and the men dashing in immaculately tailored Napoleonic War uniforms. Although the production touched only lightly on the play's darker elements, they were suggested in the autumnal leaves on the creeper climbing the house front and in the rainstorm that had the guests at Hero and Claudio's wedding arriving with dripping umbrellas. Perhaps unsurprisingly at the start of a decade that was to see such radical social changes in Britain, W. A. Darlington in the *Daily Telegraph* was conscious that Leonato and his family had been made well-to-do middle class, in contrast to the young noblemen who were their houseguests.[37]

In 1971, Ronald Eyre directed a production unequivocally set in Victorian England. The action in Leonato's house took place in an elegant conservatory with a view of immaculate green lawns beyond and costumes described by several critics as "Ruritanian comic opera." The effect, as critic Michael Billington described it, was of a "Betjemanesque" world, where "everything conspires to suggest a leisurely, sunlit, aristocratic society." Lighting "miraculously transformed" the conservatory into entrance hall, courtyard, and church.[38]

John Barton's 1976 setting of the play in late nineteenth-century British India was generally regarded as a triumph: "an ideal background for the play about the prankish practical jokes of a bored officer class and about the liberation of long-suppressed emotion."[39] A garrison town was suggested by a double tier of timber balconies, draped with beaded or cheesecloth curtains and sunblinds. Cricket could be heard being played offstage.

Sixteenth- and Seventeenth-Century Settings

For Trevor Nunn's 1968 production, Christopher Morley designed Elizabethan costumes with a twentieth-century twist: many of the fabrics suggested military camouflage in their color and pattern. The militarism of the men was emphasized, and their dance at the party at Leonato's house was an aggressive sword-dance performed in threatening visors. There was a somber and sinister air to the production, with an emphasis on the spying and eavesdropping that pervade the play. The acting area was enclosed by a severe rectangular box of translucent gauze that could be lit in a variety of ways to suggest interior and exterior locations but was always slightly sinister: "Comedy and the sinister were continually in tension."[40] Nunn is quoted as saying: "I have yet to see the play done with sufficient seriousness; 'Kill Claudio' is for real."[41]

3. Helen Mirren as Hero, Janet Suzman as Beatrice, and Rowena Cooper as Ursula in Trevor Nunn's 1968 Stratford production, with its emphasis on the spying and eavesdropping that pervade the play.

For Terry Hands' 1982 production, designer Ralph Koltai also enclosed the stage in a box, but this time it had a mirrored floor and walls constructed of perspex screens imprinted with stylized trees. The effect was not sinister but "achingly beautiful,"[42] magical and romantic. The mirrored setting suggested a self-regarding, self-loving, narcissistic society, and the Cavalier-style costumes gave the production an elegant courtliness while implying that this world was about to come to an end—Michael Billington in the *Guardian* felt that Hands had missed a trick: "Surely if Don Pedro and his chums are Cavaliers, Don John should be a Roundhead?"[43] The overall effect, however, was not elegiac but romantic—joy just tinged with melancholy. This was a highly successful production, acclaimed by critics and enjoyed by audiences. It had a long afterlife following its season at the RST: it went to Newcastle and The Barbican in 1983 and spent 1984 touring, culminating in performances in New York and Washington.

Of Bill Alexander's 1990 production it was suggested:

Two years ago, the RSC bombed badly with a vogue-ish *Much Ado About Nothing* set in some 50's no-man's-land. They now make amends with a visually seductive, socially consistent Bill Alexander production that aroused the audience to ecstasy.[44]

The production's designer, Kit Surrey, returned to the seventeenth century with an elegantly hedged English garden which "neatly suggests a hierarchical world in which everyone knows his or her place."[45] Lighting cast a golden glow: "it bathed the cast's faces in wonderful amalgams of amber, bronze, flame, white and creamy pink. It gave the evening its enchanted atmosphere—and its meaning."[46]

In 1996, Michael Boyd's production was staged in another enclosed courtyard, but its eclectic nature failed to please: "The costumes are Elizabethan enough but Tom Piper's set is decidedly odd, a mixture of 18th-century drawing-room, Guildford Cathedral and de Chirico piazza that comes complete with a tree splintering up through varnished floorboards."[47] Like the 1982 production, the set also featured mirrors and portraits, but here they were disturbing; the whole production was dark in tone, focusing on the Hero–Claudio–Don John plot as the core of the play. Even the final dance "was accompanied by music to slit your wrists to."[48] Many of the critics disliked the air of gloom, although Nicholas de Jongh found it exhilarating: "It makes it feel as if an early Shakespeare comedy is being transformed into one of his dark problem plays or late romances."[49] He alone commented on the ending of the play: the roof of the courtyard rose to reveal blue sky, and the audience saw the mirrored reflection of a small boy standing beside a sapling tree—signs that the future was assured. It was, he suggested, "*Much Ado* turned vividly inside out."[50]

1930s, 1940s, and 1950s Settings

In 1988 Di Trevis turned a materialist-feminist light on the play. Messina was a Mediterranean playground for the rich and idle; the set (designed by Mark Thompson) a pillared white-marble patio complete with swimming pools. The costumes were 1950s couture, but the decade glanced at was the materialistic 1980s. At the opening of the play, the lazy luxury of Messina was disrupted by the sound of a helicopter overhead from which a wounded soldier was winched down before the other men appeared. The gender attitudes of a patriarchal society were made very clear, and the "happy ending" of the double wedding was subverted by dressing Beatrice and Hero in black with black confetti fluttering down on them. Critics and audiences, for the most part, found this a problematic interpretation; Robert Smallwood commented: "It is difficult to go on disliking the whole of Messina's high society as much as the production seems to want us to."[51]

For Gregory Doran's 2002 production, Stephen Brimson Lewis designed a set that let the audience know instantly that it was in Sicily—"a sun-baked Sicilian piazza, which glows like a ripe tomato,"[52] with a great wall on wooden shutters and wrought-iron balconies. For some critics the opening moments were too crowd-pleasing: "an appallingly saccharine start—wheeling in a brass band, a cute schoolboy and the predictable jolly local on a bike,"[53] but the men returning from the war were black-shirted—Mussolini's troops, back from the Ethiopian campaign—and the scene was set firmly in 1930s fascist Sicily. Though the sun shone and the comedy flourished, the dark underbelly of the play was never hidden for long.

For Marianne Elliott's 2006 production, Lez Brotherston transformed the Swan Theatre into Havana. Multicolored lights were strung across the auditorium and the audience entered a Cuban nightclub alive with salsa music and cigar smoke. Smiles broke out in expectation of fun. This was early 1950s, pre-Castro Cuba; "You half expect Sky Masterson and Sarah Brown, on their whirlwind trip to Havana, to wander in from *Guys and Dolls*."[54] Elliott had chosen a Latin country for the play's hot blood and macho honor code and an era just before the changes in Western sexual mores of the 1960s which would make the Hero–Claudio plot implausible. In addition, as Michael Billington suggested, "What it offers is a plausible military context, a raffish glamour and endless opportunities, gloriously seized by Olly Fox's score, for rumbas, sambas and congas."[55] On the darker side, "The reflex sexism of this Catholic society suits the sobering aspects of a play in which an innocent girl is slandered at the altar by credulous barrack-room misogynists."[56] The change in mood in the play's second half was strongly signaled: the audience returned from the interval to find the strings of lights turned off.

Beatrice and Benedick

These roles dominate performances, and productions are remembered more for the actors who played them than for their directors or design features or for the playing of any of the other roles. Since the second half of the twentieth century was a period during which gender issues were of unprecedented interest, a variety of constructions of the gender politics of this play have been reflected in the playing of these central roles, and the role of Beatrice in particular.

1961—A New Kind of Beatrice

The actors in the 1961 production must have felt a huge weight of expectation on their shoulders: not only were they starring in the RST's opening production, but critics and audiences brought with them the golden memory of a very popular 1955 production starring Peggy Ashcroft and John Gielgud. This romantic, lyrical staging, in which Beatrice and Benedick were clearly in love from the outset, had been hugely popular—and Peggy Ashcroft was in the audience for the 1961 opening night. Geraldine McEwan and Christopher Plummer, as Beatrice and Benedick, could hardly have been more different from these earlier models. McEwan's Beatrice bore resemblances to Jane Austen's Elizabeth Bennet: she was "crackling" and "fiery." Oddly, she was criticized for a lack of poetry when the only verse Beatrice speaks is her "What fire is in mine ears?" soliloquy, but perhaps it was an absence of lyricism that troubled the critics. *The Times'* reviewer commented that "she dispenses with the airs and graces of the traditional Beatrice"; she was "hoydenish" and "a modern young woman who thoroughly enjoys the Elizabethan notion of repartee."[57] These are significant comments: the "airs and graces" had only accrued to actresses playing Beatrice from the Victorian period onward. Seventeenth- and eighteenth-century audiences, to judge from the critics' comments, had enjoyed a forceful, fiery, combative performance from their Beatrices: "every word stabbed," the critics observed approvingly, and praised the actresses' "spirit" and "vigor." In the nineteenth century, however, we find actresses in the role beings extolled as "feminine," "womanly," "refined," and "well-bred" and their raillery had become "pleasant archness."[58] Actresses were being required to tone down Beatrice's combativeness, and went on doing so, it seems, through to the 1950s. Again, 1961 was a significant date.

Christopher Plummer, a Canadian actor making his English debut, was an energetic, virile Benedick, in the young Olivier mold, according to Bernard Levin in the *Daily Express*. Where Gielgud had played a sophisticated, poised, rather intellectual Benedick, Plummer gave a far more physical, soldierly performance, which some critics found charmless.

1971, 1976, 1988, 2002 — Middle-Aged Lovers

In the sunlit Victorian 1971 production Elizabeth Spriggs and Derek Godfrey played Beatrice and Benedick approaching middle age. Elizabeth Spriggs had made a career in comic supporting roles and was a surprising choice for Beatrice. She created a cheerful, bustling forty-something spinster, constantly busy early on with small household tasks but growing visibly younger from the moment when she believed herself to be loved; he was a hearty public school type, still indulging in schoolboy behavior (at one point, Benedick's pants were thrown around by his friends). Their early verbal battles were good-natured but sad, freighted with disappointing experience; in place of the brittle exchange of barbs, they fell into comforting, familiar routines. Audiences found them very appealing.

In John Barton's 1976 production, set in late nineteenth-century India under the British Raj, Judi Dench and Donald Sinden played a couple on the brink of a lonely middle age, both slight outsiders in their social milieu. One critic wrote: "They make no attempt to be archly charming nor to hold tennis rallies . . . They swap their insults with a sort of desiccated desperation."[59] Dench, in an unbecoming wig, was "an intelligent spinster who knows she is edging toward the status of maiden aunt,"[60] while beneath Sinden's plummy mannerisms was a man who knew he was heading for the role of eccentric uncle. In Sinden's performance, "swagger and buffoonery are a camouflage for easily wounded private feelings";[61] he had moments of acute shyness. As her key to playing Beatrice, Dench took the revelation that Benedick had once won Beatrice's heart "with false dice." She played a sad, spinsterish woman who had once believed that Benedick loved her but felt she had been deceived; when she "overheard" Hero talking of Benedick's love for her, she literally skipped for joy.

In 1988 in Di Trevis' opulent, cold, materialistic 1950s Messina, Maggie Steed and Clive Merrison played another ageing couple. Steed was "a brassily-painted maypole,"[62] "an acid-tongued spinster"[63] who

> is on the point of settling into the role of eccentric maiden aunt. Everything about her, from her swooping movement and exaggerated handling of long, swishing costumes, to her advance on the mocking girls with a bared hatpin and her trick of winding up each anti-marital fusillade with a dazzling mirthless grin, comes over as a mocking parody of the feminine arts.[64]

Steed has said that she saw Beatrice as the poor relation in the household (where Hero is the heiress), who "sings for her supper" by playing the joker.[65] Merrison, too, was a joker, balding and knobbly-kneed in his Bermuda shorts, once he had taken off his military uniform, physically dominated by the taller Steed.

In Gregory Doran's acclaimed 2002 production, set in Mussolini's Sicily, Harriet Walter and Nicholas le Prévost played a couple well into middle age. Le Prévost was "a shabby roué," "a lank-haired, unshaven old louche, for whom even the plink and fizz of a soluble aspirin proves too vexatious the morning after the night before."[66] Walter, on the other hand, was an intensely glamorous older woman, "dazzlingly attractive in her Thirties outfits," with "the thoroughbred wit and presence of a Katharine Hepburn."[67] The critics were unanimous in praise of her performance:

> Walter exudes the kind of sophisticated Thirties sassiness one associates with comedies featuring cocktails and Cole Porter.

Her Beatrice can switch winningly between headgirl surliness and heartfelt hurt, and even hints at a deeply pained past with her old sparring partner Benedick.[68]

In the first scene, elegantly trousered, she jumped onto the dispatch rider's motorbike and "thereafter remained the play's moral engine."[69]

She and Gregory Doran solved the problem that very "sassy," controlled Beatrices have of her sudden melt into girly helplessness at the end of the eavesdropping scene: "And, Benedick, love on, I will requite thee, / Taming my wild heart to thy loving hand" (3.1.113–14). Hero deliberately doused her with water while watering the hedge behind which she was hiding so that she emerged unglamorously dripping and disheveled, her physical disarray mirroring her emotional confusion. (This piece of business also provided a reason for the cold she is suffering from on the morning of Hero's wedding—an idea used in the 1988 production where Maggie Steed hid in the swimming pool during the eavesdropping scene.) Walter and le Prévost were a couple who grew into an extraordinary and touching emotional closeness in the dark second half of the play.

1968, 1982—The Rebels

When Trevor Nunn directed the play in 1968 he was only twenty-eight, though he had just taken over as artistic director at the RSC. He directed Janet Suzman and Alan Howard as a very young, almost adolescent Beatrice and Benedick, boisterous, frivolous, and cynical, in rebellion against the matchmaking society around them, denying their evident attraction to each other. In spite of the Elizabethan costume, there was a suggestion of 1960s disaffection in their attitudes. Suzman was a zany Beatrice, her hair and clothes often in disarray; B. A. Young, in the *Financial Times*, thought she seemed "not altogether to have got over her Katherine in last year's *Shrew*."[70]

Sinead Cusack's Beatrice in 1982 also evoked comparisons with Katherine; one critic stated: "when she says 'I would eat his heart in the market place' you'd better believe it," before going on to suggest she was a "self-taming shrew," who comes to emotional equilibrium through love.[71] Cusack herself has said that she had some conflict

4. Derek Jacobi as Benedick and Sinead Cusack as Beatrice in Terry Hands' 1982 RSC production. Cusack played her as "A Beatrice who is very angry. A woman who has been damaged by society."

with her director, Terry Hands, over her interpretation. Young, blond, and beautiful, she had been cast for her femininity: "That's what he cast. That's what he used in his direction of me. But . . . I showed him other areas of her character. A Beatrice who is very angry. A woman who has been damaged by society."[72] Her Benedick, Derek Jacobi, played a "skittish, larky, life-and-soul-of-the-party bachelor"[73] with some camp mannerisms, who sobered up and grew up under the influence of love. The play ended on an unashamedly romantic note, with the pair left alone, dancing together and talking—the beginning of a lifelong conversation—as a red sun set behind them.

1996—Lovers in Dark Times

The dark tone of Michael Boyd's 1996 production was a challenge to Siobhan Redmond and Alex Jennings in their early exchanges: audiences expect fun from Beatrice and Benedick, and this production was not about fun. Alex Jennings played the part with "sardonic and urbane wit," "elegant nobility," and, later, "sober gravity";[74] his performance was widely regarded as the play's "one unqualified success . . . [he] seems to be taking part in a different play from everyone else—the real play. He is unashamedly charming, a smoothie who is also engagingly ridiculous."[75] Siobhan Redmond played a "restless babbling Beatrice, lightweight but intense";[76] she burst into wretched tears on hearing that Benedick loved her.

1990, 2006 — Sexual Attraction

Before the opening of Bill Alexander's 1990 production, Susan Fleetwood, who was to play Beatrice, was interviewed with her Benedick, Roger Allam. Of Beatrice she said:

> She is delicious—a wonderful, eruptive person, an oddball, like Benedick. The two don't fit into their society. Beatrice is quick, sharp, vulnerable, then there are moments when she is pure joy, when she wants to just fly for the hell of it . . . I've never worked with Roger before but we'll buzz one another up and be a treat . . . You've got to play . . . for sex—opposite Roger you couldn't do anything else.[77]

Behind her cutting one-liners, Fleetwood always suggested her intense feelings for Allam's relaxed, charming, intelligent Benedick.

Tamsin Greig came as the star name to the 2006 1950s Cuba production in The Swan. Well known as a comedienne in her television work, she found much more in the role than the comedy. A striking figure in black and white, in contrast to the sweet-pea frocks of Hero and the other young women, she dominated the stage early on. Critics reached out for comparisons to convey her style: "Greig brings to Beatrice the caustic wit and pencil-skirted style of a wise-cracking Hollywood dame like Eve Arden";[78] "Tamsin Greig makes a handsome Beatrice, who with her slit skirt, pointy shoes, cigarette holder and hands on hips has something of the tart grandeur of a downmarket Princess Margaret."[79] What she also suggested was the barely controlled frustration of a woman who was faster and brighter than anyone else around. The scene of her eavesdropping was quite as funny as Benedick's, where it is often less so, but faced with the news that Benedick loved her, she was filled with an aching vulnerability. Joseph Millson as Benedick was not overshadowed, though: "Joseph Millson's performance . . . strikes me as definitive. Handsome in voice and in person, he can carry the audience on his roar and draw it into his hush. The elements of wit, anger and vulnerability are thrillingly mixed in this actor."[80] Together they made a funny, intelligent, passionate pairing.

"Kill Claudio"

The delivery of this notoriously difficult line is often singled out for comment by the critics. In 1968, Janet Suzman yelled the line with tigerish intensity and Alan Howard yelled back "Not for the wide world!" One critic felt that they "solved the problem" of the line.[81] Many thought that Judi Dench, in 1976, delivered it beautifully (with a smothered giggle) but others complained that the line raised a laugh. Michael Billington wrote of Susan Fleetwood in 1990 that she "delivers that death-trap injunction to Benedick, 'Kill Claudio', with such intensity that not a titter runs through the house. This is real acting."[82] Billington commented on Harriet Walter's delivery of the line too: "the exchanges (in the Church scene) between Harriet Walter's Beatrice and Nicholas le Prévost's Benedick are charged with a heady mix of eroticism and violence. Walter's demand that he 'Kill Claudio' springs out of an incandescent fury that leads her to kick over the church pews."[83] Tamsin Greig in the 2006 production spilled out the line amid a torrent of tears and kisses, sometimes evoking a laugh from the audience and sometimes an awed hush.

Claudio and Hero

Technically, the Claudio–Hero plot is the play's main plot, but they are invariably overshadowed. Finding the balance between the pleasure of the Beatrice–Benedick plot and the pain of the Hero–Claudio one emerges as more of an issue in later productions. In 1961, Michael Langham made little of the pain and Michael

Billington noted the difficulties created for this part of the play by the very English setting of Ronald Eyre's 1971 production, lacking as it did "Italian ardor." The golden glow of the English garden in Bill Alexander's 1992 production similarly marginalized Hero's suffering, though Alex Kingston was a touching Hero.

In 1968, Trevor Nunn took the Hero–Claudio–Don John plot as its dark focus, and though the Claudio was generally felt by critics to be undercast, Helen Mirren was a moving Hero, playing her as barely more than a child, wide-eyed and excited at the prospect of marriage, a true lamb to the slaughter. In Barton's 1976 production, Cherie Lunghi played an appealing Hero and Richard Durden a heartless Claudio who was as "coldly frivolous" after the disgrace of Hero as he had been before. Billington observed that the two plots melded unusually well because Don John's plot against Claudio and Hero was a particularly vicious extension of the practical jokes indulged in by a heartless officer class.[84]

The cruelty of Hero's treatment, not only by Don John and Claudio but by her own father, was strongly emphasized in Di Trevis' 1988 production. Ralph Fiennes played a particularly unpleasant, smug, sycophantic Claudio, and Irving Wardle noted: "There is perhaps more substance in the production's feminist angle: as where Hero (Julia Ford) collapses in church and is immediately surrounded by a flock of sympathetic girls, while the men all retire to nurse their personal grievances."[85]

In Gregory Doran's 2002 production, the Sicilian setting supported the play's masculine honor code and the mood shifted successfully from sun-drenched comedy to the darkness of Hero's betrayal:

Doran also captures the darkness which casts such threatening shadows over this golden comedy. The great scene in which that callow gold-digger Claudio (excellent John Hopkins) accuses Hero of being a whore during their wedding ceremony is played with real psychological perception and packs a devastating and painful dramatic punch. When even Hero's loving father viciously turns on her, the eggshell surface of the comedy cracks to reveal the possibility of real tragedy.[86]

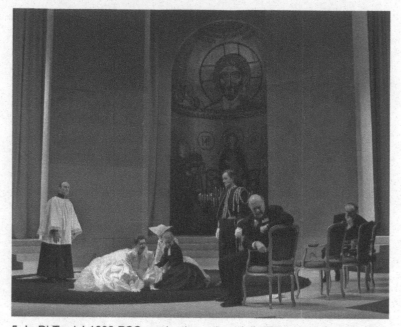

5. In Di Trevis' 1988 RSC production, when Julia Ford as Hero collapsed, she was "immediately surrounded by a flock of sympathetic girls, while the men all retire[d] to nurse their personal grievances."

John Hopkins played Claudio as a man genuinely hurt as well as wounded in his pride, and Kirsten Parker was a deeply affecting Hero, "who, in the rejection scene, retains all the dignity of a princess."[87] With a skilled director's touch, Doran later had the wan face of Hero, immured indoors, look down from an upstairs window to see her now penitent father cradling her bridal veil.

In the salsa-filled Cuban setting of 2006, director Marianne Elliott made no attempt to keep the mood light in the second half: the bright lights went out in the interval, literally darkening the atmosphere: "The pain of the wedding scene in which Morven Christie's sweet young Hero is so vilely traduced by Adam Rayner's cruel, callow Claudio achieves a bruising tragic intensity."[88]

Of all the productions, Michael Boyd's in 1996 went furthest in giving main-plot status to this thread in the play. Emily Bruni as Hero was withdrawn and unsmiling, passive in her acquiescence to an arranged marriage and traumatized by what followed.

Minor Roles

The role of Don John has been a jumping-off point for several young actors who would go on to highly successful careers both in the RSC and outside it. Several critics noted a "cankerous" performance in 1961 by a young Ian Richardson, who played Don John with a "sinister stammer,"[89] and in 1971, Richard Pasco, too, was a "canker" in the otherwise sunny Victorian garden, playing Don John as a viciously repressed homosexual. In 1996, reviewing the production which strikingly foregrounded Don John's plot against Claudio, Alastair Macaulay comments: "a very impressive young actor brings Don John to life with a nervous, laughing loutishness that is both dangerous and naïve,"[90] while de Jongh writes: "The remarkable Damian Lewis plays this villain as a suave but passionate malcontent, who puts a disarming face upon sheer evil."[91] In 1968, Don John's lieutenants, Conrad and Borachio, were played with villainous perfection by two young actors, Ben Kingsley and Patrick Stewart.

In Bill Alexander's 1990 production, critics singled out John Carlisle:

> The most complete performance of the evening comes from John Carlisle as Don Pedro. This is no princely cipher but an ageing Cavalier, shrouded in solitude, hungry for emotional contact. Mr Carlisle enters into the proxy wooing of Hero with suspicious enthusiasm and proposes to Beatrice with direct urgency. He creates a character where on the page one barely exists.[92]

The Dogberry–Verges–Watch scenes are difficult to pull off, and actors and directors often seem to be trying too hard. "Frenziedly overpitched," says Billington of Terry Hands' 1982 production.[93] David Waller played a richly comic, pompous, bucolic Dogberry in Nunn's 1968 production, in fine contrast to Clifford Rose's delicate Verges; John Woodvine's Sikh Dogberry in Barton's 1976 production was generally praised as bringing fresh comedy to Dogberry's malapropisms and self-importance. Audiences would be less comfortable with the implied racial attitudes now, and even then, as one critic commented cuttingly, "You only need to raise a finger and a Paki accent and you're home."[94] Marianne Elliott in 2006 tried to inject humor into Dogberry by casting Bette Bourne as an outrageously camp officer, accessorizing his uniform with a pink suspender belt and lipstick, making him appear like "a slightly scary low-rent drag queen."[95]

THE DIRECTOR'S CUT: INTERVIEWS WITH MARIANNE ELLIOTT AND NICHOLAS HYTNER

Marianne Elliott was born in 1967 into a distinguished theatrical family and brought up in Manchester where her father was cofounder of the Manchester Royal Exchange. She studied drama at Hull University, but spent some years working in a variety of jobs unconnected with the theater before working as a casting director and then setting up her own company, Small Talk. She was subsequently appointed artistic director at the Manchester Royal Exchange. Her production of Lillian Hellman's *The Little Foxes* with Penelope Wilton at the Donmar Warehouse in 2001 was highly praised, and she went on to become an associate director at London's Royal Court. She has directed numerous successful productions as an associate director at the National, including an adaptation of Émile Zola's *Thérèse Raquin*, Michael Morpurgo's *War Horse*, Shaw's *St. Joan*, and Samuel Adamson's *Mrs Affleck*. She was nominated for an Evening Standard theater award for her 2005 production of Ibsen's *Pillars of the Community*. Marianne directed the highly acclaimed 2006 production of *Much Ado About Nothing* in the Swan Theatre for the RSC Complete Works Festival with Tamsin Greig as Beatrice and Joseph Millson as Benedick.

Nicholas Hytner was appointed director of the National Theatre in 2003. He was born in Manchester in 1956 and, after attending Manchester Grammar School, read English at Cambridge. He was associate director of Manchester's Royal Exchange Theatre from 1985 to 1989 and at the National from 1989 to 1997. He was a visiting professor of contemporary theater at Oxford University in 2000–01, and is an honorary fellow of Trinity Hall, Cambridge. He is credited with revolutionizing the National Theatre artistically and with attracting large new audiences by producing bold, original work. He has directed many plays from the classical repertoire, including *King Lear* and *The Tempest* at the RSC and *The Winter's Tale*, *Henry V*, *The Alchemist*, and *Phèdre* at the National. His long-standing collaboration with the playwright Alan Bennett includes *The Madness of George III* and *The History Boys* at the National. His films include *The Madness of King George*, *The Crucible*, and *The History Boys*. He directed Zoë Wanamaker and Simon Russell Beale in *Much Ado About Nothing* in 2007–08.

What sort of a world was your Messina? Did you give particular attention to the element of soldiers returning from the war, the transition from the battlefield to the battle of the sexes?

Elliott: Our Messina was Cuba around 1953, just after a rebel uprising had been crushed. The soldiers are victorious and ready to celebrate, get drunk, meet girls, etc. It's party time.

I felt the setting needed to be an imperialistic and patriarchal society. Men and women are viewed and treated very differently, hence their battling. It is also a society that is rather exotic and glamorous; like Italy was viewed by the English when Shakespeare wrote the play. Hence Cuba felt right. It's a place where there's a merging between public and private places, between street and house. This helped the in and out scenes: the outside party/festival feel and the more private family scenes. Cuba is a place that can hum to the beat of music. We used the rhythms of the time, which had a feel like the Buena Vista Social Club. Ours was a world where music was very much part of the soul of the people; the atmosphere was hot, sexy, and sweaty with an air of machismo. It's tropical, it's possibly a bit wild, and it's nothing like England! Cuba is somewhere we recognize as a sophisticated, glamorous, Latino place with a holiday feel, but at that time it had a darker side. In 1953, just before the revolution, it was in a flux of change, just like the characters in the play.

Hytner: Leonato's household is made up of many women and a couple of old men. It's very deliberately a testosterone-free zone. Its femininity is more interesting, and more unusual, than the locker-room machismo of the army. An army which isn't returning home incidentally—it's a mercenary army, presumably recruited from all over Italy, commanded by a Spaniard on behalf of the Spanish crown, billeting itself temporarily before further action. It's more like the army in *Three Sisters*—disrupting a sleepy backwater—but, there's no suspicion that Messina is dead without it. We took care to create an easygoing, hospitable household, very Sicilian. Its first instinct is to throw a party. You don't get the impression that it is in any way incomplete before the army arrives. On the contrary, it seems content and at ease with itself. It's quite hard to negotiate through the first forty-five minutes without repeated gales of cheesy stage laughter.

The battle between Beatrice and Benedick seems to me to be less a battle between the sexes than a painful, and very funny, mutual baptism. They have in common a refusal to take the plunge: they cast themselves instead in the same roles in relation to the largely single-sex worlds to which they have resigned themselves. They are both their respective "prince's fool," and there is in both an underlying unhappiness with the corner they've painted themselves into. Their banter is a front for their emotional dishonesty; the "mountain of affection" is the elephant in the room and Don Pedro's therapeutic trick makes it impossible for them to ignore it. We played our gulling scene around a pool. Both jumped in it to hide. They took the plunge, literally.

The real battle is between unthinking patriarchy and the apparently irrational, instinctive female loyalty embodied by Beatrice. The evidence of their own eyes seems to favor Claudio and Don Pedro. Leonato impulsively takes their side against his daughter. Beatrice's instinctive refusal to believe them is based on something truer than the evidence: she has a genuine capacity to know—to note—those around her. She knows Hero. When Benedick joins her, it's not so much a resolution of a battle between the sexes as a union between two people who, through allowing themselves to be genuinely and fully known by each other, have the capacity to know those around them.

There is clearly a history between Beatrice and Benedick that has taken place before the play starts. Is that something you explored in rehearsal?

Elliott: We were interested in all the characters wearing metaphorical masks and creating unrealistic images of themselves, but Beatrice and Benedick specifically seemed to exist under a very polished veneer. They live carefully guarded lives, which they have cultivated—always resorting to making people laugh rather than letting anyone in. Of course, this changes during the play through the power of their love and the shock of what happens to Hero. As for their history, we felt there would be no reason for them to hate each other unless they've been burnt by each other before. There would be no reason for them to keep touting their rather vain "joker" images of themselves if they weren't trying to cover up something vulnerable inside—and/or trying to control everyone and everything around them.

Hytner: It's essential to create a past for Beatrice and Benedick. We agreed on a very specific history—not something that we intended to be legible to the audience, but a foundation for the palpable pain that they cause each other by being in each other's presence. Our assumption was that at some stage Beatrice read their deepening friendship as blossoming love; that she pushed too hard and that Benedick did a runner. Benedick, we assumed, was a greater coward than Beatrice. And the memory is still raw. These secret histories are essential actors' tools. They played their first exchange in Act 1 Scene 1 ("nobody marks you"; "Are you yet living?") not as a public performance but away from the crowd, a private acknowledgment of the disdain that masks deep hurt.

It's a commonplace that Shakespeare's marriages seem very often to be built on shaky foundations, and that Beatrice and Benedick make the marriage most likely to succeed in all of his plays. Essential, therefore, that both actors convey that they know the worst about each other and marry because of it, not in spite of it. Zoë Wanamaker and Simon Russell Beale were in an established tradition of middle-aged Beatrices and Benedicks: people who have lived, failed, resigned themselves to loneliness and, through a genuine sense of each other in the round (prompted admittedly by a trick), become capable of the compromise that long-lasting relationships require.

Did you find there were some key shifts in the balance of power between them? The "Kill Claudio" moment's a crucial one, isn't it?

Elliott: Yes, it is a crucial moment. It's difficult to do nowadays as it can engender a giggly, slightly embarrassed reaction in the audience because it is so surprising and so extreme. But Beatrice is very much a product of where she comes from. She's an incredibly strong, strident woman, but she is living in a patriarchal, warlike world where the men are fighters and their enemies are very real and immediate. She wants Benedick to be a man of action, to stop all his talk and do something about the horrendous situation.

It's also a test, of course, because although she really does believe that Claudio should be exterminated Mafia-style, she is pushing Benedick to the limit, to see how far and how deep this newly professed love for her is. She's been hurt by him before, don't forget. Of course, in this moment the lady takes all the power. Benedick has to perform a very difficult (nearly impossible) task to win her.

6. Simon Russell Beale as Benedick and Zoë Wanamaker as Beatrice argue as intellectual equals in Nicholas Hytner's 2007 National Theatre production.

Generally, we found that Benedick and Beatrice were constantly looking for the upper hand. We explored that in our production by having them always playing to the crowd. Whichever of them had the joke that got the biggest reaction had the power and the control. That reinforced their image, their veneer of being the sophisticated, witty one who could bring the other down with a damning look or word. Beatrice won these subtle little wars quite a lot, we found! But this habit of theirs is a hard one to crack, even at the end of the play!

Hytner: We were less interested in shifts in the balance of power than in their uncovering of themselves to each other. Beatrice is plainly wittier than Benedick—she gets the better of him through most of the banter. But they share a way of looking at the world even before they declare themselves to each other. The banter is a way of avoiding the truth.

"Kill Claudio" is so shockingly truthful that it always gets a laugh—in recognition, I think, of how desperately helpless a man like Benedick is bound to be in the face of such raw hatred. It's tricky (and critically de trop) to make these sorts of judgment about fictional characters, but it's worth saying that Benedick is a man of unusual integrity, a good man. Beatrice is also good—a loyal cousin and a caring niece. Her murderousness is the consequence of her love for Hero—evidence, if any were needed, of how deeply she is capable of loving. Audiences laugh because they expect Benedick to be comically wrong-footed. (There's a need to release tension too.) The play's most striking reversal of expectation is Benedick's agreement to challenge Claudio. He must know that he hasn't got a chance. Claudio is set up from the start of the play as a demon soldier. Opinions vary about Benedick, but you're inclined to believe Don Pedro when he accuses him of "Christian-like fear." So, for love of Beatrice, and out of an altruistic dismay at the injustice done to Hero, Benedick embarks on a journey that could end in his death. Simon Russell Beale took this entirely seriously. Zoë Wanamaker slowly realized the magnitude of his sacrifice.

The Hero–Claudio story line is often overshadowed by the Beatrice–Benedick one, isn't it? Berlioz left it out of his operatic

version altogether! Did you find ways of keeping it whole, giving due weight to the "romantic" lovers? Especially tough with Hero, maybe, since she has so few lines?

Elliott: It's crucial to the story that Hero is a virginal, pure, straightforward, obedient girl but, of course, this does not have the same meaning for a modern audience. It's also crucial that Claudio's character undergoes a *massive* turnaround on just a couple of lines. His sense of "honor" (a very important theme in the whole play) is upturned. His cruel and shocking behavior toward Hero in the church when he tries to protect his "honor" is finally seen as the most dishonorable thing of all. Again, a man's honor and reputation doesn't mean the same thing now. Hence the importance of setting the production in a place and period where all this is still very much alive.

We tried to serve the through-lines of Hero and Claudio honestly. While Hero does have quite a wicked sense of humor—because Beatrice is her mate she can have moments where her sense of humor is quite sharp—she also has to truly believe that being a virgin and being a young, pure, inexperienced woman who obeys her father and then her husband is what you should aspire to. I think Beatrice has slightly different opinions about that! Beatrice was older than Hero in our production. As Hero was very young we tried to show how she starts to learn about men as things happen to her. Claudio's repentance is a genuine one, or so we tried to convey; it is so deeply felt that, in a play where the gift of articulacy is rewarded, he simply can't find the words to express his shame.

The main characters are definitely Beatrice and Benedick; they're the most complex characters. Claudio and Hero are much more straightforward because they haven't had the experience of life that the other two have had. Shakespeare has less fun with them!

Hytner: But isn't that the point? Hero and Claudio are barely allowed by the playwright to talk to each other. They plainly don't get to know each other. Claudio gets an unfairly bad rap for making sure that Hero is Leonato's heir before he proposes. But he's making a conventional, sensible marriage. The problem is that although they're clearly attracted to each other, neither he nor Hero bother to note each other.

I'm very taken by the puns in the title of the play. "Nothing"—no thing (slang for "vagina"). "Noting"—the Elizabethan pronunciation of "nothing." The third is the most important. The failure to note properly, to look properly, to listen properly is what the play's about. It's there from the start: Antonio, Borachio, Leonato, Benedick, Beatrice, Don Pedro and, most disastrously, Claudio (at Hero's window) are among those who get it wrong. The main plot (Hero–Claudio) is about the terrible consequences of not looking, not engaging. It's about the folly of an attraction that is conventional and skin-deep. The Beatrice–Benedick plot is about two people who love, warts and all. The great heart-stopper ("I do love nothing in the world so well as you. Is not that strange?") is moving because it acknowledges both an evident truth and the genuine strangeness not of a *coup de foudre* (happens all the time, rarely meaningful, not particularly strange) but of their capacity to love without narcissism. They have discovered how to look, to know, to note the other and love the other, not as a projection of romantic perfection, but for who the other actually is. And how strange for Benedick to find himself not ambushed by passion but overwhelmed by the gradual realization that he's found the courage to love, and to say it. Hero and Claudio are age-appropriate, class-appropriate, and good-looking. It's not enough. Beatrice and Benedick are more than intellectual equals. They become capable of being truly vulnerable to each other (Benedick: "And how do you?" Beatrice: "Very ill too." Benedick: "Serve God, love me and mend"). Claudio and Hero never get beyond conventional pleasantries ("Lady, as you are mine, I am yours").

Their relative callowness is the point. That doesn't mean that the actors playing them should patronize them. Nor is it good enough to write Claudio off as irredeemable. He falls for a stupid trick and he behaves with naked aggression at the wedding. But so do all the other men on stage apart from Benedick. Claudio isn't alone in his failure to note properly, and although it's Hero who suffers the worst consequences of an arrogant impulsiveness that seems to be the hallmark of masculinity, Claudio is at least given an opening to grow up.

Berlioz wasn't the first (or last) great artist to love Shakespeare to death. He wrote about Shakespeare better than he set him to music.

Béatrice et Bénédict isn't the worst Shakespeare opera (far too much competition), but he blundered badly by cutting the main plot. There is terrific satisfaction in watching an unsatisfactory relationship fall apart, and it's tantalizing to sniff the possibility that they may be able to start again on a firmer footing.

Your actresses must have particularly enjoyed the women-only scenes, such as the one with Margaret and Ursula before the wedding?

Elliott: No, they found them really difficult! Particularly the gulling scene that comes after the men's and has so much pressure on it to be funny. The scene before the wedding is quite fun, though, as the women get a chance to shine a little because they're alone and Beatrice is ill. But there aren't long and interesting through-lines for Margaret and Ursula in the play. They generally have very little to say.

Hytner: You're right. They did.

Are Don John and Borachio simply Machiavellian characters, or did you find a different explanation for their actions?

Elliott: I thought Don John was understandably bereaved. For me he was a Che Guevara–type figure, which fitted with our setting the play in 1950s Cuba. He was absolutely antiestablishment and therefore unfairly treated. I did feel very passionately that in our production Don John and Borachio should have reasons for doing the things that they were doing. On a larger level, this society needs to change, and if it weren't for characters like Don John and Borachio then there would be nothing to unsettle the status quo. We had Borachio be in love with Hero. When he sees Claudio, the new young celebrity of the war, suddenly win Hero, with everyone's vocal approval, then he wants to exact revenge on him. He takes his plan to Don John, who would do anything to hurt his brother's regime.

Hytner: It's not unusual for Shakespeare to be compact in his writing of a character and to leave the actors to fill in the gaps. Imagine a draft of the play that fleshed out Don John, explored his inner life, and spent valuable stage time providing him with a history that motivated his malevolence. A decent director would reach immediately for the blue pencil. Shakespeare always knows where his plays give off heat and where they don't, where it's worth hanging around and where it's best to move on. There's too much else of interest in *Much Ado* to make more space for Don John.

So he gives the actors the responsibility to ground Don John and Borachio in emotional reality. A convincing performance gives an impression of psychological truth that may be missing in the text. Don John is plainly jealous of Claudio, resentful of his relationship with Don Pedro, and as Iago hates Cassio for the daily beauty in his life, so Don John hates Claudio for being the most popular officer in the mess. Andrew Woodall decided that Don John had once made a pass at Claudio, and that Claudio had brusquely rejected it. That appealed to me: it felt right that Don John was eaten up with self-loathing and fury that he'd allowed Claudio to note him. There's no particular textual evidence for this—but it allowed the actor to give emotional flesh where the playwright has provided a functional theatrical skeleton.

Dogberry: a difficult balancing act between, on the one hand, the plodding mind and the mixed-up words, and, on the other hand, the goodness of heart and the part played in exposing the plot?

Elliott: He's meant to be a funny character and funny characters in Shakespeare have their pressures, because there are often a lot of colloquialisms or period references that don't mean anything today. He's muddled and probably uneducated but trying to create an important image of himself. Because he gets it wrong, it's recognizably comical—hopefully. But in other ways he's the play's true hero. His actions again subvert the idea of what is "honorable." He has a clear sense of right and wrong.

Hytner: So find a good actor.

Seventy percent prose and only 30 percent verse: unusual proportions for Shakespeare. Did that make a difference to your language work with the actors?

Elliott: Shakespeare chooses such amazing words and creates such extraordinary images that unless you get behind exactly what they are, it can seem senseless. He does, however, give you little clues all the time; in the alliteration, in the sound of a word when spoken, in the meter, in the visualization of the image—all things that take a bit of time to really understand. Each word is like its own delectable sweet! But you can't stress everything. Working at the RSC, you have a lot of experts on hand to help you. We had about two weeks at the beginning of rehearsal just exploring Shakespeare's writing before we even started on the play.

Hytner: Not really. The rhetorical patterns of Shakespeare's prose are often tricky. Prose is generally longer-winded than verse, and sometimes knotted and obscure. But the intellectual, emotional, and imaginative challenges are the same.

Hero's return: a neat trick for which we're well prepared, and yet isn't there some element of magical resurrection about it—one thinks back to the *Alcestis* of Euripides and forward to the revival of Hermione's statue in *The Winter's Tale*? The problem, though, is Claudio's rather grudging participation?

Elliott: We didn't treat it as particularly magical because the audience are told beforehand that it's going to happen. Because they are better informed than Claudio, you don't see it as a piece of magic but more as a trick on him. What I was interested in doing was subverting what the society was about. Claudio started to understand that women weren't necessarily either icons or whores; he started to understand that there was much more complexity to it, and that what he had done was a horrific crime that had led to somebody's death. When Hero returned, I brought out all the girls wearing Virgin Mary masks, so that every time he saw one of them appear he was literally confronted with the Virgin Mary iconography, and had to question quite fundamentally a few things in his culture and religion. He *should* be grudging at the idea of taking a new wife—if he truly loves his dead Hero. When he discovered that it was Hero resurrected to him, then we tried to make his reaction very celebratory. He

7. Adam Rayner as Claudio confronted by "all the girls wearing Virgin Mary masks" in Marianne Elliott's 2006 Cuban *Much Ado* for the RSC.

picked her up and swung her round. But he's still learnt a very salutary lesson.

Hytner: The question rather overlooks the scene at Hero's fake tomb. Nobody could deny that Claudio's repentance is underwritten. But whenever Shakespeare calls for music, you know that he recognizes its insidious communicative power. The theatrical potential of the tomb scene is less in its text than in ritual and music. It's possible to create an event that gives Claudio space for genuine repentance. If Hero witnesses an act of true contrition (Leonato can bring her to watch surreptitiously), the resolution comes more easily.

Admittedly, Claudio in Act 5 seems to revert (at least with Benedick) to the locker room. But in nearly all of his romantic comedies, Shakespeare insists on the possibility of repentance and forgiveness. He thinks people can change. He's realistic about how hard it is, but he believes in a second chance. We're less inclined to, nowadays. Our loss.

If you were to direct the play again, would you consider following the early Quarto and Folio texts—and this edition—and giving the line "Peace! I will stop your mouth" (5.4.101) to Leonato, rather than assigning it to Benedick, as most productions have done? How might that alter this moment of resolution?

Elliott: When we rehearsed it, we were constantly chopping and changing between the different versions. If I did it again? Difficult to say, as I don't know what kind of production that would be. But I love that moment. I wanted to show they were genuinely in love and quips wouldn't serve them anymore. Benedick is stopping Beatrice gabbing away again at her usual game of verbal wit by just cutting it short with a kiss. At last! The resolution is one of love.

When you direct a play it becomes very personal. It's hard to explain how. It's not just personal to you, it's personal to everybody involved in the rehearsal room: the creative team and the actors. If I did it again I would probably, at that time of my life, be interested in different things, as I'm sure everyone else in the room would be, so we would do it with a slightly different slant. At the time I really wanted to explore the character of Beatrice, and who she was. I was fascinated by Benedick too, but really very interested in Beatrice; in the way she lived within the world, as described above, but still with a sense of her own individuality. And given that she had to fight to be so different to everyone else, how does she fall in love? And with whom? And what does that do to change her? And if it changes her, how does that change the world around her? And what does it mean anyway that the world changes? That's what I wanted to explore. Maybe if I did it again I'd be much more interested in Benedick, or the fact that Benedick and Beatrice were much older and perhaps felt they were past it, and then refound their sexiness and allure—which Nick Hytner's production portrayed so brilliantly. I'd be interested in other things. That's why theater is so alive, isn't it? It's ephemeral, of the moment. Productions shouldn't be compared. They are their own entities, produced by a particular group of people, at a particular time in history, who relate to the material as products of their time and place.

Hytner: I would consider it briefly and decide that we were right first time. There are all sorts of reasons to give the line to Leonato that look good in the study. Leonato has spent the play trying (often inef-fectually) to exert control—particularly over Beatrice. By silencing Beatrice, Benedick might be in danger of coming across as a crypto-Petruchio—better to leave Leonato with the line and allow them to end the play in perfect equality. And so on.

But in the theater, it's blindingly obvious that the line is Benedick's and that the Quarto compositor got it wrong. It's about a kiss. It's about a marriage. It's about a man and a woman. That old thing. Therefore play, music.

HARRIET WALTER ON PLAYING BEATRICE

Harriet Walter was born in 1950 and trained at the London Acad-emy of Music and Dramatic Art. Her early experience included work with the Joint Stock touring theater company, Paines Plough touring company, and the Dukes playhouse, Lancaster. She has worked with the RSC many times during her career and was made an associate artist in 1987. She has numerous television and film roles to her credit, including DI Natalie Chandler in *Law and Order: UK, Sense and Sensibility,* and *Atonement.* Apart from Beatrice in Gregory Doran's successful 2002 production of *Much Ado About Nothing,* she has played Helena in Trevor Nunn's 1981 production of *All's Well That Ends Well* and Imogen in Bill Alexander's 1987 production of *Cymbe-line* at The Other Place, as well as Lady Macbeth in Doran's 1999 production of *Macbeth,* chronicling the experience in her book *Mac-beth* in Faber and Faber's "Actors on Shakespeare" series, and a much-acclaimed Cleopatra in his 2006 production of *Antony and Cleopatra.*

There is clearly a history between Beatrice and Benedick that has taken place before the play starts. Is that something you explored in rehearsal?

We certainly discussed this, yes. We found quite a few possible sce-narios, but the most helpful thought was that at some point in the past when they were letting their guard down and verging on a loving relationship, there had been a misunderstanding whereby

Beatrice and Benedick had each interpreted the other as having rejected them. Both pretend to the world and to themselves that they were the dumper, not the dumpee. Both are too proud to admit their pain, so they revert to raillery and public scorn or teasing.

This "performance" not only acts as a much-needed shield to protect each of their egos, but it also becomes so publicly entertaining that they feel obliged to please the crowd and keep it up. They are trapped by the success of their posturing into a habit of mutual dislike. Everyone expects it of them and they have got to a point where each privately expects it of him/herself.

It is doubtful that Benedick ever got so far as to consciously think he was ever in love with Beatrice, while Beatrice, who is a little more in touch with her heart, probably did admit to loving Benedick, though by the beginning of the play this has long since been converted to strong dislike. Her comment "I know you of old" was interesting to play with an awareness of hurt inside. She skates near the edge, teasing her audience with hints. For example, in Act 2 Scene 1:

DON PEDRO: Come, lady, come, you have lost the heart of Signior Benedick.

BEATRICE: Indeed, my lord, he lent it me awhile, and I gave him use for it, a double heart for his single one: marry, once before he won it of me with false dice, therefore your Grace may well say I have lost it.

It felt to me as though she both wanted to be found out, and was, at the same time, absolutely loath to be found out. Her jokes are a brilliant mask and also a trap.

It takes the two eavesdropping scenes to reveal Beatrice and Benedick's true feelings to themselves. It is their private shock (and relief in a way) on discovering they love deep down, the bit they "privately" confess to the audience, that is moving and funny. It is also important, for all the actors involved in those duping scenes in the garden, to remember that each group *thinks* they are tricking each of the lovers into believing a lie that the other is in love with them, and neither group realizes till much later that they have in fact revealed the truth.

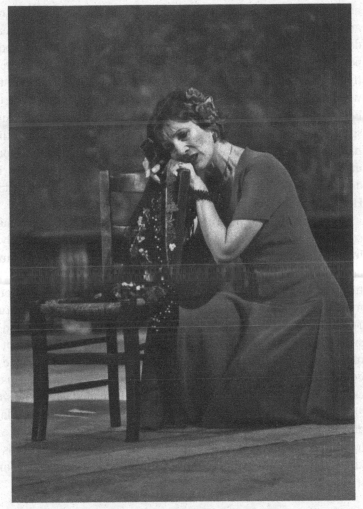

8. Harriet Walter as Beatrice in Gregory Doran's Sicilian *Much Ado* for the RSC in 2002.

Did you find there were some key shifts in the balance of power between them? The "Kill Claudio" moment's a crucial one, isn't it?

I think both Beatrice and Benedick are sticklers for equality, which is what makes their relationship at the end so sympathetic to a modern audience. The Hero–Claudio plot takes over so quickly after Beatrice and Benedick discover their love for one another that Shakespeare denies the latter couple the happy payoff scene, or at least he postpones it until Act 5 Scene 2. Instead they have to admit their love in the urgent and stressed circumstances of Hero's humiliation at the wedding. Just as Beatrice was beginning to unfurl and put her trust in Benedick, she is reminded of all that she mistrusts about the male species. There is Claudio willing to believe so quickly that his betrothed has been sleeping with another man, and Hero's own father is shockingly quick to believe hearsay above a lifetime's knowledge of his daughter. Both men love their own honor better than they ever love Hero. This is the Sicilian climate of macho honor, of *omertà*.

By setting the play in a recognizable Sicily and stressing this male code so strongly, [director] Gregory Doran helped me enormously. It justified Beatrice's defensive bloody-mindedness. It comes from a deep place of fear, however humorously expressed. In such a culture, the bonds between men are stronger than any bond between a man and a woman, and while women will bond together in mutual protection against this fact, once they marry they are expected to switch their primary loyalty to their man and children. For a mature marriage to work, a man must prove himself capable of doing the same and leaving his boyish comrades behind. This is essentially what Beatrice is demanding of Benedick when she says "Kill Claudio." I believe it is not so much that she wants to see Claudio dead, as that she wants proof that Benedick is capable of rejecting and criticizing this worst aspect of male behavior. She needs to know that he can distance himself from his past allegiances and truly commit to her.

The Hero–Claudio story line is often overshadowed by the Beatrice–Benedick one, isn't it? Berlioz left it out of his operatic version altogether! Did you find ways of helping your director to keep it whole, to give due weight to the "romantic" lovers? Especially tough with Hero, maybe, since she has so few lines?

The distinctive and very modern aspect of the relationship between Beatrice and Benedick is that from the moment they admit their love to one another they are free to respect one another's strength of character. In each of them, submitting to love was linked with an idea of loss of power and control. But having had such a long drawn-out and often antagonistic courtship, they can be said to really know one another and to have seen the worst of one another. This is very different from the untested and idealistic love between Claudio and Hero, who have really only fallen in love with one another's image and social suitability. Shakespeare deliberately contrasts these two types of relationship and each plot elucidates the other.

Was it a particular pleasure to play the women-only scenes?

This is an interesting question. In fact the women-only scenes are quite difficult to find the tone for. Aside from a general ease of atmosphere, the plotting is less obviously funny than in the all-male scenes. Dare I wonder whether it has something to do with Shakespeare himself not quite knowing what women get up to or talk about when men aren't around? Aside from the delightful scene between Katherine and Alice in *Henry V*, most of Shakespeare's successful all-female scenes either have a girl posing as a boy, as in *Twelfth Night*, or they are between a wiser older woman and a younger (*Othello*, *All's Well*). All-girlie scenes are harder for him to write and therefore harder to play. Having said that, it was very noticeable that the hierarchy changes distinctly in Hero's household when there are no men about. Hero becomes the dominant female. She has the highest social status and the actress gets a chance to play a sparky character, very different from the subdued trophy bride and favorite daughter she is forced to play in public.

Seventy percent prose and only 30 percent verse: unusual proportions for Shakespeare. Did that make a difference to your language work on this play?

Yes. Beatrice only speaks in verse at the end of Act 3 Scene 1. It is also her only soliloquy. I therefore took it that this was a moment to reveal her deepest feelings and romantic aspirations—things she wouldn't dream of revealing to anyone "inside" the play. As actors we are always asked to note where the language changes from verse to prose or to rhyming. There are no hard-and-fast rules as to what Shakespeare means by these changes, but if an actor observes them, a kind of reason is revealed inside us via the different rhythms and notes that are sounded in our subconscious. We note the changes and try and justify or explain them later. It is better that way round.

Hero's return: a neat trick for which we're well prepared, and yet isn't there some element of magical resurrection about it—one thinks back to the *Alcestis* of Euripides and forward to the revival of Hermione's statue in *The Winter's Tale*? The problem, though, is Claudio's rather grudging participation?

Yes. In each of these cases what is required is a solemnity, an almost religious ritual to match the scale of the conversion of the wrong-doer and to earn the audience's forgiveness. In our production, Gregory Doran recognized that Claudio's rehabilitation can seem very glib and speedy, and wanted to make his contrition at Hero's supposed graveside as true and as heartfelt as possible. He gave the scene more time and gravity than usual, and Claudio's grief was played (by John Hopkins) with moving sincerity. Despite these best efforts, I think the play leaves us all with a big worry for the future of Claudio and Hero's partnership, in contrast to our pleasure in the coming together of the less romantic, less deluded Beatrice and Benedick.

If you were to play the part again, how would you feel if the director followed the early Quarto and Folio texts—and this edition—and gave the line "Peace! I will stop your mouth" (5.4.101) to Leonato, rather than assigning it to Benedick, as most productions have done? If Leonato more or less forces Benedick to stop Beatrice's mouth with a kiss, how might that alter the moment of resolution? Might it get round the problem you have when Benedick speaks the line, whereby Beatrice is effectively, if only momentarily, suffocated with the kiss (something that seems more *Othello* than *Much Ado*)?

I am convinced that it is better to give the line to Benedick, and I don't find it is a sinister suffocation at all. Rather, it seems to be a restoration of their usual banter but with love behind it now. Their power struggles are over. Beatrice no longer feels the need to have the last word. They have a wonderful confidence in one another. It is playable the other way, of course, but is not so dramatically compact or eloquent. I am glad most productions have disobeyed the early Quarto and Folio texts.

What interesting connections and contrasts did you discover in the process of playing this Shakespearean lead, as opposed to others such as Innogen in *Cymbeline*, Helen in *All's Well That Ends Well*, and Cleopatra or even Lady Macbeth?

I have a tendency to seek dissimilarities rather than similarities between the characters I have played, so I haven't given much thought to the links. The most obvious thing that springs to mind in retrospect is that Beatrice does not drive the plot to the extent of Lady Macbeth or Cleopatra or Innogen or Helena. This is partly to do with her position in the household as a sort of poor relation, and partly because she reveals herself through a lot of prose banter rather than arias of great poetry. The great soliloquies give an actor a special sort of command of the stage and of the audience. Beatrice, as befits her place in the community, has to win her points through wit, through ducking and diving and dancing and then, when Benedick offers her first taste of unfettered power—"Come, bid me do anything for thee"—she surprises everyone (including herself) with the depth of passion she feels: "Kill Claudio." Cleopatra or Lady Macbeth would probably have been instantly obeyed. Beatrice gets a greater reward than obedience. Benedick goes as far as his integrity will allow and challenges Claudio to a duel. The play, being a comedy, lets us all off the hook, but Beatrice has found an ally who loves her but is still his own man. Perfect.

SHAKESPEARE'S CAREER
IN THE THEATER

BEGINNINGS

William Shakespeare was an extraordinarily intelligent man who was born and died in an ordinary market town in the English Midlands. He lived an uneventful life in an eventful age. Born in April 1564, he was the eldest son of John Shakespeare, a glove-maker who was prominent on the town council until he fell into financial difficulties. Young William was educated at the local grammar in Stratford-upon-Avon, Warwickshire, where he gained a thorough grounding in the Latin language, the art of rhetoric, and classical poetry. He married Ann Hathaway and had three children (Susanna, then the twins Hamnet and Judith) before his twenty-first birthday: an exceptionally young age for the period. We do not know how he supported his family in the mid-1580s.

Like many clever country boys, he moved to the city in order to make his way in the world. Like many creative people, he found a career in the entertainment business. Public playhouses and professional full-time acting companies reliant on the market for their income were born in Shakespeare's childhood. When he arrived in London as a man, sometime in the late 1580s, a new phenomenon was in the making: the actor who is so successful that he becomes a "star." The word did not exist in its modern sense, but the pattern is recognizable: audiences went to the theater not so much to see a particular show as to witness the comedian Richard Tarlton or the dramatic actor Edward Alleyn.

Shakespeare was an actor before he was a writer. It appears not to have been long before he realized that he was never going to grow into a great comedian like Tarlton or a great tragedian like Alleyn. Instead, he found a role within his company as the man who patched up old plays, breathing new life, new dramatic twists, into tired repertory pieces. He paid close attention to the work of the university-educated dramatists who were writing history plays and tragedies for the public stage in a style more ambitious, sweeping, and poetically grand than anything that had been seen before. But he may also have noted that what his friend and rival Ben Jonson would call "Marlowe's mighty line" sometimes faltered in the mode of comedy. Going to university, as Christopher Marlowe did, was all well and good for honing the arts of rhetorical elaboration and classical allusion, but it could lead to a loss of the common touch. To stay close to a large segment of the potential audience for public theater, it was necessary to write for clowns as well as kings and to intersperse the flights of poetry with the humor of the tavern, the privy, and the brothel: Shakespeare was the first to establish himself early in his career as an equal master of tragedy, comedy, and history. He realized that theater could be the medium to make the national past available to a wider audience than the elite who could afford to read large history books: his signature early works include not only the classical tragedy *Titus Andronicus* but also the sequence of English historical plays on the Wars of the Roses.

He also invented a new role for himself, that of in-house company dramatist. Where his peers and predecessors had to sell their plays to the theater managers on a poorly paid piecework basis, Shakespeare took a percentage of the box-office income. The Lord Chamberlain's Men constituted themselves in 1594 as a joint stock company, with the profits being distributed among the core actors who had invested as sharers. Shakespeare acted himself—he appears in the cast lists of some of Ben Jonson's plays as well as the list of actors' names at the beginning of his own collected works—but his principal duty was to write two or three plays a year for the company. By holding shares, he was effectively earning himself a royalty on his work, something no author had ever done before in England. When the Lord Chamberlain's Men collected their fee for performance at court in the Christmas season of 1594, three of them went along to the Treasurer of the Chamber: not just Richard Burbage the tragedian and Will Kempe the clown, but also Shakespeare the scriptwriter. That was something new.

The next four years were the golden period in Shakespeare's career, though overshadowed by the death of his only son, Hamnet, aged eleven, in 1596. In his early thirties and in full command of both his poetic and his theatrical medium, he perfected his art of comedy, while also developing his tragic and historical writing in new ways. In 1598, Francis Meres, a Cambridge University graduate with his finger on the pulse of the London literary world, praised Shakespeare for his excellence across the genres:

> As Plautus and Seneca are accounted the best for comedy and tragedy among the Latins, so Shakespeare among the English is the most excellent in both kinds for the stage; for comedy, witness his *Gentlemen of Verona*, his *Errors*, his *Love Labours Lost*, his *Love Labours Won*, his *Midsummer Night Dream* and his *Merchant of Venice*; for tragedy his *Richard the 2*, *Richard the 3*, *Henry the 4*, *King John*, *Titus Andronicus* and his *Romeo and Juliet*.

For Meres, as for the many writers who praised the "honey-flowing vein" of *Venus and Adonis* and *Lucrece*, narrative poems written when the theaters were closed due to plague in 1593–94, Shakespeare was marked above all by his linguistic skill, by the gift of turning elegant poetic phrases.

PLAYHOUSES

Elizabethan playhouses were "thrust" or "one-room" theaters. To understand Shakespeare's original theatrical life, we have to forget about the indoor theater of later times, with its proscenium arch and curtain that would be opened at the beginning and closed at the end of each act. In the proscenium arch theater, stage and auditorium are effectively two separate rooms: the audience looks from one world into another as if through the imaginary "fourth wall" framed by the proscenium. The picture-frame stage, together with the elaborate scenic effects and backdrops beyond it, created the illusion of a self-contained world—especially once nineteenth-century developments in the control of artificial lighting meant that the auditorium could be darkened and the spectators made to focus on the lighted stage. Shakespeare, by contrast, wrote for a bare platform stage with a standing audience gathered around it in a courtyard in full daylight. The audience were always conscious of themselves and their fellow spectators, and they shared the same "room" as the actors. A sense of immediate presence and the creation of rapport with the audience were all-important. The actor could not afford to imagine he was in a closed world, with silent witnesses dutifully observing him from the darkness.

Shakespeare's theatrical career began at the Rose Theatre in Southwark. The stage was wide and shallow, trapezoid in shape, like a lozenge. This design had a great deal of potential for the theatrical equivalent of cinematic split-screen effects, whereby one group of characters would enter at the door at one end of the tiring-house wall at the back of the stage and another group through the door at the other end, thus creating two rival tableaux. Many of the battle-heavy and faction-filled plays that premiered at the Rose have scenes of just this sort.

At the rear of the Rose stage, there were three capacious exits, each over ten feet wide. Unfortunately, the very limited excavation of a fragmentary portion of the original Globe site, in 1989, revealed nothing about the stage. The first Globe was built in 1599 with similar proportions to those of another theater, the Fortune, albeit that the former was polygonal and looked circular, whereas the latter was rectangular. The building contract for the Fortune survives and allows us to infer that the stage of the Globe was probably substantially wider than it was deep (perhaps forty-three feet wide and twenty-seven feet deep). It may well have been tapered at the front, like that of the Rose.

The capacity of the Globe was said to have been enormous, perhaps in excess of three thousand. It has been conjectured that about eight hundred people may have stood in the yard, with two thousand or more in the three layers of covered galleries. The other "public" playhouses were also of large capacity, whereas the indoor Blackfriars theater that Shakespeare's company began using in 1608—the former refectory of a monastery—had overall internal dimensions of a mere forty-six by sixty feet. It would have made for a much more intimate theatrical experience and had a much smaller capacity, probably of about six hundred people. Since they paid at least sixpence a head, the Blackfriars attracted a more select or "private" audience. The atmosphere would have been closer to that of an indoor performance before the court in the Whitehall Palace or at Richmond. That Shakespeare always wrote for indoor production at court as well as outdoor performance in the public theater should make us cautious about inferring, as some scholars have, that the opportunity provided by the intimacy of the Blackfriars led to a significant change toward a "chamber" style in his last plays—which, besides, were performed at both the Globe and the Blackfriars. After the occupation of the Blackfriars a five-act structure seems to have become more important to Shakespeare. That was because of artificial lighting: there were musical interludes between the acts, while the candles were trimmed and replaced. Again, though, something similar must have been necessary for indoor court performances throughout his career.

Front of house there were the "gatherers" who collected the money from audience members: a penny to stand in the open-air yard, another penny for a place in the covered galleries, sixpence for the prominent "lord's rooms" to the side of the stage. In the indoor "private" theaters, gallants from the audience who fancied making themselves part of the spectacle sat on stools on the edge of the stage itself. Scholars debate as to how widespread this practice was in the public theaters such as the Globe. Once the audience were in place and the money counted, the gatherers were available to be extras onstage. That is one reason why battles and crowd scenes often come later rather than early in Shakespeare's plays. There was no formal prohibition upon performance by women, and there certainly were women among the gatherers, so it is not beyond the bounds of possibility that female crowd members were played by females.

The play began at two o'clock in the afternoon and the theater had to be cleared by five. After the main show, there would be a jig— which consisted not only of dancing, but also of knockabout comedy (it is the origin of the farcical "afterpiece" in the eighteenth-century theater). So the time available for a Shakespeare play was about two and a half hours, somewhere between the "two hours' traffic" mentioned in the prologue to *Romeo and Juliet* and the "three hours' spectacle" referred to in the preface to the 1647 Folio of Beaumont and

Fletcher's plays. The prologue to a play by Thomas Middleton refers to a thousand lines as "one hour's words," so the likelihood is that about two and a half thousand, or a maximum of three thousand lines made up the performed text. This is indeed the length of most of Shakespeare's comedies, whereas many of his tragedies and histories are much longer, raising the possibility that he wrote full scripts, possibly with eventual publication in mind, in the full knowledge that the stage version would be heavily cut. The short Quarto texts published in his lifetime—they used to be called "Bad" Quartos—provide fascinating evidence as to the kind of cutting that probably took place. So, for instance, the First Quarto of *Hamlet* neatly merges two occasions when Hamlet is overheard, the "Fishmonger" and the "nunnery" scenes.

The social composition of the audience was mixed. The poet Sir John Davies wrote of "A thousand townsmen, gentlemen and whores, / Porters and servingmen" who would "together throng" at the public playhouses. Though moralists associated female playgoing with adultery and the sex trade, many perfectly respectable citizens' wives were regular attendees. Some, no doubt, resembled the modern groupie: a story attested in two different sources has one citizen's wife making a post-show assignation with Richard Burbage and ending up in bed with Shakespeare—supposedly eliciting from the latter the quip that William the Conqueror was before Richard III. Defenders of theater liked to say that by witnessing the comeuppance of villains on the stage, audience members would repent of their own wrongdoings, but the reality is that most people went to the theater then, as they do now, for entertainment more than moral edification. Besides, it would be foolish to suppose that audiences behaved in a homogeneous way: a pamphlet of the 1630s tells of how two men went to see *Pericles* and one of them laughed while the other wept. Bishop John Hall complained that people went to church for the same reasons that they went to the theater: "for company, for custom, for recreation . . . to feed his eyes or his ears . . . or perhaps for sleep."

Men-about-town and clever young lawyers went to be seen as much as to see. In the modern popular imagination, shaped not least by *Shakespeare in Love* and the opening sequence of Laurence Olivier's

Henry V film, the penny-paying groundlings stand in the yard hurling abuse or encouragement and hazelnuts or orange peel at the actors, while the sophisticates in the covered galleries appreciate Shakespeare's soaring poetry. The reality was probably the other way around. A "groundling" was a kind of fish, so the nickname suggests the penny audience standing below the level of the stage and gazing in silent openmouthed wonder at the spectacle unfolding above them. The more difficult audience members, who kept up a running commentary of clever remarks on the performance and who occasionally got into quarrels with players, were the gallants. Like Hollywood movies in modern times, Elizabethan and Jacobean plays exercised a powerful influence on the fashion and behavior of the young. John Marston mocks the lawyers who would open their lips, perhaps to court a girl, and out would "flow / Naught but pure Juliet and Romeo."

THE ENSEMBLE AT WORK

In the absence of typewriters and photocopying machines, reading aloud would have been the means by which the company got to know a new play. The tradition of the playwright reading his complete script to the assembled company endured for generations. A copy would then have been taken to the Master of the Revels for licensing. The theater book-holder or prompter would then have copied the parts for distribution to the actors. A partbook consisted of the character's lines, with each speech preceded by the last three or four words of the speech before, the so-called "cue." These would have been taken away and studied or "conned." During this period of learning the parts, an actor might have had some one-to-one instruction, perhaps from the dramatist, perhaps from a senior actor who had played the same part before, and, in the case of an apprentice, from his master. A high percentage of Desdemona's lines occur in dialogue with Othello, of Lady Macbeth's with Macbeth, Cleopatra's with Antony, and Volumnia's with Coriolanus. The roles would almost certainly have been taken by the apprentice of the lead actor, usually Burbage, who delivers the majority of the cues. Given that apprentices lodged with their masters, there would have been ample

9. Hypothetical reconstruction of the interior of an Elizabethan playhouse during a performance.

opportunity for personal instruction, which may be what made it possible for young men to play such demanding parts.

After the parts were learned, there may have been no more than a single rehearsal before the first performance. With six different plays to be put on every week, there was no time for more. Actors, then, would go into a show with a very limited sense of the whole. The notion of a collective rehearsal process that is itself a process of discovery for the actors is wholly modern and would have been incomprehensible to Shakespeare and his original ensemble. Given the number of parts an actor had to hold in his memory, the forgetting of lines was probably more frequent than in the modern theater. The book-holder was on hand to prompt.

Backstage personnel included the property man, the tire-man who oversaw the costumes, call boys, attendants, and the musicians, who might play at various times from the main stage, the rooms above, and within the tiring-house. Scriptwriters sometimes made a nuisance of themselves backstage. There was often tension between the acting companies and the freelance playwrights from whom they purchased scripts: it was a smart move on the part of Shakespeare and the Lord Chamberlain's Men to bring the writing process in-house.

Scenery was limited, though sometimes set pieces were brought on (a bank of flowers, a bed, the mouth of hell). The trapdoor from below, the gallery stage above, and the curtained discovery space at the back allowed for an array of special effects: the rising of ghosts and apparitions, the descent of gods, dialogue between a character at a window and another at ground level, the revelation of a statue or a pair of lovers playing at chess. Ingenious use could be made of props, as with the ass's head in *A Midsummer Night's Dream*. In a theater that does not clutter the stage with the material paraphernalia of everyday life, those objects that are deployed may take on powerful symbolic weight, as when Shylock bears his weighing scales in one hand and knife in the other, thus becoming a parody of the figure of Justice who traditionally bears a sword and a balance. Among the more significant items in the property cupboard of Shakespeare's company, there would have been a throne (the "chair of state"), joint stools, books, bottles, coins, purses, letters (which are brought onstage, read, or referred to on about eighty occasions in the complete works), maps, gloves, a set of stocks (in which Kent is put in *King Lear*), rings, rapiers, daggers, broadswords, staves, pistols, masks and vizards, heads and skulls, torches and tapers and lanterns that served to signal night scenes on the daylit stage, a buck's head, an ass's head, animal costumes. Live animals also put in appearances, most notably the dog Crab in *The Two Gentlemen of Verona* and possibly a young polar bear in *The Winter's Tale*.

The costumes were the most important visual dimension of the play. Playwrights were paid between £2 and £6 per script, whereas Alleyn was not averse to paying £20 for "a black velvet cloak with sleeves embroidered all with silver and gold." No matter the period of the play, actors always wore contemporary costume. The excitement for the audience came not from any impression of historical accuracy, but from the richness of the attire and perhaps the transgressive thrill of the knowledge that here were commoners like themselves strutting in the costumes of courtiers in effective defiance of the strict sumptuary laws whereby in real life people had to wear the clothes that befitted their social station.

To an even greater degree than props, costumes could carry symbolic importance. Racial characteristics could be suggested: a breastplate and helmet for a Roman soldier, a turban for a Turk, long robes for exotic characters such as Moors, a gabardine for a Jew. The figure of Time, as in *The Winter's Tale*, would be equipped with hourglass, scythe, and wings; Rumour, who speaks the prologue of *2 Henry IV*, wore a costume adorned with a thousand tongues. The wardrobe in the tiring-house of the Globe would have contained much of the same stock as that of rival manager Philip Henslowe at the Rose: green gowns for outlaws and foresters, black for melancholy men such as Jaques and people in mourning such as the Countess in *All's Well That Ends Well* (at the beginning of *Hamlet*, the prince is still in mourning black when everyone else is in festive garb for the wedding of the new king), a gown and hood for a friar (or a feigned friar like the duke in *Measure for Measure*), blue coats and tawny to distinguish the followers of rival factions, a leather apron and ruler for a carpenter (as in the opening scene of *Julius Caesar*—and in *A Midsummer Night's Dream*, where this is the only sign that Peter Quince is a carpenter), a cockle hat with staff and a pair of sandals for a pilgrim or palmer (the disguise assumed by Helen in *All's Well*), bodices and kirtles with farthingales beneath for the boys who are to be dressed as girls. A gender switch such as that of Rosalind or Jessica seems to have taken between fifty and eighty lines of dialogue—Viola does not resume her "maiden weeds," but remains in her boy's costume to the end of *Twelfth Night* because a change would have slowed down the action at just the moment it was speeding to a climax. Henslowe's inventory also included "a robe for to go invisible": Oberon, Puck, and Ariel must have had something similar.

As the costumes appealed to the eyes, so there was music for the ears. Comedies included many songs. Desdemona's willow song, perhaps a late addition to the text, is a rare and thus exceptionally poignant example from tragedy. Trumpets and tuckets sounded for ceremonial entrances, drums denoted an army on the march. Background music could create atmosphere, as at the beginning of

Twelfth Night, during the lovers' dialogue near the end of *The Merchant of Venice*, when the statue seemingly comes to life in *The Winter's Tale*, and for the revival of Pericles and of Lear (in the Quarto text, but not the Folio). The haunting sound of the hautboy suggested a realm beyond the human, as when the god Hercules is imagined deserting Mark Antony. Dances symbolized the harmony of the end of a comedy—though in Shakespeare's world of mingled joy and sorrow, someone is usually left out of the circle.

The most important resource was, of course, the actors themselves. They needed many skills: in the words of one contemporary commentator, "dancing, activity, music, song, elocution, ability of body, memory, skill of weapon, pregnancy of wit." Their bodies were as significant as their voices. Hamlet tells the player to "suit the action to the word, the word to the action": moments of strong emotion, known as "passions," relied on a repertoire of dramatic gestures as well as a modulation of the voice. When Titus Andronicus has had his hand chopped off, he asks "How can I grace my talk, / Wanting a hand to give it action?" A pen portrait of "The Character of an Excellent Actor" by the dramatist John Webster is almost certainly based on his impression of Shakespeare's leading man, Richard Burbage: "By a full and significant action of body, he charms our attention: sit in a full theater, and you will think you see so many lines drawn from the circumference of so many ears, whiles the actor is the centre. . . ."

Though Burbage was admired above all others, praise was also heaped upon the apprentice players whose alto voices fitted them for the parts of women. A spectator at Oxford in 1610 records how the audience were reduced to tears by the pathos of Desdemona's death. The puritans who fumed about the biblical prohibition upon crossdressing and the encouragement to sodomy constituted by the sight of an adult male kissing a teenage boy on stage were a small minority. Little is known, however, about the characteristics of the leading apprentices in Shakespeare's company. It may perhaps be inferred that one was a lot taller than the other, since Shakespeare often wrote for a pair of female friends, one tall and fair, the other short and dark (Helena and Hermia, Rosalind and Celia, Beatrice and Hero).

We know little about Shakespeare's own acting roles—an early allusion indicates that he often took royal parts, and a venerable tradition gives him old Adam in *As You Like It* and the ghost of old King Hamlet. Save for Burbage's lead roles and the generic part of the clown, all such castings are mere speculation. We do not even know for sure whether the original Falstaff was Will Kempe or another actor who specialized in comic roles, Thomas Pope.

Kempe left the company in early 1599. Tradition has it that he fell out with Shakespeare over the matter of excessive improvisation. He was replaced by Robert Armin, who was less of a clown and more of a cerebral wit: this explains the difference between such parts as Lancelet Gobbo and Dogberry, which were written for Kempe, and the more verbally sophisticated Feste and Lear's Fool, which were written for Armin.

One thing that is clear from surviving "plots" or storyboards of plays from the period is that a degree of doubling was necessary. *2 Henry VI* has over sixty speaking parts, but more than half of the characters only appear in a single scene and most scenes have only six to eight speakers. At a stretch, the play could be performed by thirteen actors. When Thomas Platter saw *Julius Caesar* at the Globe in 1599, he noted that there were about fifteen. Why doesn't Paris go to the Capulet ball in *Romeo and Juliet*? Perhaps because he was doubled with Mercutio, who does. In *The Winter's Tale*, Mamillius might have come back as Perdita and Antigonus been doubled by Camillo, making the partnership with Paulina at the end a very neat touch. Titania and Oberon are often played by the same pair as Hippolyta and Theseus, suggesting a symbolic matching of the rulers of the worlds of night and day, but it is questionable whether there would have been time for the necessary costume changes. As so often, one is left in a realm of tantalizing speculation.

THE KING'S MAN

The new king, James I, who had held the Scottish throne as James VI since he had been an infant, immediately took the Lord Chamberlain's Men under his direct patronage. Henceforth they would be the King's Men, and for the rest of Shakespeare's career they were favored with far more court performances than any of their rivals.

There even seem to have been rumors early in the reign that Shakespeare and Burbage were being considered for knighthoods, an unprecedented honor for mere actors—and one that in the event was not accorded to a member of the profession for nearly three hundred years, when the title was bestowed upon Henry Irving, the leading Shakespearean actor of Queen Victoria's reign.

Shakespeare's productivity rate slowed in the Jacobean years, not because of age or some personal trauma, but because there were frequent outbreaks of plague, causing the theaters to be closed for long periods. The King's Men were forced to spend many months on the road. Between November 1603 and 1608, they were to be found at various towns in the south and Midlands, though Shakespeare probably did not tour with them by this time. He had bought a large house back home in Stratford and was accumulating other property. He may indeed have stopped acting soon after the new king took the throne. With the London theaters closed so much of the time and a large repertoire on the stocks, Shakespeare seems to have focused his energies on writing a few long and complex tragedies that could have been played on demand at court: *Othello*, *King Lear*, *Antony and Cleopatra*, *Coriolanus*, and *Cymbeline* are among his longest and poetically grandest plays. *Macbeth* only survives in a shorter text, which shows signs of adaptation after Shakespeare's death. The bitterly satirical *Timon of Athens*, apparently a collaboration with Thomas Middleton that may have failed on the stage, also belongs to this period. In comedy, too, he wrote longer and morally darker works than in the Elizabethan period, pushing at the very bounds of the form in *Measure for Measure* and *All's Well That Ends Well*.

From 1608 onward, when the King's Men began occupying the indoor Blackfriars playhouse (as a winter house, meaning that they only used the outdoor Globe in summer?), Shakespeare turned to a more romantic style. His company had a great success with a revived and altered version of an old pastoral play called *Mucedorus*. It even featured a bear. The younger dramatist John Fletcher, meanwhile, sometimes working in collaboration with Francis Beaumont, was pioneering a new style of tragicomedy, a mix of romance and royalism laced with intrigue and pastoral excursions. Shakespeare experimented with this idiom in *Cymbeline* and it was presumably with his blessing that Fletcher eventually took over as the King's Men's company dramatist. The two writers apparently collaborated on three plays in the years 1612–14: a lost romance called *Cardenio* (based on the love-madness of a character in Cervantes' *Don Quixote*), *Henry VIII* (originally staged with the title "All Is True"), and *The Two Noble Kinsmen*, a dramatization of Chaucer's "Knight's Tale." These were written after Shakespeare's two final solo-authored plays, *The Winter's Tale*, a self-consciously old-fashioned work dramatizing the pastoral romance of his old enemy Robert Greene, and *The Tempest*, which at one and the same time drew together multiple theatrical traditions, diverse reading, and contemporary interest in the fate of a ship that had been wrecked on the way to the New World.

The collaborations with Fletcher suggest that Shakespeare's career ended with a slow fade rather than the sudden retirement supposed by the nineteenth-century Romantic critics who read Prospero's epilogue to *The Tempest* as Shakespeare's personal farewell to his art. In the last few years of his life Shakespeare certainly spent more of his time in Stratford-upon-Avon, where he became further involved in property dealing and litigation. But his London life also continued. In 1613 he made his first major London property purchase: a freehold house in the Blackfriars district, close to his company's indoor theater. *The Two Noble Kinsmen* may have been written as late as 1614, and Shakespeare was in London on business a little over a year before he died of an unknown cause at home in Stratford-upon-Avon in 1616, probably on his fifty-second birthday.

About half the sum of his works were published in his lifetime, in texts of variable quality. A few years after his death, his fellow actors began putting together an authorized edition of his complete *Comedies, Histories and Tragedies*. It appeared in 1623, in large "Folio" format. This collection of thirty-six plays gave Shakespeare his immortality. In the words of his fellow dramatist Ben Jonson, who contributed two poems of praise at the start of the Folio, the body of his work made him "a monument without a tomb":

And art alive still while thy book doth live
And we have wits to read and praise to give . . .
He was not of an age, but for all time!

SHAKESPEARE'S WORKS:
A CHRONOLOGY

1589–91	*? Arden of Faversham* (possible part authorship)
1589–92	*The Taming of the Shrew*
1589–92	*? Edward the Third* (possible part authorship)
1591	*The Second Part of Henry the Sixth*, originally called *The First Part of the Contention Betwixt the Two Famous Houses of York and Lancaster* (element of coauthorship possible)
1591	*The Third Part of Henry the Sixth*, originally called *The True Tragedy of Richard Duke of York* (element of coauthorship probable)
1591–92	*The Two Gentlemen of Verona*
1591–92; perhaps revised 1594	*The Lamentable Tragedy of Titus Andronicus* (probably cowritten with, or revising an earlier version by, George Peele)
1592	*The First Part of Henry the Sixth*, probably with Thomas Nashe and others
1592/94	*King Richard the Third*
1593	*Venus and Adonis* (poem)
1593–94	*The Rape of Lucrece* (poem)
1593–1608	*Sonnets* (154 poems, published 1609 with *A Lover's Complaint*, a poem of disputed authorship)
1592–94/ 1600–03	*Sir Thomas More* (a single scene for a play originally by Anthony Munday, with other revisions by Henry Chettle, Thomas Dekker, and Thomas Heywood)
1594	*The Comedy of Errors*
1595	*Love's Labour's Lost*

1595–97	*Love's Labour's Won* (a lost play, unless the original title for another comedy)
1595–96	*A Midsummer Night's Dream*
1595–96	*The Tragedy of Romeo and Juliet*
1595–96	*King Richard the Second*
1595–97	*The Life and Death of King John* (possibly earlier)
1596–97	*The Merchant of Venice*
1596–97	*The First Part of Henry the Fourth*
1597–98	*The Second Part of Henry the Fourth*
1598	*Much Ado About Nothing*
1598–99	*The Passionate Pilgrim* (20 poems, some not by Shakespeare)
1599	*The Life of Henry the Fifth*
1599	"To the Queen" (epilogue for a court performance)
1599	*As You Like It*
1599	*The Tragedy of Julius Caesar*
1600–01	*The Tragedy of Hamlet, Prince of Denmark* (perhaps revising an earlier version)
1600–01	*The Merry Wives of Windsor* (perhaps revising version of 1597–99)
1601	"Let the Bird of Loudest Lay" (poem, known since 1807 as "The Phoenix and Turtle" [turtle-dove])
1601	*Twelfth Night, or What You Will*
1601–02	*The Tragedy of Troilus and Cressida*
1604	*The Tragedy of Othello, the Moor of Venice*
1604	*Measure for Measure*
1605	*All's Well That Ends Well*
1605	*The Life of Timon of Athens*, with Thomas Middleton
1605–06	*The Tragedy of King Lear*
1605–08	? contribution to *The Four Plays in One* (lost, except for *A Yorkshire Tragedy*, mostly by Thomas Middleton)

1606	*The Tragedy of Macbeth* (surviving text has additional scenes by Thomas Middleton)
1606–07	*The Tragedy of Antony and Cleopatra*
1608	*The Tragedy of Coriolanus*
1608	*Pericles, Prince of Tyre*, with George Wilkins
1610	*The Tragedy of Cymbeline*
1611	*The Winter's Tale*
1611	*The Tempest*
1612–13	*Cardenio*, with John Fletcher (survives only in later adaptation called *Double Falsehood* by Lewis Theobald)
1613	*Henry VIII (All Is True)*, with John Fletcher
1613–14	*The Two Noble Kinsmen*, with John Fletcher

FURTHER READING
AND VIEWING

CRITICAL APPROACHES

Bloom, Harold, ed., *Modern Critical Interpretations: William Shakespeare's Much Ado About Nothing* (1988). Excellent collection of critical essays offering variety of interpretations.

Callaghan, Dympna, ed., *A Feminist Companion to Shakespeare* (2000). Includes a short essay on *Much Ado*—"Gender, Class, and the Ideology of Comic Form: *Much Ado About Nothing* and *Twelfth Night*"—by Mihoko Suzuki which focuses on class/gender relations.

Clamp, Mike, *Cambridge Student Guide: Much Ado About Nothing* (2002). Useful commentary with basic critical and contextual information.

Everett, Barbara, "*Much Ado About Nothing*: The Unsociable Comedy," in *English Comedy*, ed. Michael Cordner, Peter Holland, and John Kerrigan (1994), pp. 68–84. Intricately grounded reading.

Howard, Jean E., "Renaissance Antitheatricality and the Politics of Gender and Rank in *Much Ado About Nothing*," in *Shakespeare Reproduced: The Text in History and Ideology*, ed. Jean E. Howard and Marion F. O'Connor (1987), pp. 163–87. Strong political reading.

Mangan, Michael, *A Preface to Shakespeare's Comedies 1594–1603* (1996). Part 1 gives a broad overview of the role of comedy; part 2 offers a basic critical discussion of individual plays—*Much Ado* is on pp. 179–201.

Wynne-Davies, Marion, ed., *New Casebooks: Much Ado About Nothing and The Taming of the Shrew* (2001). Selection of five modern critical essays focusing on gender politics and early modern society; number four by Penny Gay discusses post–Second World War productions in relation to the changing social climate, reproduced from her *As She Likes It: Shakespeare's Unruly Women* (1994).

THE PLAY IN PERFORMANCE

Branagh, Kenneth, *Much Ado About Nothing by William Shakespeare* (1993). Screenplay of Branagh's film with notes and photographs.

Cox, John F., ed., *Shakespeare in Production: Much Ado About Nothing* (1997). Excellent introductory account of the play's stage history.

Mason, Pamela, *Text and Performance: Much Ado About Nothing* (1992). Part 1 offers a useful overview of the play; part 2 discusses important productions from 1949 to 1990.

Raccah, Dominique, and Maria Macaisa, eds., *Shakespeare in Performance: Much Ado About Nothing* (2007). Useful student guide with accompanying CD.

Reeves, Saskia, *Actors on Shakespeare: Much Ado About Nothing* (2003). Entertaining, thoughtful account of the author's experience of playing Beatrice in Cheek by Jowl's 1998 production.

AVAILABLE ON DVD

Much Ado About Nothing directed by Joseph Papp (1980, DVD 2002). Film of 1973 New York Shakespeare Festival production: updates the play to 1910 America with Sam Waterston as Benedick and Kathleen Widdoes as Beatrice; Dogberry and the Watch are played as Keystone Kops. Lively and entertaining, but divided the critics.

Much Ado About Nothing directed by Stuart Burge (1984, DVD 2006). Lackluster version for the BBC television Complete Shakespeare series.

Much Ado About Nothing directed by Kenneth Branagh (1993, DVD 2003). Lush romantic version set in gorgeous Tuscan landscape. Very popular box-office success.

REFERENCES

1. *Much Ado* was not one of Shakespeare's plays listed in Francis Meres' commonplace book *Palladis Tamia* (1598), but Will Kempe left the Chamberlain's Men in 1599, which suggests that the play was written between these dates, a theory borne out by stylistic and linguistic evidence.
2. Robert Latham and William Matthews, eds., *The Diary of Samuel Pepys*, Volume 3 (1970), p. 32. This diary entry may have referred to the premiere on 15 February 1662 or a later performance on 17 December in the same year.
3. Arthur Murphy, *The Life of David Garrick, Esq.*, Volume I (1801), p. 389.
4. Charles E. L. Wingate, "Beatrice," in his *Shakespeare's Heroines on the Stage* (1895), pp. 31–50.
5. Georg Christoph Lichtenberg, *Lichtenberg's Visits to England*, ed. and trans. Margaret L. Marc and W. H. Quarrell (1938), quoted in George Winchester Stone, Jr., and George M. Kahrl, "Garrick's Greatest Comic Roles," in *David Garrick: A Critical Biography* (1979), pp. 473–514.
6. Jeffrey Kahan, *Much Ado About Nothing: Shakespeare in Performance* (2007), p. 8.
7. Clement Scott, "Much Ado About Nothing," in *From "The Bells" to "King Arthur"* (1897), pp. 247–58.
8. Vincent Sternroyd and Harcourt Williams, "Irving as Benedick," in *We Saw Him Act: A Symposium on the Art of Sir Henry Irving*, ed. H. A. Saintsbury and Cecil Palmer (1939, repr. 1969), pp. 229–38.
9. Vincent Sternroyd in Sternroyd and Williams, "Irving as Benedick," pp. 229–38.
10. Scott, "Much Ado About Nothing," pp. 247–58.
11. Ellen Terry, *The Story of My Life* (1908). Can be downloaded at www.gutenberg.org/etext/12326.
12. Terry, *The Story of My Life*, VIII, "Work at the Lyceum."
13. F. H. Mares in the introduction to his Cambridge edition of *Much Ado About Nothing* (1988), pp. 1–52.
14. J. C. Trewin, *Shakespeare on the English Stage 1900–1964* (1964).
15. G. B. Shaw, in a letter to Ellen Terry, 3 June 1903, in *Ellen Terry and Bernard Shaw: A Correspondence*, ed. Christopher St. John (1932), pp. 293–94.

16. *The Times*, London, 23 April 1904.
17. G. B. Shaw, *Saturday Review*, 11 February 1905.
18. *The Times*, London, 22 July 1955.
19. John Gielgud, "1946–1954," in *Gielgud: An Actor and His Time* (1980), pp. 157–87.
20. Brooks Atkinson, *New York Times*, 8 August 1957.
21. Henry Hewes, *Saturday Review*, 24 August 1957.
22. V. S. Pritchett, *New Statesman*, 6 September 1958.
23. *The Times*, London, 27 August 1958.
24. Alan Brien, *Spectator*, 5 September 1958, pp. 305–6.
25. Brooks Atkinson, *New York Times*, 26 June 1958.
26. Penelope Gilliatt, "Prodigals: Shakespeare in Italy," in her *Unholy Fools, Wits, Comics, Disturbers of the Peace: Film & Theatre* (1973), pp. 330–33.
27. *The Times*, London, 17 February 1965.
28. B. A. Young, *Financial Times*, 17 February 1965.
29. Mel Gussow, *New York Times*, 18 August 1972.
30. Stanley Kauffman, *New Republic*, 9 September 1972, pp. 20, 33–34.
31. H. R. Coursen, "Anachronism and Papp's *Much Ado*," in *Shakespeare on Television: An Anthology of Essays and Reviews*, ed. J. C. Bulman and H. R. Coursen (1988), pp. 151–55.
32. Leslie Bennetts, *New York Times*, Section 2, 10 July 1988, pp. 1, 5.
33. Page R. Laws, *Theatre Journal*, 54, no. 2 (2002), pp. 305–7.
34. Markland Taylor, *Variety*, 388, no. 7 (30 September–6 October 2002), p. 36.
35. Martha Tuck Rozett, *Shakespeare Bulletin*, 21, no. 3 (Fall 2003), pp. 131–33.
36. Kenneth Branagh, *Introduction to Much Ado About Nothing, by William Shakespeare, with Screenplay, Introduction, and Notes on the Making of the Movie* (1993), pp. vi–xvi.
37. W. A. Darlington, *Daily Telegraph*, 5 April 1961.
38. Michael Billington, *Guardian*, 29 May 1971.
39. Michael Billington, *Guardian*, 9 April 1976.
40. J. F. Cox, *Shakespeare in Production: Much Ado About Nothing* (1997), p. 71.
41. Ralph Berry, *On Directing Shakespeare: Interviews with Contemporary Directors* (1977), p. 78.
42. Michael Coveney, *Financial Times*, 28 April 1982.
43. Michael Billington, *Guardian*, 21 April 1982.
44. Michael Billington, *Guardian*, 12 April 1990.
45. Billington, *Guardian*, 12 April 1990.

46. Benedict Nightingale, *The Times*, London, 11 April 1990.
47. Benedict Nightingale, *The Times*, London, 29 November 1996.
48. Charles Spencer, *Daily Telegraph*, 29 November 1996.
49. Nicholas de Jongh, *Evening Standard*, 27 November 1996.
50. De Jongh, *Evening Standard*, 27 November 1996.
51. Robert Smallwood, *Shakespeare Quarterly*, 40 (1989), p. 84.
52. Patrick Marmion, *Mail on Sunday*, 4 August 2002.
53. Kate Bassett, *Independent on Sunday*, 19 May 2002.
54. Paul Taylor, *Independent*, 25 May 2006.
55. Michael Billington, *Guardian*, 19 May 2006.
56. Taylor, *Independent*, 25 May 2006.
57. *The Times*, London, 5 April 1961.
58. Cox, *Much Ado About Nothing*, p. 69.
59. Peter Lewis, *Daily Mail*, 9 April 1976.
60. Don Chapman, *Oxford Mail*, 15 October 1968.
61. Chapman, *Oxford Mail*, 15 October 1968.
62. Maureen Paton, *Daily Express*, 15 April 1988.
63. Don Chapman, *Oxford Mail*, 14 April 1988.
64. Irving Wardle, *The Times*, London, 14 April 1988.
65. Maggie Steed in *Players of Shakespeare 3*, ed. Russell Jackson and Robert Smallwood (1993), pp. 42–52.
66. Marmion, *Mail on Sunday*, 4 August 2002.
67. Paul Taylor, *Independent*, 15 May 2002.
68. Ian Johns, *The Times*, London, 5 August 2002.
69. Marmion, *Mail on Sunday*, 4 August 2002.
70. B. A. Young, *Financial Times*, 15 October 1968.
71. Billington, *Guardian*, 21 April 1982.
72. Sinead Cusack in Carol Rutter's *Clamorous Voices* (1988), p. xvi.
73. Billington, *Guardian*, 21 April 1982.
74. Alastair Macaulay, *Financial Times*, 29 November 1996.
75. Charles Spencer, *Daily Telegraph*, 3 August 1996.
76. Macaulay, *Financial Times*, 29 November 1996.
77. Susan Fleetwood, interviewed with her Benedick, Roger Allam, *Leicester Mercury*, 6 April 1990.
78. Billington, *Guardian*, 19 May 2006.
79. Nicholas de Jongh, *Evening Standard*, 19 May 2006.
80. Alastair Macaulay, *Financial Times*, 23 May 2006.
81. Chapman, *Oxford Mail*, 15 October 1968.
82. Billington, *Guardian*, 12 April 1990.
83. Michael Billington, *Guardian*, 10 May 2002.

84. Billington, *Guardian*, 9 April 1976.
85. Wardle, *The Times*, 14 April 1988.
86. Spencer, *Daily Telegraph*, 3 August 2002.
87. Spencer, *Daily Telegraph*, 3 August 2002.
88. Charles Spencer, *Daily Telegraph*, 22 May 2006.
89. W. A. Darlington, *Daily Telegraph*, 5 April 1961.
90. Macaulay, *Financial Times*, 29 November 1996.
91. De Jongh, *Evening Standard*, 27 November 1996.
92. Billington, *Guardian*, 12 April 1990.
93. Billington, *Guardian*, 21 April 1982.
94. Peter Lewis, *Daily Mail*, 9 April 1976.
95. Christopher Hart, *Sunday Times*, London, 21 May 2006.

ACKNOWLEDGMENTS AND PICTURE CREDITS

Preparation of "*Much Ado* in Performance" was assisted by a generous grant from the CAPITAL Centre (Creativity and Performance in Teaching and Learning) of the University of Warwick for research in the RSC archive at the Shakespeare Birthplace Trust. The Arts and Humanities Research Council (AHRC) funded a term's research leave that enabled Jonathan Bate to work on "The Director's Cut."

Picture research by Michelle Morton. Grateful acknowledgment is made to the Shakespeare Birthplace Trust for assistance with picture research (special thanks to Helen Hargest) and reproduction fees.

Images of RSC productions are supplied by the Shakespeare Centre Library and Archive, Stratford-upon-Avon. This library, maintained by the Shakespeare Birthplace Trust, holds the most important collection of Shakespeare material in the UK, including the Royal Shakespeare Company's official archive. It is open to the public free of charge.

For more information see www.shakespeare.org.uk.

1. Directed by John Gielgud (1949) Angus McBean © Royal Shakespeare Company
2. Directed by Douglas Seale (1958) Angus McBean © Royal Shakespeare Company
3. Directed by Trevor Nunn (1968) Tom Holte © Shakespeare Birthplace Trust
4. Directed by Terry Hands (1982) Joe Cocks Studio Collection © Shakespeare Birthplace Trust
5. Directed by Di Trevis (1988) Joe Cocks Studio Collection © Shakespeare Birthplace Trust
6. Directed by Nicholas Hytner (2007) © Donald Cooper/photostage.co.uk

7. Directed by Marianne Elliott (2006) Simon Annand © Royal Shakespeare Company
8. Directed by Gregory Doran (2002) Jonathan Dockar-Drysdale © Royal Shakespeare Company
9. Reconstructed Elizabethan playhouse © Charcoalblue

With new commentary, as well as definitive
text and cutting-edge notes from the RSC's
William Shakespeare: Complete Works,
the first authoritative, modernized edition of
Shakespeare's First Folio in more than 300 years.

Hamlet

Love's Labour's
Lost

A Midsummer
Night's Dream

Richard III

The Tempest

Also available in hardcover
William Shakespeare: Complete Works